P9-CKN-492

DEC - 9 2004

WITHDRAWN

JUL 01

DAVID O. McKAY LIBRARY
BYU-IDAHO

PROPERTY OF:
DAVID O. McKAY LIBRARY
BYU-IDAHO
REXBURG ID 83460-0405

Introduction to Formal Grammars

M. Gross · A. Lentin

Introduction to Formal Grammars

With a Preface by Noam Chomsky

Translated by M. Salkoff

With 75 Figures

Springer-Verlag New York · Heidelberg · Berlin 1970

Maurice Gross
André Lentin
Morris Salkoff
Institut Blaise Pascal, Paris

Translation of
Notions sur les Grammaires formelles
© Gauthier-Villars, Paris, 1967

This work is subject to copyright. All rights are reserved, whether the whole or part of
the material is concerned, specifically those of translation, reprinting, re-use of illustra-
tions, broadcasting, reproduction by photocopying machine or similar means, and
storage in data banks. Under § 54 of the German Copyright Law where copies are
made for other than private use, a fee is payable to the publisher, the amount of the
fee to be determined by agreement with the publisher.

© by Springer-Verlag Berlin · Heidelberg 1970. Library of Congress Catalog Card
Number 76-98261. Printed in Germany.

Title No. 1630

Foreword

The present work originates in a course given by the authors during the last few years in various university departments and institutions, among which we should like to mention: the *Centre de Linguistique Quantitative* of the *Faculté des Sciences de Paris*, created at the instance of the late Professor Favard; the *Chaire d'Analyse Numérique* of the *Faculté des Sciences de Paris* (Professor René de Possel), curriculum of *Troisième Cycle*; the *Chaire de Physique Mathématique* of the University of Toulouse (Professor M. Laudet), for the degree *Diplôme d'Etudes Approfondies* in the section *"Traitement de l'Information"*; the department of linguistics of the University of Pennsylvania[1] (Professor Z. S. Harris); the *Institut de Programmation* of the *Faculté des Sciences de Paris* for the courses in the *troisième niveau*.

Written for purely didactic purposes, this *Introduction to Formal Grammars* makes no pretense to any scientific originality. Large portions of it have been borrowed from the fundamental and "classic" works cited in the bibliography, such as that of M. Davis, *Computability and Unsolvability* [9], and those of N. Chomsky, among others *Formal Properties of Grammars* [6]. Ineluctably, there are numerous borrowings made during a course, and the authors would like to acknowledge their debt to J. Pitrat for his lectures given in the *Centre de Linguistique Quantitative* mentioned above, and to M. Nivat for his work in connection with codes[2] and transduction.

The theory of formal grammars is presently being studied by people of varied backgrounds and interests. This heterogeneity of audience forced us to choose, and we have chosen for the simplest style. This has occasionally led us to sacrifice a perfect mathematical rigor for a more intuitive presentation. For these same reasons, we have relegated certain somewhat technical proofs to the exercises, and for some others refer the reader to the appropriate reference in the bibliography.

---

[1] Contract NSF: Transformations and Discourse Analysis Project.
[2] Contract USAF 61 (052)-945.

Preface

In the traditional study of language, an important distinction was made between "particular grammar" and "universal grammar", the first being concerned with the idiosyncratic properties of specific languages, the second, with the general features of any human language. A concern for this distinction has reappeared in the foreground of research in the past few years, and this resurgence of interest has coincided with the initiation of serious research in a branch of mathematical linguistics that is sometimes called "algebraic linguistics", to distinguish it from statistical investigations of language or the study of probabilistic models for performance. The coincidence of these developments is quite natural, in several respects. Algebraic linguistics is the study of formal properties of natural language, abstracted from the specific realization in particular languages. So defined, it is really quite indistinguishable from universal grammar, although in practice there has been a division of labor between the more empirically oriented studies of universal grammar and the strictly mathematical studies of formal structures suggested by linguistic research. The existence of this division is in part a sign of the immaturity of the field, in part a reflection of the differing motivations and research interests of particular investigators. If the division can be substantially narrowed, a true theory of mathematical linguistics may emerge which studies in a purely abstract way the class of systems defined by the principles of universal grammar — the class of "possible human languages".

A second reason for the coincidence of the rise of algebraic linguistics and the revived interest in universal grammar can be found in the development of the study of language in the modern period. Over a century ago, the study of *grammaire générale et raisonnée* entered into a decline and its value and significance were seriously questioned as scholars turned to historical and comparative study, and, later, to study of language within the very fruitful "structuralist" or "descriptivist" traditions. The older studies of *grammaire générale et raisonnée* were held to be too speculative, not firmly enough grounded in linguistic fact. It was felt that they seriously underestimated the possible variety of language structures and that they imposed, arbitrarily, a model of language structure that distorted the actual phenomena of particular languages. Some scholars went so far as to maintain that languages can differ without limit and that there are no general conditions of any significance that restrict and constrain the form of any possible human language. At the same time, attention shifted to sound structure, which had by no means been neglected in the classical linguistic tradition but which had been regarded as ancillary to the investigation of the deeper syntactic properties of language. A major concern of the classical tradition was a property of language that might be called its "creative aspect", that is, the fact that a language provides recursive mechanisms that permit the expression of infinitely many thoughts, feelings, intentions, and so on, independently of any control by external stimuli or identifiable internal states. The "creative aspect" of language was in effect denied by many modern students of a behaviorist orientation, who came to view a language as a system of habits, a network of stimulus-response connections, or something of the sort; by others, for example, de Saussure, it was not denied, but was assigned to *parole*, and regarded as either peripheral, or else definitely beyond the scope of the study of language, and not subject to strict linguistic rule.

Certainly at least one reason, perhaps the major reason, for this shift of interest and modification of doctrine lay in the fact that available technique and understanding of formal processes did not make it possible to study the recursive mechanisms of syntax in any clear and productive way. In fact, it was not until a generation ago that the proper concepts were developed and sharpened, in the course of investigation of foundations of mathematics. With the new understanding of recursive mechanisms and the nature of algorithms that has developed in the past thirty years, it becomes possible to return to the study of the creative aspect of language use, and to attempt to formulate, in a precise way, the mechanisms that each language makes available for the free and unbounded use of language. The study of these mechanisms is now generally referred to as "generative grammar"; the generative grammar of a language is understood as the system of rules and processes that characterize the potentially infinite class of sentences of a natural language and that assign to each of these objects a structural description representing its significant phonetic, syntactic, and semantic properties. Thus the study of generative grammar became feasible as a result of developments in mathematics, and it is therefore not surprising that interest in formal properties of grammars, in algebraic linguistics, was a natural outgrowth of this new approach to the study of language.

There is much to be said about these matters, but I think it is fairly clear that the skepticism of structural and descriptive linguistics with respect to the possibilities for a *grammaire générale et raisonnée* was unwarranted, and that, in fact, the classical tradition was probably much too conservative in the extent to which it postulated restrictive conditions and constraints that govern the form of any human language. Speculating, I think it is not unreasonable to assume that the linguistics of the next generation will reveal that each natural language is a specific realization of a highly restrictive schema that permits grammatical processes and structures of a very limited variety, and that there are innumerable

"imaginable" languages that violate these restrictions and that are, therefore, not possible human languages in a psychologically important sense,
even though they are quite able, in principle, to express the entire content
of any possible human language. If this is true, then a mathematical study
of universal grammar, in the sense described earlier, may well become
the central domain of linguistic theory. It is too early to know whether
these hopes can be realized, but they seem not unreasonable, given what
we know and are coming to know today.

I would like to stress again that there is still a significant gap between
the mathematical and the empirical investigations that fall within the
domain of what ultimately may become a mathematical theory of universal grammar. The schema for grammatical description that seems
empirically motivated by the facts of particular languages specifies a class
of systems that are for the moment, much too complex for fruitful and
far-reaching mathematical investigation; furthermore, it must be borne
in mind that any proposals that can be made today concerning this
universal schema are both highly tentative and also somewhat loose in
important respects. At the same time, there have been interesting and
suggestive studies of much more restricted schemata for grammatical
description — the theory of so-called "context-free languages" is the
primary example — but these systems are surely empirically inadequate.
A mathematical theory of universal grammar is therefore a hope for the
future rather than a present reality. The most that one can say is that
present research appears to be tending in the direction of such a theory.
To me it seems that this is one of the most exciting areas of study today,
and that if it proves successful, it may place the study of language on an
entirely new footing in coming years.

Noam Chomsky

Table of Contents

Part I

Logical and Algebraic Preliminaries

Chapter I.   Words — Monoids — Languages   1
Chapter II.   General Definition of Formal Systems 16
Chapter III. Combinatorial Systems 31
Chapter IV.   Algorithms — Turing Machines 43
Chapter V.   Computability   Decidability . . .   56
Chapter VI.   Combinatorial Systems and Turing Machines;
              Undecidable Problems 71

Part II

Some Important Classes of Languages

Chapter VII.   Context-Free Languages 81
Chapter VIII. Undecidable Properties of CF-Grammars 94
Chapter IX.   Push-Down Automata 106
Chapter X.   Kleene Languages and Finite Automata 118
Chapter XI.   Languages Defined by Systems of Equations . . . 132
Chapter XII.   Context-Sensitive Grammars. Linear Bounded
               Automata 148

Part III

The Algebraic Point of View

Chapter XIII. Homomorphisms of Monoids 157
Chapter XIV. More about Kleene Languages 167
Chapter XV.   More about Context-Free Languages 183
Chapter XVI. Algebraic Languages 196

Appendix

Transformational Grammars 217

Bibliography of Transformational Grammars 229
Annotated Bibliography 229

PART I

Logical and Algebraic Preliminaries

Chapter I

Words — Monoids — Languages

1.1. The Free Monoid

1.1.0. Mathematics and Metamathematics

When we read or write a mathematical text, we employ a certain number of marks and conventions which are more or less well-defined and more or less expressed — if not simply left understood — and which enable mathematicians to understand each other.

The same mark has different uses: do the parentheses have the same rôle in expressions like

$$\text{the function } f(x)\dots$$

$$y = (m+1)\, x^2 - 2\, m\, x + 2\, m - 3 \dots$$

$$\text{the pair } (x, y)\dots?$$

Why does the distributivity of multiplication with respect to addition enable one to write:

$$(a+b)(c+d) = a\,c + a\,d + b\,c + b\,d,$$

whereas, when speaking of an operation ∘ which is distributive with respect to an operation ∗, one would write more carefully:

$$(a*b) \circ (c*d) = (a \circ c) * (a \circ d) * (b \circ c) * (b \circ d)?$$

Such questions are beyond the scope of ordinary mathematics and fall in the domain of *metamathematics*.

In general the mathematics student, or the user of mathematics, makes little distinction between a *mathematical concept* and the *metamathematical procedure* of definition and notation associated with this concept. The confusion between function and formula is "classical"....
Moreover, the very fact of mistaking form for substance, *syntax* for *semantics*, or an expression for its meaning, is frequently of help in reconstructing the meaning of an incorrect or ambiguous expression.

It is clear that a machine does not possess this background of knowledge and habits which leads a person to choose the correct interpretation: in order to communicate a message to the machine, we are obliged to employ a language which is rigorously defined down to its minutest detail.

It is therefore necessary for us to refer to the work of logicians, who, rather conveniently for our purposes, didn't wait for the era of the electronic machine to take *metamathematics* as the *domain of mathematical study*!

By so doing we shall avoid rediscovering, at great pains, well-known results. To begin with, we shall study the phenomenon of "writing" in its most direct application: the use of signs arranged one after the other to form words and, perhaps, to express something. This is the aim of the first chapter.

1.1.1. The Base Elements

We take a non-empty set $\mathfrak{A}$ which we call the *base set* and whose elements we call *base elements*. In order to represent these elements we associate each of them with some printed mark (or material symbol) which will be its *written name*; in order to speak about these elements we attribute to each one of them a *spoken name*. Of course, we see to it that two different elements do not receive the same name.

Example 1. $\mathfrak{A}$ contains just one element which is represented by the mark | and designated by the English word "stick".

Example 2. $\mathfrak{A}$ contains two elements which are represented by the marks ■ and □ respectively, and designated by the words "black" and "white".

The mark used to designate the base set (in the present case, the mark $\mathfrak{A}$) cannot be used to name an element of that set.

1.1.2. Finite Strings

We consider now those entities which traditionally are called "arrangements with repetition of elements of $\mathfrak{A}$". These are in fact *finite strings* (completely ordered) whose elements are *occurrences* of the elements of $\mathfrak{A}$. In order to provide such a string with a graphic representation, we may arrange the occurrences of the marks associated with the elements of $\mathfrak{A}$ on some linear medium (a line of a notebook, a paper ribbon, magnetic tape ...). In a book, unless otherwise stated, the printed string is oriented from left to right.

Example. If the base set $\mathfrak{A}$ contains three elements which are represented by a, b, and c, then by writing

bacaba

we represent a string composed of six elements of $\mathfrak{A}$: the first element of the string is an occurrence of the element named b, etc.

It is useful to introduce by convention an *empty* string which contains no occurrences.

For writing and referring to strings, we shall use symbols and quotation marks respectively, provided that neither the symbols nor the quotation marks have already been used to represent base elements. In the preceding example, it is perfectly justified to write:

$$A = \text{'b a c a b a'},$$

$$B = \text{'a c c c a b'}.$$

In particular, we choose a symbol, say E, to represent the empty string:

$$E = \text{' '}.$$

The great pains which we have taken in this exposition of writing will give the reader some insight into the use of a *metalanguage* to describe a language. We shall return to this topic later.

The *degree* of a string is defined as an integer equal to the number of occurrences in the string, the degree of the empty string being zero. The degree is written by means of vertical lines:

$$|\text{b a c a b a}| = 6, \qquad |A| = 6.$$

The degree with respect to one or more symbols is defined similarly: 'b a c a b a' is of degree 3 in a, and of degree 1 in c.

1.1.3. Concatenation of Strings

Having defined the set $\mathfrak{A}$, we consider the set $\mathfrak{A}^*$ of finite strings composed of occurrences of elements of $\mathfrak{A}$. Given a string A and a string B, in that order, we can associate with the ordered pair (A, B) the string C which is obtained by writing one after the other the occurrences of A and then those of B. C is said to have been obtained by concatenating B after A. We can also write:

$$C = AB.$$

Example. For:

$$A = \text{'b a c a'} \qquad \text{and} \qquad B = \text{'a c'}$$

$$AB = \text{'b a c a a c'} \qquad \text{and} \qquad BA = \text{'a c b a c a'}.$$

The degree of a string obtained by concatenation is the sum of the degrees of its components.

It is clear that concatenation is an operation which is defined everywhere and is associative (but not commutative), having as its neutral element the empty sequence.

In algebra, a set which has an associative operation defined everywhere and which has a neutral element is called a *monoid*[1]. If the operation of concatenation is defined for it, the set $\mathfrak{A}^*$ becomes the *free monoid on* $\mathfrak{A}$ and the elements of $\mathfrak{A}$ are the *generators* of the latter.

Examples. If $\mathfrak{A} = \{a\}$, the free monoid is isomorphic to the set of powers of a letter a (with associative multiplication).

If $\mathfrak{A} = \{0, 1\}$, the words of $\mathfrak{A}^*$ can also be read as binary integers, and concatenation can be interpreted as a complex arithmetical operation.

1.1.4. Problems of Terminology

The usage, which is not yet standardized, depends on the authors and the domain to which the theory of formal grammars is applied: artificial languages, logic, natural languages....

When we study programming languages, we shall say that the base set is an *abstract alphabet* made up of *abstract letters* and that it is represented (under certain conditions) by a *concrete alphabet* made up of *concrete letters*; we shall say that finite strings are *abstract words* which can be represented by *concrete words*.

Thus, the language ALGOL utilizes an alphabet of 116 letters. An abstract letter is defined by a set of properties which characterizes it: one letter, which plays the rôle of the open parenthesis of an instruction, is written by means of the concrete letter "**begin**"[2]; another, which corresponds to the logical relation of implication, is written by means of the concrete letter "⊃". It would be fetichistic to take, implication, for example, to be the little drawing above. Note that a different concrete alphabet is used on punched tape, and yet another one when the information is in the computer.

In applications to natural languages, it turns out that the base set is made up of letters or of *phonemes*, and the strings are *words*. The base set can also be a *vocabulary* whose elements are *words* (in the linguistic sense); the strings of words are then given names like *phrases*, *sentences*, etc. There too it is necessary to make the distinction between the printed word and what it refers to: it is well known that the word "dog" doesn't bite.

In the same way one must distinguish between the letter "a" considered as one of the base elements and the single-letter word 'a', as for example in the sentence: "The empty word a has degree zero". On the other hand, in those theories concerned only with the formal properties of words, with no reference to meaning, there is no need to make the distinction between a letter and the single-letter word made up of this letter: this is the case in the algebraic theory of the free monoid.

---

[1] That is, a semigroup having a neutral element.

[2] The letter "**begin**" is part of the international alphabet ALGOL which is defined in the report ALGOL 60.

1.2. Word Calculus

1.2.1. Thue Relations

In what follows (for the sake of clarity) the concrete alphabet will be the lower-case latin alphabet (or a part of that alphabet); words will be indicated by capital letters, and the empty word by E.

The word 'touamotou' contains two *occurrences* of the word '*tou*': the first occurrence is in the initial section (or left factor) of the word 'touamotou', and the second is in the terminal section (or right factor) of this word. The word 'tananarive' contains two contiguous occurrences of the word 'na'. General definitions related to these concepts can be easily formulated.

Let P and Q be two different words (one or the other of which may be empty). Suppose A contains an occurrence of P so that it can be written in the form

$$A = XPY;$$

then it is possible to associate with this word a word B obtained by substituting an occurrence of Q for the occurrence of P.

Example. If P and Q are the words 'ara' and 'ru' respectively, then to the word 'parade' there corresponds the word 'prude'.

In the present chapter we shall consider the case where, if one has the right to replace every occurrence of P by an occurrence of Q, then we agree that we have the right to replace every occurrence of Q by an occurrence of P. We then write

$$P \sim Q; \tag{1}$$

in the preceding example we have

$$\text{'ara'} \sim \text{'ru'}.$$

Several relations of the type (1) may obtain simultaneously between the words. In this case the relations constitute a system, for example

$$\text{'ara'} \sim \text{'ru'}; \quad \text{'e'} \sim \text{'igm'}.$$

These relations, introduced and studied by the Norwegian mathematician Thue, give rise to what is called the *associative calculus*.

If the word B is derived from the word A by the application of just one relation, we shall call A and B contiguous. This notation is justified by the fact that A is also derived from B by the application of only one relation. Thus in the example we are using, we see that

'paradigm' is contiguous to 'parade'

'parade' is contiguous to 'prude'.

On the other hand, 'paradigm' is not contiguous to 'prude'. To obtain a transitive relation, we must permit several applications of the relations of the type $P \sim Q$. To be more precise, we make the following definition:

Definition. Let $\mathfrak{A}$ be an alphabet and $R: P_1 \sim Q_1, \ldots, P_n \sim Q_n$ a system of Thue relations. We say that the word B_0 is in relation with the word B_p if there exists a series of words $B_0, \ldots, B_p$ such that B_i is contiguous to B_{i-1} for $i = 1, \ldots, p$. Furthermore, we agree conventionally that every word is related to itself. Under these conditions the relation "is related to" is an equivalence relation. For this reason, and to conform to established usage, we shall speak henceforth of *equivalent* words.

Thus, in our example

'paradigm' is equivalent to 'prude'.

To indicate this equivalence relation, we shall use the symbol "$\approx$". Thus

'paradigm'$\approx$'prude'.

We now give a theorem whose proof follows directly.

Theorem. *For every word* X *and for every word* Y, *the equivalence*

$$A \approx B \quad implies \quad XAY \approx XBY.$$

1.2.2. The Word Problem

Given an associative calculus defined by an alphabet $\mathfrak{A}$ and the Thue relations

$$P_1 \sim Q_1, \ldots, P_n \sim Q_n.$$

Thue posed the following fundamental problem, known as the "*word problem*".

Given an arbitrary pair of words, determine whether or not they are equivalent.

1.2.3. Particular Cases

We begin with two definitions which will be frequently used. The string $\tilde{A}$ is called the *mirror image* of the string A if $\tilde{A}$ has the same occurrences as A, but in reverse order. Thus,

$$A = \text{'roma'}, \qquad \tilde{A} = \text{'amor'}.$$

The string A is *symmetric* (or is a *palindrome*) if it coincides with its mirror image. For example,

$$B = \text{'deed'}, \qquad C = \text{'madamimadam'}.$$

Now consider the case where we have

$$\mathfrak{A} - \{a, b\}; \qquad a\,a \sim E; \qquad b\,b \sim E.$$

(These relations are called *nilpotent*.) Reducing a word is equivalent to forming a new word which is contiguous to the first, but shorter than it. Starting from a given word and forming a chain of words by successive reductions, we end up with an irreducible word which may also be the empty word.

Example. Let us start with the word

$$A = a\,b\,a\,a\,a\,a\,b\,b\,a\,b\,a\,b\,b\,b\,b\,a\,a\,b.$$

A first chain of reductions is shown in the following schema:

$$A \approx a\,b\,a\,a\,a\,a\,\underset{\substack{1\ 1\\2\ 2\\3\quad 3}}{b}\,b\,a\,b\,a\,\underset{\substack{6\ 6\\5\quad 5}}{b}\,b\,b\,a\,a\,b,$$

$$A \approx a\,b\,a\,b\,a.$$

There are many other ways of going about the reduction, for example

$$A \approx a\,b\,a\,a\,a\,a\,b\,b\,a\,b\,a\,b\,b\,b\,b\,a\,a\,b,$$

$$A \approx a\,b\,a\,b\,a.$$

Intuition suggests that this irreducible result does not depend on the way the reductions are carried out. This has been verified in the preceding example; we leave the proof to the reader as an exercise. In other words, in each equivalence class there exists one and only one irreducible word which it is natural to consider as the *canonical representative* of the class.

In such a case the word problem can be solved: given two words, they are equivalent if and only if they have the same equivalent irreducible word. This latter can be found in a straightforward way by a mechanizable procedure.

But the case is not always so favorable. For the same alphabet {a, b}, let us consider, for example, the rules:

$$a\,a\,a \sim a\,a; \qquad a\,b\,a \sim a\,a; \qquad b\,a\,b \sim b\,b; \qquad b\,b\,b \sim b\,b.$$

Starting with the word 'a b a b a', we can form successively a a a, and then a a, or a b b a. These two words are equivalent and irreducible, but different.

The word problem can be solved when there exist invariants which characterize a class. But such *invariants* do not necessarily exist. If we try to decide whether a given word S is equivalent to a word T, then the first 'universal' method which comes to mind consists of methodically forming all the words contiguous to S, then successively all the words contiguous to each one of these, etc.; in short, the *enumeration* of all the words equivalent to S after one operation, then after two, three, and so forth. However many operations are carried out, if T has not yet been reached, one may hope to find it after yet another operation: the "universal and naive" method therefore gives no guarantee of a final decision.

Does there exist a universal method capable of solving the word problem? We shall prove that the answer to this question is negative, after having clarified the concept of the method, or better, the algorithm required.

1.2.4. The Monoid of Classes

Let us suppose that the following hypotheses are available, for a given associative calculus:

$$S \approx S' \quad \text{and} \quad T \approx T';$$

then we have successively (in view of the theorem stated in § 1.2.1.):

$$ST \approx S'T \approx S'T',$$

hence the lemma:

Lemma. $ST \approx S'T'$.

Word concatenation is an operation which is stable under the equivalence defined by Thue relations. This equivalence is called Thue-equivalence.

When an equivalence relation is compatible on the right and on the left with an operation, it is called a congruence. The preceding lemma can therefore be restated in the following way:

A Thue-equivalence is a congruence on the free monoid.

We will now cite a widely used theorem from algebra which we shall then apply to the case at hand.

Theorem. *A congruence $\Re$, defined on a set M with an associative operation, determines a set of classes, or quotient set $M/\Re$ with an induced operation which is also associative.*

If the original operation had a neutral element, the class of that element is neutral for the induced operation.

For the proof of this fundamental theorem, we refer the reader to exercise 1.4.4. So far as the free monoid and the Thue-equivalence is concerned, we deduce the following theorem:

Theorem. *The classes defined on a free monoid by a Thue-equivalence form a monoid for the operation induced by concatenation.*

Example.

$$\mathfrak{A} = \{a, b\}; \quad a\,a \sim E; \quad b\,b \sim E.$$

This is the example which was studied in § 1.2.3 from the point of view of word equivalence.

The classes can be represented canonically by reduced words in which two consecutive occurrences are occurrences of different letters. If we order the reduced words first by increasing length and then in alphabetical order, we obtain the classes:

$$\text{E, a, b, a b, b a, a b a, b a b, a b a b, ...}$$

Given two classes in a certain order, we apply the following rules in order to obtain the representative of the compound class:

1. Concatenate in the given order the class representatives;
2. Examine the occurrences at their juncture;
3. If the letters are different: the operation is finished.
   If not, cross out the two occurrences of the same letter;
4. If the result is E, the operation is finished.
   If not, go to 2.

It is clear that the neutral class is obtained if and only if the canonical representatives are mirror images of each other.

Every class can have a unique left and right inverse; from this we obtain the pairs of inverses:

$$\text{E, E; a, a; b, b; a b, b a; a b a, a b a; b a b, b a b; a b a b, b a b a; ....}$$

A class represented by a palindromic reduced word is its own inverse. The reader will recognize that, in the case under discussion, the monoid of classes is a group. As for the kernel of the mapping (the set of words of the class E), it comprises the palindromic words of even length, but it also contains others obtained by concatenating these palindromes:

$$\text{b a a b   a b b a   b b,   for example.}$$

1.3. Languages

1.3.1. Definition

Every subset of the free monoid $\mathfrak{A}^*$ of finite strings constructed from the base set $\mathfrak{A}$ is called a *formal language* defined on the base set $\mathfrak{A}$. For brevity, we shall simply say *language* instead of *formal language*.

Examples. For any $\mathfrak{A}$, the set of words of even degree is a language; the set of words of odd degree is another. The first is closed under concatenation, the second is not.

For any $\mathfrak{A}$, the set of palindromes is a language which is not closed under concatenation (unless $\mathfrak{A}$ contains only one letter).

1.3.2. An Important Case: The Dyck Languages

Consider a correct mathematical computation, or a program written
in a language like ALGOL. There are symbols which go by twos: open
parenthesis, close parenthesis; open bracket, close bracket; open braces,
close braces; open scalar product chevron, close chevron; begin, end; etc.
If in the text of the computation or of the program, we take out everything
which is not a symbol of this sort, a new text is obtained which obeys
strict rules.

Example. From the correctly written formula:

$$\{[(a+b)(c+d)-(a'+b')(c'+d')]^6-(a\,b\,c\,d-a'\,b'\,c'\,d')^3\}^2$$
$$-\{[(a\,a'+b\,b'+c\,c'+d\,d')^6+(a\,b\,c\,d\,a'\,b'\,c'\,d')^{\frac{3}{2}}]+A\}^2.$$

we obtain

$$\{[()()()()]()\}\{[()()]\}.$$

The "texts" of this kind give an idea of what is called a *restricted
Dyck language*. The importance of these languages lies, at least in part,
in their relation to the *parenthesized structures* which are found in
natural languages and in "artificial" or technical languages: mathematics, logic, programming languages, etc.

We shall now give some precise definitions.

Definitions. Let $\mathfrak{A} = \{a, a', b, b' \ldots\}$ be an alphabet made up of $2n$
letters paired by twos: a and a', b and b', etc.; let E be the empty word;
let the Thue relations be:

$$a\,a' \sim E; \qquad b\,b' \sim E, \ldots.$$

A word X belongs to the restricted Dyck language on $\mathfrak{A}$ if and only if it
is equivalent to the empty word.

The Dyck language (non-restricted) is defined in a similar way by
taking the relations

$$a'\,a' \sim a'\,a \sim E, \qquad b\,b' \sim b'\,b \sim E, \ldots.$$

Examples.

a b b' a' c c' belongs to the restricted Dyck language.

a' a b' c c' b belongs to the Dyck language.

1.3.3. Operations on Languages

Let $\mathfrak{A}$ be an alphabet, and $\mathfrak{A}^*$ the free monoid on $\mathfrak{A}$; since the (formal)
languages on $\mathfrak{A}$ are the subsets of $\mathfrak{A}^*$, it is possible to define set-theoretic
operations in the *set of the subsets of* $\mathfrak{A}^*$, which we call $\mathfrak{P}(\mathfrak{A}^*)$. We now
give the fundamental operations.

Union of Languages. Given two languages L_1 and L_2, the set of words found in one (at least) of the two languages is called the union of these languages and is designated by $L_1 \cup L_2$. This operation is just set union; it is commutative and associative:

$$L_1 \cup L_2 = L_2 \cup L_1$$

$$(L_1 \cup L_2) \cup L_3 = L_1 \cup (L_2 \cup L_3).$$

Intersection of Languages. Under the same conditions, the set of words which belongs to both languages at once is called the intersection of these languages and is designated by $L_1 \cap L_2$. This operation is set intersection; it is commutative and associative.

Complementation. The complement of the language L with respect to $\mathfrak{A}^*$ is the set of words of $\mathfrak{A}^*$ which do not belong to L. It is designated by $\mathfrak{A}^* \backslash L$. $\mathfrak{A}^*$ itself is a language whose complement is the empty language. It is worth noting that a language which contains the empty word E is not empty!

Example.

$$\mathfrak{A} = \{a, b\} \quad \text{and} \quad L = \{a^m b^n \mid m \geq 1, n \geq 1\}.$$

$\mathfrak{A}^* \backslash L = L_1 \cup L_2 \cup L_3$, where L_1 designates the set of words which begin with b, L_2 the set of words which begin with $a^m b^n a$, and

$$L_3 = \{a\}^*.$$

Product of Languages. In the same way, the set of words obtained by taking a word of L_1 and concatenating on its right a word of L_2 is called the product of the two languages and is designated by $L_1 L_2$:

$$L_1 L_2 = \{X_1 X_2 \mid X_1 \in L_1 \text{ and } X_2 \in L_2\}.$$

This operation is not the cartesian product. It is not commutative, but it is associative.

Examples. Let $\mathfrak{A} = \{a, b, c\}$. Consider the language $\{a\}$ which contains just one word: the single letter 'a'; let us designate this language by $\{a\}$. Then the product

$$\{a\}\, \mathfrak{A}^*$$

is the set of words which begin with a. More generally

$$\mathfrak{A}\, \mathfrak{A}^*$$

is the set of words which begin with a letter of $\mathfrak{A}$, i.e., the set of *non-empty words*:

$$\mathfrak{A}\, \mathfrak{A}^* = \mathfrak{A}^* \backslash \{E\}.$$

Star (or Kleene) Operation. Since the taking of a product is an associative operation, it is possible to form the successive powers of a language L:

$$L^2 = LL; \qquad L^3 = (LL)L = L(LL); \qquad \text{etc.}$$

Consider the union (following S. C. Kleene):

$$E \cup L \cup L^2 \cup L^3 \cup \cdots \cup L^n \cup \ldots$$

extending over all the successive powers of L. The result is a language designated by L^*.

Example. We can consider the alphabet

$$\mathfrak{A} = \{a, b, \ldots\}$$

as the language made up of single-letter words. Then $\mathfrak{A}^2$ is the set of two-letter words, $\mathfrak{A}^3$ the set of three-letter words, etc. Hence

$$E \cup \mathfrak{A} \cup \mathfrak{A}^2 \cup \mathfrak{A}^3 \ldots$$

is the set of all the words on $\mathfrak{A}$, that is, $\mathfrak{A}^*$, if we give the star the meaning given it by Kleene.

This fact explains the notation adopted to designate the free monoid.

Mirror Image Operation. Given a language $L \subset \mathfrak{A}^*$, the language obtained by taking the mirror image of every word of L is designated by $\tilde{L}$:

$$\tilde{L} = \{\tilde{X} \mid X \in L\}.$$

This operation is involutory (its square is the identity operation):

$$\tilde{\tilde{L}} = L.$$

Furthermore, it is related to the product by the relation:

$$\widetilde{LM} = \tilde{M}\tilde{L}.$$

Example. The language $\mathfrak{A}^* \tilde{\mathfrak{A}}^*$ coincides with $\mathfrak{A}^*$ since $\tilde{\mathfrak{A}}^* = \mathfrak{A}^*$ and $E \in \mathfrak{A}^*$.

1.4. Exercises

1.4.1.

What implicit convention have we used in writing, with regard to the empty word:

$$E = ' \ '?$$

Obtain a copy of the ALGOL 60 report and study the status of the blank space in the language ALGOL.

1.4.2.

Is it conceivable to say that an alphabet $\mathfrak{A}$ contains an "empty letter"?

1.4.3.

Take the alphabet: $\mathfrak{A} = \{a, b, c, x, \equiv, \times\}$. Consider the word

$$`a \times b \times c \equiv x'.$$

Does this writing have a meaning if a, b, c, and x are interpreted as the names of numbers, $\times$ as multiplication and $\equiv$ as equality?

Same question, interpreting a, b, c and x as free vectors in Euclidian space and $\times$ as the vectorial product. From this comparison what can one conclude about concatenation?

1.4.4.

Consider a set $S = \{A, B, C, \ldots\}$ and an operation on it (written by means of a period). An equivalence is defined on this set which is compatible on the right and on the left with this operation − i.e., a *congruence*.

1. The class of the element A is designated by $\bar{A}$, that of B by $\bar{B}$, etc. Show that the class of the compound $A \cdot B$ depends only on $\bar{A}$ and $\bar{B}$. Deduce from this that the compound class of two classes can be defined by the rule: $\bar{A} \cdot \bar{B} = \overline{A \cdot B}$.

2. Verify the associativity $(\bar{A} \cdot \bar{B}) \cdot \bar{C} = \bar{A} \cdot (\bar{B} \cdot \bar{C})$ by going back to S, i.e., by taking a *representative* in each class.

3. Take E to be neutral in S for the operation; let $\bar{E}$ be its class. Show that $\bar{A} \cdot \bar{E} = \bar{E} \cdot \bar{A} = \bar{A}$. Go back to S by taking a representative for A.

1.4.5.

Consider the following system of relations on the alphabet $\{a, b, c\}$:

$$a\,a \sim E; \qquad b\,b \sim E; \qquad a\,b \sim b\,a.$$

Can the word problem be solved for this case? Show that the monoid of classes is isomorphic to a simple group and characterize the latter.

1.4.6.

Given the alphabet $\{a, b, c\}$ and the relations

$$(1)\, a\,a\,a \sim E; \qquad (2)\, b\,a \sim a\,b; \qquad (3)\, c\,a \sim a\,c.$$

What can be said about the words 'a a b a c a' and 'a b c'? More generally, can the word problem be solved *for the particular case of this calculus?*

1.4.7.

Consider the words A, B, C, D such that $AB = CD$ and $|A| \leq |C|$. Show that there exists a word X such that $C = AX$ and $B = XD$.

1.4.8.

A word M is called *periodic* if it can be obtained by concatenating identical words. The shortest word capable of generating M is called the *pattern* of the word.

Consider now two words U and V such that $UV = VU$. Show that U and V are periodic and have the same pattern. One way of obtaining the solution is the following. Prove that

$$\underbrace{U \ldots U}_{k \text{ times}} . \underbrace{V \ldots V}_{l \text{ times}} = \underbrace{V \ldots V}_{l \text{ times}} . \underbrace{U \ldots U}_{k \text{ times}}$$

obtains for all integers. Introduce the least common multiple for the degree of U and the degree of V, choose k and show that U and V are periodic. Indicate what can be said about the pattern.

1.4.9.

1. Given words A and B such that A^m and B^n have a common initial segment of degree $|A| + |B|$. Show that A and B are periodic and have the same pattern (use the result of the preceding exercise).

2. Deduce from this that if $A^m = B^n$ with $m \geq 1$, A and B are periodic and have the same pattern.

3. Show that if A is not empty there exists an integer k and a non-periodic (primitive) word B such that $A = B^k$.

1.4.10.

Using the preceding exercises, show that if there exist for the primitive (non-periodic) words A and B two powers A^m and B^n having a common initial segment of degree $|A| + |B|$, then $A = B$.

1.4.11.

Discuss the equation $A\tilde{X} = XB$.

1.4.12.

Given an alphabet $\mathfrak{A}$, consider a function φ whose arguments are on the set of words and whose values are on or in the set of words. We would like this function to define an endomorphism for the structure of the monoid, or in other words:

$$\varphi(P \cdot Q) = \varphi(P) \cdot \varphi(Q),$$

where "$\cdot$" means concatenation.

Show that φ is determined by the values which it takes on the set of single-letter words; describe a few simple classes of such functions.

1.4.13.

Given the alphabet $\mathfrak{A} = \{a, b\}$ and the relations $a\,a\,a \sim E$; $b\,b\,b\,b \sim E$; $a\,b\,b \sim b\,b\,a$; $a\,b\,a\,b\,a \sim E$; $b\,a\,b\,a\,b \sim E$. The words can be placed on the nodes of a tree structure with root E, in alphabetical order:

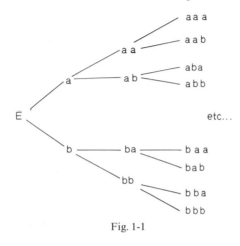

Fig. 1-1

Then every word for which an equivalent has already been written is deleted (e.g., $a\,a\,a \approx E$; then $b\,b\,a \approx a\,b\,b$, etc.). Represent the classes canonically; study the quotient monoid and the kernel.

1.4.14.

Consider functions whose arguments are on a free monoid and whose values are in this monoid. Find those functions α having the property:

$$\alpha(P \cdot Q) = \alpha[\alpha(P) \cdot \alpha(Q)].$$

Note that we have already given an example of such a function in § 1.2.3.

1.4.15.

The following is a game of patience that can be played with a deck of 32 cards:

lay out the cards in a single row;

if a card lies between two cards of the same suit or the same value, it can be removed;

if two cards of the same suit or the same value lie between two cards of the same suit or the same value, they can be removed.

Study the theory of this game of patience.

Chapter II

General Definition of Formal Systems

2.0.

In this chapter we shall describe the concept of a *formal system* and illustrate it by presenting a "variant" of the propositional calculus from a formal point of view. The full significance of this example will be lost if the reader does not already have some intuitive idea of what the propositional calculus is. We shall therefore begin by giving a brief outline of this theory.

2.1. An Intuitive Presentation of the Propositional Calculus

2.1.1. Propositions

"Monsieur Jourdain is one of the characters of the Bourgeois Gentil-homme", "Two and two are five": these two sentences in quotes are *propositions*. The first one is true, so its logical value is *true*; the second one is false, so its logical value is *false*. "It's raining", "The integer n is a prime number" are propositional variables which, according to the circumstances, can take the value true or false. Conventionally, *true* is represented by 1 and *false* by 0 (some authors invert these). The propositional variables are therefore Boolean variables: we shall return to this.

The propositional calculus is not concerned with the more difficult problem of the analysis of propositions; it considers whole, unanalyzed propositions and manipulates and combines them by means of various logical operations which we will now review. The propositions and the propositional variables will be represented by letters like p, q, etc.

2.1.2. Conjunction

Under any conditions, the proposition "It's raining and it's windy" is considered true if and only if rain and wind occur together: this is the *conjunction* of "It's raining" *and* "It's windy". More exactly, the *conjunction* of two propositions (or propositional variables) p and q is a proposition (or propositional variable) written $(p \wedge q)$ whose logical value for the four possible cases is given by the following table:

p	q	$(p \wedge q)$
0	0	0
0	1	0
1	0	0
1	1	1

Other notations for "$\wedge$": "&", "·", or nothing.

2.1.3. Disjunction

In the same way we introduce disjunction, which has the following values:

p	q	$(p \vee q)$
0	0	0
0	1	1
1	0	1
1	1	1

The disjunction $(p \vee q)$ is considered true if and only if at least one of the two propositions is true. It corresponds to the inclusive English *or* in a sentence like: "He is stupid or mean", where it is understood that he may be both at the same time.

Another notation for " $\vee$ ": " $+$ ".

2.1.4. Negation

With every proposition (or propositional variable) p can be associated the proposition $\neg p$, its *negation*, having the following values:

p	$\neg p$
0	1
1	0

Other notations: $\bar{p}$, $\sim p$, $\llcorner p$.

2.1.5. Implication

The proposition $(p \supset q)$ can be associated with every couple p, q in the following way:

p	q	$(p \supset q)$
0	0	1
0	1	1
1	0	0
1	1	1

Since the propositions p and q are not analyzed and their content is of no significance here, and since the only available datum is the logical value of each of them, the implication just defined has no connection either to any relation of cause and effect, or to a proof of q from p. There is therefore no reason to confuse the operator $\supset$ of "$(p \supset q)$" with the meta-implication "$p \Rightarrow q$".

2 Gross/Lentin, Formal Grammars

Examples.

p: Napoleon died in Sainte-Hélène.

q: Caesar had a mustache.

   $(p \supset q)$ has the same value as q.

p: Two and two are five.

q: 12 is a prime number.

   $(p \supset q)$ has the value 1.

p: The moon is made of Swiss cheese.

q: 17 is prime.

   $(p \supset q)$ has the value 1.

p: 17 is prime.

q: 16 is prime.

   $(p \supset q)$ has the value 0.

There is no paradox here, as will be clear from what follows.

Modus Ponens. If we know somehow — and the origin of this knowledge is not the question here — that p has value 1 and that $(p \supset q)$ has value 1, then we can conclude that q has value 1.

2.1.6. Logical Equivalence

Starting with two propositions (or propositional variables) p and q, the proposition $(p \equiv q)$ is constructed so that:

p	q	$(p \equiv q)$
0	0	1
0	1	0
1	0	0
1	1	1

This is the proposition: "p is equivalent to q", or "p has the same logical value as q". Just as in implication, the content of the two propositions in question plays no rôle in logical equivalence.

2.1.7. Classification of Logical Expressions

We take as variable a finite or infinite number of propositions p, q, ..., and form expressions by successively applying the operations $\wedge$, $\vee$, $\neg$, $\supset$, $\equiv$.

Examples.

$$(p \vee p) \wedge q$$

$$(p \supset q) \vee (q \supset p).$$

1. There are expressions which have the value 1 for any value of their variables.

Examples.

$$(p \vee \neg p); \qquad (p \supset p);$$

also, because of the apparently disconcerting nature of the "implication":

$$(p \supset (q \supset p)) \dots \text{N.B.!}$$

Such expressions are called *tautologies*.

2. There are expressions which have the value 0 for any value of their variables.

Examples.

$$(p \wedge \neg p)$$

$$((p \vee \neg p) \supset (p \wedge \neg p)).$$

Such expressions are *contradictions*

3. There are expressions which sometimes have value 0 and sometimes value 1, according to the values of their variables.

Example.

$$((p \supset q) \vee (p \wedge q)),$$

for, if we call this proposition r, then we have

p	q	r
1	1	1
1	0	0

The search for tautologies is interesting because tautologies are as useful in logic as the classical identities are in algebra.

Example.

$$(\neg q \supset \neg p) \supset (p \supset q) \text{ is a tautology}$$

(this can be shown by constructing a truth table). This tautology gives rise to the *rule of contraposition*.

Tautological Equivalence. We shall write r = s to mean that the proposition (r ≡ s) is a tautology.

Examples.

$$((p \vee q) \vee m) = (p \vee (q \vee m))$$

$$((p \wedge q) \wedge m) = (p \wedge (q \wedge m))$$

$$(p \supset q) \quad = (\neg p \vee q) \dots \text{N.B.}$$

$$(p \equiv q) \quad = (p \supset q) \wedge (q \supset p).$$

2*

The relation $=$ expresses the fact that under all circumstances the two expressions have the same logical value: it is an equivalence relation in the algebraic meaning of the term, a relation which can be considered to be an equality.

The constant *true* is tautologically equivalent to every tautology. Example: $(p \vee \neg p) = true$. The constant *false* is tautologically equivalent to every contradiction. Example: $(p \wedge \neg p) = false$.

2.1.8. De Morgan's Laws

It is easily shown that the following are two tautological equivalences:

$$\neg(p \vee q) = (\neg p \wedge \neg q)$$

$$\neg(p \wedge q) = (\neg p \vee \neg q).$$

These are De Morgan's Laws. For the sake of brevity, we shall write "$\bar{p}$" instead of "$\neg p$".

For every variable or expression r, s, t, we have:

1. $(r \vee r) = r; (r \wedge r) = r$: idempotence;
2. $(r \vee s) = (s \vee r); (r \wedge s) = (s \wedge r)$: commutativity;
3. $r \vee (s \vee t) = (r \vee s) \vee t; r \wedge (s \wedge t) = r \wedge (s \wedge t)$: associativity;
4. $\big(r \vee (r \wedge s)\big) = r = \big(r \wedge (r \vee s)\big)$: absorption;
5. $\big(r \vee (s \wedge t)\big) = \big((r \vee s) \wedge (r \vee t)\big)$
   $\big(r \wedge (s \vee t)\big) = \big((r \wedge s) \vee (r \wedge t)\big)$: distributivity;
6. $(r \vee \bar{r}) = true; (r \wedge \bar{r}) = false;$
7. $\overline{r \vee s} = (\bar{r} \wedge \bar{s}); \overline{r \wedge s} = (\bar{r} \vee \bar{s})$: duality;
8. $(\bar{\bar{r}}) = r$: involution.

The relations 1. to 7. suffice to show that, by the very definition of a Boolean algebra, the *propositional calculus* gives the set of logical expressions the structure of a Boolean algebra. More precisely, these are expressions obtained from a denumerable set of variables p, q, ..., by applying the unary operation "$\neg$" and the binary operations "$\wedge$" and "$\vee$" an arbitrary number of times, and by taking the tautological equivalence as the equality sign.

2.1.9. Set-Theoretic Interpretation

Let us take a family of sets P, Q, ..., and interpret the propositional variables as follows:

$x \in P, x \in Q, ...$ which all contain the same x.

Then $(p \wedge q)$ can be interpreted as $x \in P \cap Q$.

And $(p \vee q)$ can be interpreted as $x \in P \cup Q$, etc.

The propositional calculus then has the following interpretation: its set theory image is the algebra of those sets constructed from P, Q, ..., first by union and intersection. Then a universal set $\mathfrak{U}$ is introduced which contains P, Q, ..., and which corresponds to *true*. Complementation with respect to $\mathfrak{U}$ corresponds to negation; the empty set $\varnothing$, which is the complement of $\mathfrak{U}$, corresponds to *false*.

2.1.10. Variants

A calculus equivalent to the preceding can be formulated by taking a different set of fundamental operations. The most interesting variant consists in utilizing only the operations $\neg$ and $\supset$. Since

$$(p \supset q) = (\neg p \vee q) \quad \text{and} \quad \neg\neg p = p,$$

we have

$$(p \vee q) = (\neg p \supset q).$$

For $(p \wedge q)$ the formula of de Morgan can be used.

Note also that all the fundamental operations can be expressed by means of just one — carefully chosen one — of De Morgan's Laws (see the exercises).

2.1.11. Exercises

1. Given the propositions: 'It's hot $\equiv$ c', 'It's raining $\equiv$ p' and 'The air is dry' $\equiv$ s', describe the following statements in symbols:

    a) 'It's raining and it's hot'.

    b) 'It's hot but the air isn't dry'.

    c) 'The air is humid or it's hot'.

    d) 'It's not raining or the air is dry'.

2. Given that the proposition 'It's cold and the air is humid' is true, study the value of the preceding propositions.

3. If p stands for 'The tide is high' and q for 'The tide is rising', translate the following into English:

    a) $p \wedge q$ e) $\overline{p \wedge q}$

    b) $p \wedge \bar{q}$ f) $\overline{p \vee q}$

    c) $\bar{p} \wedge \bar{q}$ g) $\overline{\bar{p} \vee \bar{q}}$.

    d) $p \vee \bar{q}$

Use these translations to simplify the symbolic notation of these propositions, wherever this is possible.

4. If p stands for 'I have a turntable' and q for 'I have records', translate and simplify: $(\overline{\bar{p} \vee \bar{q}}) \wedge \bar{p}$.

5. Starting with two variables or expressions, "p W q" is formed as follows:

p	q	p W q
0	0	0
0	1	1
1	0	1
1	1	0

This corresponds to the exclusive *or*. Give a set theory interpretation of this operation. Is the operation associative?

6. Same question for the operation

p	q	p|q
0	0	1
0	1	1
1	0	1
1	1	0

which is the operation of Sheffer, or *incompatibility*.

Prove the following tautological equivalences:

$$\neg p = p|p \qquad\qquad (p \wedge q) = (p|q)|(p|q)$$
$$(p \vee q) = (p|p)|(q|q) \qquad\qquad (p \supset q) = p|(q|q).$$

2.2. The Concept of a Formal System

2.2.0.

Historically, the concept of a formal system was preceded by that of an axiomatized theory. Since the former evolved from the latter, we shall briefly describe the concept of an axiomatic theory. Euclid's "Elements" were already partially axiomatized, but the axiomatic point of view did not emerge clearly until the end of the nineteenth century.

2.2.1. Axiomatized Theory

The logical consistency of a mathematical theory is one thing, its adequacy for the description of some physical model is quite another: mathematicians became aware of this simple truth when it became necessary to explain the existence of both Euclidian and non-Euclidian geometries. To found and develop a mathematical theory logically, the "nature" of the entities which are treated therein must be disregarded (or rather, the nature of the entities which, from outside the theory, motivated the creation of the theory). On the other hand, the fundamental relations which obtain between these entities must be very carefully specified by means of *axioms*.

"Imagine that there exist entities called points, others called lines, and still others called planes", wrote Hilbert in his *Grundlagen*; in the course of conversations, he added, "instead of points, lines and planes, one could equally well speak of tables, chairs and beerglasses." The essence of the matter lies in the axioms:

1.1. A line is a set of points.

1.2. Any two points determine a line to which they belong.

1.3. Two points which belong to a line determine that line.

1.4. Every line contains at least two points.

1.5. There exist at least three points which do not lie on the same line.

Theorems can be deduced from these axioms, for example:

Theorem. *Two different lines have at most one point in common.*

The way in which theorems are deduced in an axiomatic theory is generally cloaked in silence: the rules of logic are nothing more than 'common sense'; they can be learned by the method of example; and, in any case, they are 'evident', for example:

If the proposition A is true, the negation of A is false.

For a long time, the study of the rules of logic was left to "logicians" who did not all know mathematics (and whose research was considered sterile). This situation changed when mathematicians began to study mathematical entities whose character was no longer intuitively evident, so that the simple logic of common sense was no longer sufficient to grasp them.

The move from a 'naïve axiomatic theory' to the point of view of 'formal systems' is made when one realizes that the very concept of "rules of logic" is somewhat vague and must be made precise. But then the case becomes analogous to the one encountered at the level of the axioms: just as it was arbitrary to choose Euclid's axiom rather than Lobatchevski's, so there will remain something arbitrary in the way of choosing one set of rules of deduction rather than another for the construction of various formal systems.

2.2.2. Metalanguage

A formal system manipulates a language L, defined on a certain alphabet $\mathfrak{A}$, by means of axioms and rules of deduction. This will all be made clear in due time; for the moment, we note that, in order to speak of the elements of a formal system, the rules that they obey, etc., some language of communication must be used, and this language will contain the names of entities, the names of relations, etc. We shall use the English language as it is defined in dictionaries and grammars, and we will fill it out with other symbols than those which appear in the formal system.

Example. A formal system is defined on the alphabet $\mathfrak{A} = \{a, b, c\}$; one of its rules is concatenation. In order to speak of the words of this formal system we will use names like 'a b a c a', formed by the quotes «'» and «'», or names like A, B, etc. Note that ordinary English quotes have been used to form a name by citation, and that special quotes have been used to cite these special symbols.

To indicate the operation of concatenation, the sign "." will be used; we will write, for example: if A = 'a b a c a' and if B = 'b a', then A.B = 'a b a c a b a'. Note also the use of the sign "="; it signifies that what is written to the left and to the right of it are two *names* for the *same* entity.

All the preceding is intended to suggest to the reader what a *meta-language* is. Some authors use this word for a certain more formal system of signs, but which also requires an explanation, or a less formal one, which is used to describe a system in some meta-metalanguage. Still other authors call metalanguage that combination of language of communication and special signs which together allow of the description of a formal system. We shall generally adhere to this second point of view in order to avoid introducing a hierarchy of metalanguages, which is too subtle for our purposes.

The *metalinguistic* symbols which we shall use will therefore be defined by means of English sentences which will be as clear as possible. These symbols will therefore be, in essence, abbreviations.

Example. The alphabet of the system is

$$\mathfrak{A} = \{0, 1, 2, 3, 4, 5, 6, 7, 8, 9, +, -\}.$$

We would like to define two sets of words, namely, the set "integers without sign" and the set "integers". To formulate the required rules, we shall use a metalinguistic variable D whose values are on the set $\{0, 1, \ldots, 9\}$, a metalinguistic variable IWS whose values are on the set "integers without sign", and a variable I whose values are on the set "integers".

We will use the brackets "⟨" and "⟩" to set off the occurrences of the variables, the symbol "|" for one of the meanings of English "or" (the reader can decide which), and finally the symbol ": : =". This last symbol means that it is possible to rewrite what is on its left by any of the choices indicated to its right. Note also that we use the "classical" typographical arrangement to indicate concatenation (without any special symbol).

With this in mind, here are the rules:

Rule 1: $\langle IWS \rangle :: = \langle D \rangle | \langle IWS \rangle \langle D \rangle$

Rule 2: $\langle I \rangle :: = \langle IWS \rangle | + \langle IWS \rangle | - \langle IWS \rangle.$

Applying Rule 1, we obtain, for example:

$$\langle IWS \rangle :: = 3; \qquad \langle IWS \rangle :: = 35;$$

applying Rule 2 gives, for example

$$\langle I \rangle :: = -35.$$

Imagine that the alphabet of a formal system contains the letter "$\wedge$" and that a rule stipulates "If A and B are words of type θ, then the word $A \cdot \wedge \cdot B$ is a word of type θ". The English expression "if ... then" is perfectly clear in such a case. One might find it a bit long and consider replacing it by a *metalinguistic sign* like "$\Rightarrow$". At this point, the reader may be surprised that, after having inveighed against the vague and inadequate character of the "logic of common sense", we include in the metalanguage the "if ... then" $-$ disguised, if necessary, as "$\Rightarrow$" $-$, the "inclusive or", etc.

The answer is that a "language" must be used to communicate thought, but we limit the use of the metalanguage to the description of the rules. The "logic of common sense" is not used for deduction, but only for understanding and applying a "rule of the game". Furthermore, it is not our intention to *found* some mathematical theory, in the philosophical meaning of the term; our only purpose is to make our procedure perfectly precise. In order to decide whether this rather modest objective has been reached, we have an objective criterion at our disposal: the objective has been reached if all the machines constructed to apply the rules always give the same results under the same conditions.

2.2.3. Syntax and Meaning

Clearly, formal systems are not usually constructed for mere esthetical reasons or for pure pleasure; most frequently, a formal system is conceived as an idealized image of something else $-$ call it "a theory" $-$ with respect to which it takes on meaning. The formal system therefore formalizes the theory of which it is the *syntax*, whereas the theory gives the system an *interpretation*. The well-formed words (the correct sentences) of the system have meaning in the theory; conversely, to every proposition which has a meaning in the theory there should correspond in the system a class of well-formed words (correct sentences).

The question of the adequacy of a formal system for describing a theory is a problem in scientific methodology whose study must be conducted rationally, but which may fall beyond the limits of mathematics. We shall illustrate these rather general statements by reviewing the propositional calculus from a much more formal point of view.

2.3. A Formalized Variant of the Propositional Calculus

2.3.1. The Alphabet

There exists a denumerable set of abstract mathematical entities which make up an abstract alphabet. These entities are in a one-to-one correspondence with the typographic symbols which constitute the alphabet $\mathfrak{A}$:

$$\mathfrak{A} = \{], [, \neg, \supset, a_1, \ldots, a_n, \ldots\}.$$

Comments: } and { are in the metalanguage;] and [are the names for formal parentheses; $\neg$ is the name for formal negation; $\supset$ is the name for formal implication.

The a_i are the names of elementary objects called *atoms*, which form a denumerable set.

2.3.2. Formulae

In the monoid $\mathfrak{A}^*$, we shall first separate off a subset representing a (formal) language which corresponds to the set of concrete formulae (and these represent the abstract formulae). These rules, in effect, represent the "correct use" of parentheses and symbols.

The following are the rules concerning the set (F) of formulae:

F 1. Every atom is a formula;

F 2. If the word X is a formula, then the word $\neg X$ is also a formula;

F 3. If the words X and Y are formulae, then the word $[X \supset Y]$ is also a formula;

F 4. Every formula can be obtained from the atoms by applying the procedures F 2 and F 3 a certain number of times.

Here, X and Y are metalinguistic variables. In the formulation of these rules, we have deviated somewhat from strict usage.

Examples. a_1 is a formula, by F 1; a_2 is a formula, by F 1; $[a_1 \supset a_2]$ is a formula, by F 3; $\neg[a_1 \supset a_2]$ is a formula, by F 2; a_3 is a formula, by F 1; $[\neg[a_1 \supset a_2] \supset a_3]$ is a formula, by F 3 and the preceding example.

The set of formulae can be constructed by iteration, in order of increasing degree. The formulae of degree 1 are the atoms, and since there is no length-decreasing rule, all the formulae contain at least one atom. Then there are the formulae of degree 2:

$$\neg a_1, \neg a_2, \ldots, \neg a_n, \ldots$$

After these, there come the formulae of degree 3: $\neg\neg a_1, \ldots, \neg\neg a_n, \ldots$; then those of degree 4: $\neg\neg\neg a_1, \ldots, \neg\neg\neg a_n, \ldots$; those of degree 5:

$\neg\neg\neg\neg a_1, \ldots, \neg\neg\neg\neg a_n, \ldots$ and $[a_1 \supset a_1], [a_1 \supset a_2], \ldots, [a_n \supset a_p], \ldots$ etc.

Given a word $M \in \mathfrak{A}^*$, it is therefore possible to decide whether M is a formula. If M contains no atoms, M is not a formula. If M contains atoms, all the formulae of degree less than or equal to the degree of M are constructed by iteration. Then M is a formula if and only if it is to be found in this list. It is clear that this procedure is "mechanizable"; however, there is no point in discussing here whether or not such a procedure is "convenient" or "efficient".

Examples. $\neg[[$ is not a formula (there are no atoms). $[\neg a_2 \supset a_2]$ is a formula, for, starting with a_2 we have successively: a_2; $\neg a_2$; $\neg\neg a_2$; $\ldots a_2, [a_2 \ldots a_2], \neg\neg\neg\neg\neg a_2; \neg[a_2 \supset a_2]; [\neg a_2 \supset a_2],$ $[a_2 \supset \neg a_2]$.

2.3.3. The Set of Primitive Theses

We shall now consider another (formal) language, included in the preceding, which is called the set of *theses*. The theses correspond to what were called tautologies in the non-formal presentation.

We first define *primitive theses* by the following conventions: if the words X, Y, Z are formulae, then:

T 1. $[X \supset [Y \supset X]]$ is a primitive thesis;

T 2. $[[\neg X \supset \neg Y] \supset [Y \supset X]]$ is a primitive thesis;

T 3. $[[X \supset [Y \supset Z]] \supset [[X \supset Y] \supset [X \supset Z]]]$ is a primitive thesis;

T 4. All primitive theses are of the form T 1, T 2, or T 3.

If we consider the theses as *axioms*, then the preceding expressions, which are part of the metalanguage, are *axiom schemata*.

It is easily verified that the primitive theses are formulae by virtue of F 2 and F 3. It is also clear that, given a word M, it can be decided whether or not this word is a primitive thesis.

2.3.4. Some Comments on the Choice of Primitive Theses

We have already noted the "quasi-paradoxical" nature of the implication in T 1. We have also noted that T 2 gives rise to contraposition. We now remark the following: if we start with the concept of truth, it is clear that $\neg(\neg p) = p$, and we may write indifferently: $[\neg X \supset \neg Y] \supset [Y \supset X]$, or $[Y \supset X] \supset [\neg X \supset \neg Y]$. But this is not the case if we do not bring in the concept of truth from the very beginning (i.e., if we have some other interpretation in mind).

The choice of T 3 is technically rather convenient. Starting with the primitive theses, we form the theses by choosing a rule of deduction *a priori*.

2.3.5. The Rule of Deduction

If the words X and $[X \supset Y]$ are theses, then the word Y is also a thesis. It follows easily that the theses are necessarily formulae.

 Comment: Note that this rule is nothing more than the rule of *modus ponens*.

2.3.6. Examples of Deduction

As an example, we shall prove that $[a_1 \supset a_1]$, or more generally, $[X \supset X]$, is a thesis. To this end, we shall construct a thesis in which $[a_1 \supset a_1]$ is to be found in a position where *modus ponens* can be applied.

 (1) a_1 is a formula, by F 1.

 (2) The word $[a_1 \supset a_1]$, which will be called M, is a formula by (1) and F 3.

 (3) The word $[a_1 \supset M]$ is then a formula, by (1), (2), and F 3.

 (4) The word $[a_1 \supset M]$ is a thesis by (1) and T 1.

 (5) The word $[a_1 \supset [M \supset a_1]]$ is a thesis, by (1), (2), and T 1.

 (6) The word $[[a_1 \supset [M \supset a_1]] \supset [[a_1 \supset M] \supset [a_1 \supset a_1]]]$ is a thesis, by (1), (2), and T 3.

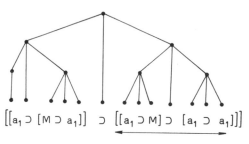

Fig. 2-1

 (7) The section of Fig. 2-1 underlined by an arrow is a thesis by *modus ponens*.

 (8) $[a_1 \supset a_1]$ is a thesis, by (4), (7), and *modus ponens*.

 In the same way, it can be shown for any formula X that $[X \supset X]$ is a thesis.

2.3.7. Conclusion

By following *a rule of the game*, we have built a "system" which consists of two nested parts, and a meaning can be attributed to this system: it formalizes the "intuitive propositional calculus", hence it formalizes, after a fashion, the "logic of common sense". Note that the system thus built is independent of the interpretation given it; we have given it an interpretation, but there is no reason why it cannot be given a different one.

It remains to show how the semantic interpretation, namely, the use of truth values, can be incorporated rigorously, starting with the formal system; we shall not do this here.

2.4. Definition of Formal Systems

2.4.0.

We shall now systematize what has been presented thus far.

2.4.1. Formal Systems

A logistic system[1] is a mathematical structure defined by a quadruple of sets:

$$\mathfrak{S} = \langle \mathfrak{X}, \mathfrak{F}, \mathfrak{A}, \mathbf{R} \rangle.$$

1. $\mathfrak{X}$ is a denumerable alphabet whose letters can be considered to have been numbered;

2. $\mathfrak{F}$ is a (formal) language on $\mathfrak{X}$, which is called the set of formulae. We have: $\mathfrak{F} \subset \mathfrak{X}^*$.

3. $\mathfrak{A}$ is a subset of $\mathfrak{F}$ which is called the set of axioms. It can be defined by means of axiom schemata.

4. $\mathbf{R}$ is a set of rules of deduction to be specified below.

2.4.2. The Rules of Deduction

Consider the cartesian product $\mathfrak{F} \times \cdots \times \mathfrak{F}$ having n factors ($n \geq 1$) and whose elements are the ordered n-tuples of formulae. A rule of deduction $\mathfrak{R}$ is a rule which allows us to associate a certain unique formula x with certain of these n-tuples $\langle y_1, y_2, \ldots, y_n \rangle$. More precisely, a rule $\mathfrak{R}$ is defined by a subset of the cartesian product $\mathfrak{F}^n \times \mathfrak{F}$, and its *domain* is a subset of $\mathfrak{F}^n$. During the application of the rule, $y_1, \ldots, y_n$ are the *antecedents*, x is the *consequence*, and all these formulae are the *arguments* of the rule.

2.4.3. Particular Cases

It may be that $\mathfrak{X}$ is finite, $\mathfrak{F}$ coincides with $\mathfrak{X}^*$ and that there is but one axiom: this is the case for the *combinatorial systems* which we shall study later. There may be no axioms at all, i.e., $\mathfrak{A}$ is empty: this is the case for the Markov algorithms.

---

[1] Following the terminology proposed by J. Porte in "Recherches sur la théorie générale des systèmes formels et sur les systèmes connectifs", Paris, Gauthier-Villars, 1965.

2.4.4. Deducibility

Let $\Phi = \langle f_1, f_2, \ldots, f_k \rangle$ be an ordered k-tuple of formulae. If there exists a rule $\Re$ and a formula x such that $\Phi \Re x$ obtains, x is said to be an *immediate consequence* of Φ. The set **R** of relations of deduction therefore defines the relation of *immediate deducibility*. We shall write $\Phi \mathbf{R} x$ if and only if there exists a relation $\Re$ with $\Phi \Re x$. This relation is defined in the cartesian product of the set of series of formulae by the set of formulae.

Consider now all the series obtained by taking occurrences of elements of Φ or axioms: we obtain a set E_0 of formulae. Consider all the immediate consequences of the sequences formed with the help of E_0, and add them to E_0: we obtain a set E_1. Continuing in this way, every formula so obtained is a *consequence of* Φ. By choosing a series of formulae which enable us to go from Φ to y, we obtain a deduction of y from Φ.

We shall write $\Phi \underset{\mathfrak{S}}{\vDash} y$ if and only if y is deducible from Φ in $\mathfrak{S}$.

Remarks.

a) Only the elements of Φ have a role here; their order is irrelevant. The set of elements of Φ is called the set of *premisses*.

b) If a set Ψ contains the elements of Φ and if $\Phi \underset{\mathfrak{S}}{\vDash} y$, then clearly $\Psi \underset{\mathfrak{S}}{\vDash} y$ also obtains: "premisses can be added on".

c) Immediate deducibility implies deducibility.

d) Every formula can be deduced from itself.

2.4.5. The Theses of the System

The formulae which can be deduced from the axioms alone are called the theses of a system. One characteristic property of the theses is that they can be deduced from every set of premisses *including the empty set*. Then $\varnothing \underset{\mathfrak{S}}{\vDash} y$ will be abbreviated as $\underset{\mathfrak{S}}{\vdash} y$.

2.4.6. Exercises

1. Prove that immediate deducibility implies deducibility and that every formula can be deduced from itself.

2. Let a formal system be defined which has the same alphabet, the same set of formulae and the same rule of deduction as the system which was constructed for the exposition of the propositional calculus. The axiom schemata are the following:

T 1 $[X \supset [Y \supset X]]$,
T 2 $[[X \supset [Y \supset Z]] \supset [[X \supset Y] \supset [X \supset Z]]]$,
T 3 $[\neg X \supset [X \supset Y]]$.

Decide whether the following formulae are theses or not:

(1) $[[Y \supset Z] \supset [[X \supset Y] \supset [X \supset Z]]]$,

(2) $[X \supset [[X \supset Y] \supset Y]]$,

(3) $[[X \supset Y] \supset [Y \supset Z] \supset [X \supset Z]]$.

3. In the system of exercise 2, can the formula $[Y \supset [X \supset Z]]$ be deduced from the formula $[X \supset [Y \supset Z]]$?

4. In § 2.3.1 we considered an *infinite* alphabet. Show that the definition can be so modified that the alphabet is finite.

5. In § 2.2.1 several axioms concerning the concepts of point and straight line were given. With the help this time of *semantic* considerations, i.e., considerations which involve the content, the *model* of a system, show that the axiom "two points which lie on a straight line determine that line" is not a consequence of the axiom "any two points determine a straight line on which they lie".

To show this, first replace the word "point" by the word "gizmo" and the word "straight line" by the word "widget". Then find an interpretation of a gizmo and a widget which will satisfy the second axiom above, but not the first.

Chapter III
Combinatorial Systems

3.0.

Combinatorial systems are formal systems of a particular kind; as their name indicates, they are of interest in the study of those mechanisms which involve problems of a *combinatorial* nature that deal in particular with the words of a free monoid. We shall begin with a presentation of the concepts which allow the rules of deduction in a combinatorial system to be formulated.

In this book, we shall consider the free monoid defined on the alphabet: $\mathfrak{A} = \{a_i \mid 1 \leq i \leq n\}$; in the examples, lower-case latin letters will be used. Also, we use E for the empty word, and |A| for the degree of word A.

3.1. The Definition of Combinatorial Systems

3.1.1. Productions

When speaking of the word calculus, we introduced relations like 'a r a' ~ 'r u' which could be taken in either direction. In this chapter, our point of view changes: an *orientation* will be systematically introduced into our rules.

We define productions (or rewriting rules) by means of a couple $(G, \bar{G})$ and write

$$G \rightarrow \bar{G}$$

or

$$P G Q \rightarrow P \bar{G} Q. \tag{1}$$

P, Q, G, and $\bar{G}$ are elements of $\mathfrak{A}^*$, G and $\bar{G}$ define the productions, and P and Q are variables that range over those parts of the word to which the production applies. Let X be such a word; if X can be analyzed as

$$X = P G Q, \qquad \text{for every } P, Q,$$

then the production $G \rightarrow \bar{G}$ applies, and

$$Y = P \bar{G} Q$$

is called the *consequence of the word* X with respect to the production (1).

The associated production

$$P \bar{G} Q \rightarrow P G Q$$

is the inverse production of (1).

(1) is actually a production schema, rather than a single production. Since P and Q are variables, (1) corresponds in fact to an arbitrary number of productions.

3.1.2. Definitions

In order to define a combinatorial system, the following must be given:

1. A *finite* alphabet $\mathfrak{A}$, called the alphabet of the system, and if need be, an auxiliary alphabet $\mathfrak{B}$ to be used in writing the productions.

2. A distinguished, non-empty word, called the *axiom* of the system.

3. A finite number of production schemata.

From the preceding, it is seen that a combinatorial system is a formal system in which:

1. All the words on $\mathfrak{A}$, and if $\mathfrak{B}$ is used, on $\mathfrak{A} \cup \mathfrak{B}$, are formulae;

2. The set of primitive theses is reduced to a single word, the axiom;

3. The rules of deduction are given by the productions.

We shall illustrate with examples after defining certain particular systems.

3.1.3. Different Types of Productions

Productions of the type

$$P G Q \rightarrow P \bar{G} Q$$

will be called *semi-Thue*[1] productions; their inverses are also semi-Thue productions. We shall use the following shortened notation for the semi-Thue productions:

$$G \to \bar{G}$$

without introducing any ambiguity.

Productions of the type

$$G P \to P \bar{G}$$

are called *normal* productions. In this case, the variable must appear explicitly. Their inverses are said to be *anti-normal;* we have

$$P \bar{G} \to G P.$$

We shall however take

$$|G| \, |\bar{G}| \neq 0.$$

Example. Let $G = $ 'off', $\bar{G} = $ 'back'. For $P = $ 'set', the normal production $G P \to P \bar{G}$ yields 'offset' → 'setback'. The antinormal production $P \bar{G} \to G P$, under these same conditions, gives 'setback' → 'offset'.

3.1.4. Special Systems

A semi-Thue system contains only semi-Thue productions.

A Thue system is a semi-Thue system which has an inverse production for each of its productions.

A normal system has only normal productions.

A Post system is a system having only normal productions and their inverses.

3.1.5. Examples of Thue Systems

Example 1. The alphabet of the system is $\mathfrak{A} = \{a, b\}$. The auxiliary alphabet is $\mathfrak{B} = \{s\}$. The axiom is the word 's'. There are two semi-Thue productions:

$$s \to a \, b; \tag{1}$$

$$s \to a \, s \, b. \tag{2}$$

The word   s   has the consequence   asb,   by (2).
The word   asb   has the consequence   aasbb,   by (2).
The word   aasbb has the consequence   aaasbbb,   by (2).
The word aaasbbb has the consequence aaaabbbb, by (1).

Note that this last word is written entirely in the alphabet of the system and can have no consequence. The way that the word 'aaaabbbb'

---

[1] The term Thue production is reserved for the case where the rules of transformation are not oriented. This is why we use the prefix 'semi'.

has been reached can be represented by the following tree:

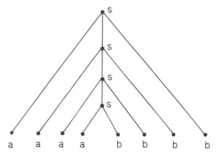

a   a   a   a   b   b   b   b   Fig. 3-1

The possibility of associating a tree with the successive formation of the words, which "grow from each other" according to the rules, arises when the left sides of the productions contain words of one letter only. If we were to introduce, for example, the production

$$a\,a\,b\,b \rightarrow b\,a, \tag{3}$$

it would no longer be possible to develop a tree.

Example 2. In this example we shall use the following terminology: vocabulary (instead of alphabet), sentence (instead of word), etc. The terminal vocabulary of the system is:

$$r = \{the, a, child, banana, picks, eats\}.$$

The auxiliary vocabulary is

S,   for sentence;
NP, for noun phrase;
VP, for verb phrase;
Art, for article;
N,   for noun;
V,   for verb.

The axiom of the system is the string 'S'. The productions are semi-Thue productions:

$$S \rightarrow NP\ VP; \tag{1}$$

$$NP \rightarrow Art\ N; \tag{2}$$

$$VP \rightarrow V\ NP; \tag{3}$$

$$Art \rightarrow the; \tag{4}$$

$$Art \rightarrow a; \tag{4a}$$

$$N \rightarrow child; \tag{5}$$

$$N \rightarrow banana; \tag{5a}$$

$$V \rightarrow picks; \tag{6}$$

$$V \rightarrow eats. \tag{6a}$$

The first three rules correspond, *grosso modo*, to the rules of English syntax: "in order to make a sentence, write a noun phrase followed by a verb phrase", "in order to make a noun phrase, write an article followed by a noun", etc. The other rules make it possible to set the value of a grammatical category equal to a particular word of that category.

The reader may verify that the application of the rules above leads to the following tree (which may be constructed for the reasons given in example 1):

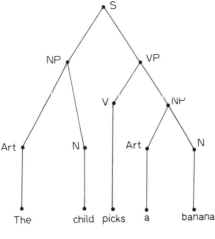

Fig. 3-2

We have obtained the sentence "The child picks a banana" which has no consequence.

In a similar fashion we may obtain sentences like "A child eats the banana" or "The banana picks the child". The former is an ordinary English sentence, and the latter might be found in a book like "Alice in Wonderland".

Example 3. The alphabet is {s, b, c}; the axiom is 's'; the semi-Thue productions are:

$$s \rightarrow s\,b; \tag{1}$$

$$s \rightarrow c; \tag{2}$$

$$c\,b\,b \rightarrow b\,b\,s. \tag{3}$$

Because of production (3) it is not possible to represent by a tree any sequence of words which are derived from each other. But it is possible to represent by means of a directed graph the appearance of each of the successive words.

The number of the production used is indicated on each line of the graph; production (1) is directed to the left, production (2) to the right, and production (3) is directed down:

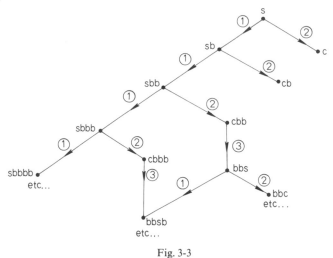

Fig. 3-3

Note that there are two different paths leaving s and arriving at b b s b.

3.1.6. Proof; Theorems

Let Γ be a combinatorial system and let there be given a finite sequence of words: $X_1, X_2, \ldots, X_m(\Sigma)$, where X_1 is the distinguished word
(the axiom) of the system and each word X_j, for $1 < j \le m$, is a consequence
of X_{j-1} with respect to a production of Γ. We will say that the sequence
(Σ) is a *proof* in Γ and that the last word of (Σ) is a *theorem* of Γ. Under
these conditions, it is clear why the distinguished word, which is the
origin of every proof, is called the *axiom* of the system.

The move from word X_{j-1} to word X_j constitutes a step in the proof
(Davis calls each word X_j a step, which seems less natural). Instead of
'proof of a theorem' we may also speak of the *derivation of a word* (or of
a sentence if the base set is called a vocabulary). It may happen that a
proposition concerning all the words of the system or all the words of a
certain class is proven. If any misunderstanding is possible, such a
proposition will be called a *metatheorem*: it is stated in a *metalanguage*,
with respect to the system.

Example 1. Consider again the first example of § 3.1.5. The alphabet
is {a, b}, the axiom is 's', and the productions are s → a b; s → a s b. The
theorem a a a a b b b b was proven and illustrated with a tree.

The proposition "all the words of the system not containing the
letter s can be obtained by concatenating to a word made up of occurrences of a a word of the same length made up of occurrences of b"
is a metatheorem.

Example 2. In the third example of § 3.1.5, illustrated by the graph of Fig. 3-3, the word 'b b s b' is a theorem for which two distinct proofs were given. A proposition like "there exist an infinite number of theorems in this system which have two proofs" is a metatheorem.

3.1.7. Monogenic Systems

A combinatorial system is called *monogenic* if every theorem has at most *one* consequence with respect to the productions of the system. Monogenicity excludes then the existence of a word X such that:

1. X can be decomposed in two distinct ways into PGQ and $P'G'Q'$,

2. there exist in Γ two productions whose left members are precisely PGQ and $P'G'Q'$.

Example 1. The system in example 1 of § 3.1.5 is not monogenic since the word s has two distinct consequences, namely a b and a s b. The system having the alphabet {a, b, c}, the auxiliary alphabet {s, t, u}, the axiom 's' and the productions:

$$s \to a\,t\,b;$$
$$a\,t\,b \to a\,a\,u\,b\,b;$$
$$u \to c$$

is a monogenic system comprising only a finite number of theorems.

Example 2. The system having the alphabet {a, b, s}, the axiom 's', and the production $s \to a\,s\,b$ is a monogenic system comprising an infinite number of theorems.

3.1.8. Ambiguity

From the most general point of view possible, we shall consider two proofs of a theorem to be different if they differ from each other by the words that they contain or by the order of these words (or by both). The terminal word (sentence) of a proof is ambiguous if there exist at least two different proofs of it. In the applications, we may introduce various stronger or weaker concepts of ambiguity.

Example. In example 3 of § 3.1.5 such a situation was encountered: the word b b s b had two paths leading to it. The following is another example.

Consider the system defined by the alphabet $\mathfrak{A} = \{a, b, c, s\}$, the axiom s, and the productions:

$$s \to a\,s; \qquad (1)$$

$$s \to s\,b; \qquad (2)$$

$$s \to a\,s\,b; \qquad (3)$$

$$s \to c. \qquad (4)$$

The theorem a c b is ambiguous. In effect, we have:

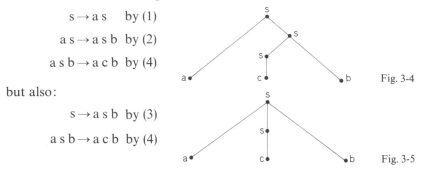

$s \rightarrow a\, s$ by (1)

$a\, s \rightarrow a\, s\, b$ by (2)

$a\, s\, b \rightarrow a\, c\, b$ by (4)

Fig. 3-4

but also:

$s \rightarrow a\, s\, b$ by (3)

$a\, s\, b \rightarrow a\, c\, b$ by (4)

Fig. 3-5

3.2. Normal Systems

3.2.0. Normal System

A *normal system* is defined by:

    1. An alphabet $\mathfrak{A} = \{a_i | 1 \leq i \leq n\}$;

    2. An axiom A;

    3. v normal productions (production schemata):

$$\{G_j\, P \rightarrow P\, \bar{G}_j | 1 \leq j \leq v\}$$

where $A, G_j, \bar{G}_j$ are words of the free monoid generated by $\mathfrak{A}$.

Example. The alphabet is $\{a, b\}$, the axiom is 'a', and the production schemata are: $a\, P \rightarrow P\, b\, b\, a$, $b\, P \rightarrow P\, a\, b\, a$. A proof: $a \rightarrow b\, b\, a \rightarrow b\, a\, a\, b\, a$.

3.2.1. Normal System Canonically Associated with a Semi-Thue System

For simplicity of notation, we shall adopt a system whose alphabet contains only three letters, but it is easily verified that this choice in no way affects the generality of the proof. Consider then a semi-Thue (S T) system defined by the following:

    Alphabet: $\mathfrak{A} = \{a, b, c\}$;

    Axiom: A;   (S T)

    Productions: $P\, G_i\, Q \rightarrow P\, \bar{G}_i\, Q$, $1 \leq i \leq m$.

We will now construct from the system (S T) a normal system (N) having the same axiom A and whose theorems can be grouped into theorems associated by a certain equivalence in such a way that:

Every theorem of (S T) is a theorem of (N); every theorem of (N) belongs to an association class in which a theorem of (S T) appears.

Fig. 3-6 below illustrates this system-to-system correspondence.

To construct (N) we shall first double the alphabet by introducing the primed letters a', b', c'. To each word M written with $\mathfrak{A}$ there now corresponds the word M' obtained by adding primes; we take E'=E.

This enables us to define (N), as follows:

Alphabet: $\mathfrak{B} = \{a, b, c, a', b', c'\}$;

Axiom: A;

Productions. They can be divided into three types: (N)

(1) a P → P a', and analogous ones;

(2) a' P → P a, and analogous ones;

(3) G_i P → P $\overline{G}_i'$, $1 \leq i \leq m$.

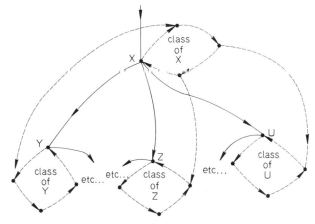

Fig. 3-6. X, Y, Z, theorem of (ST); ⟶ semi-Thue productions; --→ normal productions

Associated Words. The productions of type (1) and (2) shift a letter through a word, from the far left to far right, on the condition that the prime is changed (i.e., prime the letter if it is unprimed, and take off the prime if it is primed). Let then u, v, w, ... be variables representing letters of $\mathfrak{B}$, and $\hat{u}, \hat{v}, \hat{w}, ...$ variables which are oppositely primed with respect to the preceding letters, respectively. Let us start with a word like w u u v, and successively apply to it the one production possible, either of type (1) or of type (2). We obtain the following cyclic schema by (1) or (2):

$$
\begin{array}{l}
\text{w u u v} \longleftarrow \\
\quad \text{u u v } \hat{w} \\
\quad\quad \text{u v } \hat{w} \; \hat{u} \\
\quad\quad\quad \text{v } \hat{w} \; \hat{u} \; \hat{u} \\
\quad\quad\quad\quad \hat{w} \; \hat{u} \; \hat{u} \; \hat{v} \\
\quad\quad\quad\quad\quad \hat{u} \; \hat{u} \; \hat{v} \text{ w} \\
\quad\quad\quad\quad\quad\quad \hat{u} \; \hat{v} \text{ w u} \\
\quad\quad\quad\quad\quad\quad\quad \hat{v} \text{ w u u} \\
\quad\quad\quad\quad\quad\quad\quad\quad \text{w u u v} \longleftarrow
\end{array}
$$

Fig. 3-7

In this way we define an equivalence class made up of *associated words*. In particular, starting from a word M on $\mathfrak{A}$, we reach the word M′ which is one of its associates: to see this, it suffices in Fig. 3-7 to interpret the presence (absence) of a circumflex accent as the presence (absence) of a prime.

Note then that the associates of any word of $\mathfrak{A}^*$, and those only, are of the form PQ′ or P′Q, with P, Q ∈ $\mathfrak{A}^*$. We shall call words of this kind *regular*.

Direct Proposition. We shall now prove that the theorems of a semi-Thue system (ST) are also theorems of a normal system (N). The following lemma is immediately seen:

Lemma 1. *Every associate of a theorem of (N) is a theorem of (N).*

In effect, the associates of a theorem are derived from the latter by productions of (N). Note now that the proposition which is to be established is true for the axiom A, which is common to the two systems. Since all the theorems derive from A, it suffices to show that the property is preserved under the productions of (ST).

Let us suppose that the theorem X of (ST) is a theorem of (N). In order for X to have a consequence in (ST), it must be possible to write it in one of the forms $X = P G_i Q$. It then generates the theorem $P \overline{G}_i Q = \overline{X}$. But, by virtue of Lemma 1, the word $G_i Q P'$, an associate of X, is a theorem of (N). If the appropriate production of (3) is applied to this last word, we obtain the word $Q P' \overline{G}_i'$ which is another theorem of (N). This word is an associate of $P \overline{G}_i Q$ which, by virtue of Lemma 1, is therefore a theorem of (N).   Q.E.D.

Reciprocal Proposition. Every theorem of (N) is regular and is an associate of a theorem of (ST).

We shall proceed in the much the same way as above. The axiom A of (N) is regular and it is the associate of a word of (ST), namely, itself. It suffices then to show that the two properties (of regularity and association) are preserved under the productions of (N). It is evident that these properties are preserved for productions of type (1) or (2). Let us examine the effect of productions of type (3).

Suppose the two properties hold for the theorem $G_i P$. Since we have $G_i \neq E$, the regularity of $G_i P$ implies that it can be written in the form $G_i P_1 P_2'$ with P_1 and P_2 in (ST). The only possible associate in (ST) of $G_i P$ is $P_2 G_i P_1$ and by our hypothesis it is necessarily a theorem of (ST). It follows from this that $P_2 \overline{G}_i P_1$ is also a theorem of (ST); but $P_2 \overline{G}_i P_1$ is associated with $P_1 P_2' \overline{G}_i'$ which is regular.

We have now shown that $P \overline{G}_i'$, obtained from $G_i P$ by means of a production of type (3) in (N), preserves the two properties of being regular and an associate of a theorem of (ST). This concludes the proof.

Summary. Given a semi-Thue system with alphabet {a, b, c, ...}, we can associate with it a normal system with alphabet {a, a', b, b', c, c', ...} such that the theorems of the semi-Thue system are just those theorems of the associated system which do not contain primed letters.

3.3. Exercises

Exercises 1, 2, and 3 deal with ambiguity.

1. Consider the system: $\mathfrak{A} = \{a, b, c\}$; Axiom: 'a'; Productions $a \rightarrow b$; $b \rightarrow c$ and $c \rightarrow a$. Is the system monogenic? Is the theorem 'c' ambiguous?

Conclusion. Does monogenicity exclude ambiguity?

2. In the example of § 3.1.8, the word 'a c b' is ambiguous because of the possibility of *branchings* from s. Consider now the system: $\mathfrak{A} = \{a, b, s\}$; Axiom: 's'; productions $s \rightarrow a b$; $s \rightarrow a s b$. Is the system monogenic? Are the theorems ambiguous?

Conclusion. Is the presence of possible branch points a sufficient condition for there to be ambiguity?

3. A system contains productions of the form $a \rightarrow a$ and $b \rightarrow E$. On the basis of this example criticize the very general definition of ambiguity which we have given.

Give a second criticism on the basis of the system: $\mathfrak{A} = \{A, B, C, b, c\}$; axiom: A; productions: $A \rightarrow B C$; $B \rightarrow b$; $C \rightarrow c$.

4. Carry out the construction of (N) for the (ST) system given by:

$$\mathfrak{A} = \{a, b, c\}; \quad \text{axiom: 'c'}; \quad \text{productions: } P c Q \rightarrow P a c b Q.$$

3.4. "Non-Influence" of the Alphabet

3.4.0.

It is known to be possible to code an alphabet by means of the letters of another alphabet which are fewer in number than those of the first alphabet. The Morse code is an example of a reduction to three elementary signs, namely, the dit, the dah, and a separating space. In certain codings, a symbol is associated with this space, in others the space is made 'by itself'.

A binary code is used in computing machines; if the words contain n binary occurrences, 2^n letters can be coded. However, it will be noted that the organization of the memory into memory cells introduces separators.

3.4.1. Binary Coding

It is therefore possible to associate with every combinatorial system (S) an equivalent system $(\hat{S})$ written in the alphabet {0, 1}. Here is one way of doing this.

Let $\mathfrak{A} = \{a_1, \ldots, a_n\}$ be the alphabet of (S). We set

$\hat{a}_i = $ '1 0 0 ... 0 1'   with $i+1$ symbols "0", or for short:

$\hat{a}_i = $ '1 0^{i+1} 1'.

With the word $M = a_{i_1} \ldots a_{i_p}$ we associate the word: $\hat{M} = \hat{a}_{i_1} \ldots \hat{a}_{i_p}$, and the empty word $\hat{E}$ with the empty word E.

This procedure maps the monoid $\mathfrak{A}^*$ onto a subset $\mathfrak{M}^*$ of $\{0, 1\}^*$; the mapping of $\mathfrak{A}^*$ into $\mathfrak{M}^*$ is injective. More precisely, given a word of $\{0, 1\}$ we can:

1. decide whether it belongs to $\mathfrak{M}^*$,

2. if it is in $\mathfrak{M}^*$, find the unique word M from which it comes.

We shall say that a word written in the alphabet $\{0, 1\}$ is well-formed if it is in $\mathfrak{M}^*$, i.e., if it comes from a word of $\mathfrak{A}^*$.

3.4.2. The Construction of ($\hat{S}$).

If (S) is defined by the axiom A and the productions

$$P\,G_i\,Q \rightarrow P\,\bar{G}_i\,Q \qquad i = 1, \ldots, m$$

we take the axiom $\hat{A}$ and the productions

$$\hat{P}\,\hat{G}_i\,\hat{Q} \rightarrow \hat{P}\,\hat{\bar{G}}_i\,\hat{Q} \qquad i = 1, \ldots, m.$$

Proposition 1. If M is a theorem of (S), then $\hat{M}$ is a theorem of ($\hat{S}$). In effect, we see that if $M_1, \ldots, M_q, M$ is a proof of M in (S), then $\hat{M}_1, \ldots, \hat{M}_q, \hat{M}$ is a proof of $\hat{M}$ in ($\hat{S}$).   Q.E.D.

Proposition 2. Every theorem of ($\hat{S}$) is well-formed. This is a property of the axiom and is preserved under the productions.   Q.E.D.

Proposition 3. Every theorem of ($\hat{S}$) comes from a theorem of (S). Since it is well-formed, a theorem of ($\hat{S}$) is of the form $\hat{M}$ with $M \in \mathfrak{A}^*$ and this is true of all the theorems that enter into its proof. The proof of $\hat{M}$ in ($\hat{S}$) thus furnishes us with a proof of M in (S).   Q.E.D.

3.4.3. Decidability of a Combinatorial System

Using Gödel's techniques of arithmetization and construction of predicates, it can be shown that the set of theorems of a combinatorial system is recursively denumerable. This property leaves open the question of whether the set of theorems is recursive; if it is, the system is said to be *decidable*.

The alphabet has no effect on the decidability of a system in the sense that to every system (S) there can be associated the system ($\hat{S}$) whose alphabet contains just two symbols and for which the decision problem has the same answer.

3.4.4. Exercises

1. What can be said about $(\hat{S})$ in the following cases: (S) is a semi-Thue, a Thue, a normal, or a Post system?

2. Find a more economical coding than $\hat{a}_i = 1\,0^{i+1}\,1$ by showing that it is not necessary to have two markers.

3. Code the alphabet $\{a, b, c, d\}$ by replacing a, b, c and d by 0, 10, 110, and 111 respectively. Is a symbol of separation necessary? Same question for the coding $0\,0, 0\,1, 1\,0, 1\,1$, and again for the coding $0, 1, 10, 11$.

Chapter IV

Algorithms   Turing Machines

4.1. Algorithms

4.1.1. The Concept of an Algorithm

In grade school we study "the four operations". Once having learnt and understood multiplication, the schoolboy knows how to do all multiplications: he has memorized an algorithm. Intuitively, an algorithm is a set of rules which enable every particular case of an operation, which corresponds to a certain kind of operation, to be carried out mechanically. One can also say that an algorithm is a mechanical procedure which, when applied to a certain class of symbols (input symbols), ultimately produces an *output* symbol.

Example 1. *Differentiation of polynomials.*

1. Take a monomial of the polynomial (if there are any; otherwise write "finished");
2. Take the exponent of the variable and
a) multiply it by the coefficient and take this result as the new coefficient;
b) reduce it by 1 and take this as the new exponent;
3. Go back to 1.

Example 2. *Dictionary Look-up.*

1. Take the first letter of the word and find the section in the dictionary which begins with this letter;
2. Take the first three letters of the word and find the first of the pages, in the section just found in 1., whose words begin with these three letters;

3. Starting at this page, look at each of the words of the dictionary and compare them with the word to be found until this latter has been found, or one is certain not to be able to find it;

4. Examine the dictionary equivalents when the word has been found;

5. If the word has not been found, take a more complete dictionary and go back to 1.

The procedures given in these two examples are mechanical — in the intuitive meaning of this word — but would require much more detail if we wanted to have them carried out by some unintelligent agent; many of the operations that must be done have not been mentioned. In order to make the concept of an algorithm more precise, a certain number of characteristics seem to be essential (H. Rogers, Jr.):

a) An algorithm is a set of instructions of *finite size* (where its size may be measured in terms of the number of symbols required to state the rules, for example);

b) An operator (human, mechanical, optical, etc. or electronic) responds to the instructions and carries out the computation;

c) Certain devices (pencil and paper, toothed wheels, magnetic memories, etc.) allow the various steps of the computation to be executed, stored and brought back again;

d) *The procedures are essentially discrete* (although the objects treated by these procedures may have a continuous character);

e) The set of *elementary operations* to be carried out is perfectly determined (it will be called *deterministic*): at each step there is just one possible way of going on to the next step.

The analogy of this concept with the pair "electronic computer, program" is clear:

a) corresponds to the program;

b) corresponds to the electronic computer in which the program is executed;

c) corresponds to the computer's memory;

d) corresponds to the numerical ('digital') — and not analog — character of the computer;

e) corresponds to the mechanical, deterministic character of the machine execution of a program.

4.1.2. Algorithms and Formal Grammars

The concept of an algorithm plays a rôle in formal linguistics in the following way. We have defined a (formal) language L on an alphabet $\mathfrak{A}$ (or on a vocabulary $\mathfrak{B}$); L is a set of words (or sentences) which belong to the free monoid $\mathfrak{A}^*$ (or $\mathfrak{B}^*$) generated by $\mathfrak{A}$ (or by $\mathfrak{B}$). The language L represents the set of permitted words (or the permitted sentences), i.e., the syntactically correct ones. The set of words which are not permitted (or the incorrect sentences) is represented by $\mathfrak{A}^*\backslash L$.

The goal of a grammar is therefore to specify the rules which generate a well-formed word (a correct sentence) or which recognize whether a sequence of letters (words) is or is not a well-formed word (a correct sentence). In other words, the goal of a grammar is to characterize the words (sentences) which belong to a language. A formal grammar is therefore an algorithm (a set of rules characterizing a language).

If we refer now to the concept of algorithm as defined in § 4.1.1, we can take the input symbols to be the names 1, 2, ..., n, ... of whole numbers and also take each input of a whole number to correspond to the output of a word (sentence) of the language defined by the algorithm — or grammar — which *enumerates* the words (sentences) of a language.

Example 1. The alphabet is $\mathfrak{A} = \{0, 1, 2, 3, 4, 5, 6, 7, 8, 9\}$; a word belongs to L if and only if this word is the decimal representation of a prime number. One possible algorithm can be based on the sieve of Eratosthenes.

Example 2. The alphabet is $\mathfrak{A} = \{1, 2, 3, 4, 5, 6, 7, 8, 9\}$; the language L is defined in the following way. Consider the infinite decimal representation of the number π. A sequence is a word of L if and only if it is contained between two successive occurrences of 0 in this representation. The algorithm is derived from the computation of π.

4.1.3.

Another type of algorithmic problem which arises naturally is the following:

Given a string of occurrences of letters (words), decide whether it is or is not a well-formed word (a correct sentence).

Example. A programming language comprises basic symbols and rules given by a manual (which, if it serves its purpose correctly, constitutes the grammar of the language). A correct program is a correct sentence of this language, and vice-versa.

The compilation of a program for any given machine is an operation that is rather difficult to define formally; roughly speaking, it can be considered as a "translation" from one language to another: to correct sequences of the input language there correspond correct sequences of the output language. The compiler contains a *check* of the correctness of the syntax of the input program. This check constitutes an algorithm with two possible output symbols (which may be represented by "correct" and "not correct"); the appearance of one of them excludes the appearance of the other.

One can easily see that an algorithm of enumeration does not guarantee the existence of an algorithm for recognition of correctness. In example 1, § 4.1.2, it can be decided whether a number is prime or not. In Example 2, although the question is easy to formulate, there does not presently exist — at least, not to our knowledge — an algorithm which gives the answer. It may well be proven one day that it is impossible to construct such an algorithm.

Up to this point, we have given only an intuitive definition of what we mean by an algorithm. This concept can be formalized, and has been formalized in numerous ways which have proved to be equivalent. Among others, one can use for this purpose the combinatorial systems which we have already presented, or the Turing machines which we shall study in this chapter.

4.1.4. Computability

The concept of a Turing machine is intended to formalize the intuitive concept of computability (hence, the intuitive concept of an algorithm). The point of departure is a psychological concept of computability: an agent, a human being in general, is given certain data and rules for processing these data; he is required to reach a result which depends on the data. It frequently happens that a human being can say whether the desired result is computable or not, for this person possesses a certain computational experience which is based on the examples he may already have encountered. Thus, for example, he might say:

1. The number π is not computable since it contains an *infinite* number of decimals;

2. The approximate (lower) rounded value of π to within 10^{-n} is computable when n is given.

But there are cases where it is not obvious if one can say whether the result asked for is computable or not.

Note that this concept of computability disregards the limitations inherent in men and machines. Some computations may require a number of memory elements greater than the number of elementary particles of our galaxy and a computation time of the order of billions of centuries. Nevertheless, independently of these material limitations, we can see or prove whether a certain computation really enables us to reach a result after a *finite* number of steps. A number of mathematical studies have been undertaken to obtain a more realistic concept of computability, but, in any case, mathematical theories dealing with computability are not intended for *practical* computation, e.g., for numerical analysis. Also, we shall see that certain problems, which appear to be "computable" intuitively, in fact are not — not even within the rather general concept of computability as formalized by Turing machines.

4.2. Turing Machines

4.2.0. Purpose

As we have said, we are seeking a formalization of the concept of computability. One way of reaching this goal is to use a computing machine, but, since we would like to give as many things as possible a mathematical form, this machine will have to be as simple as possible. The idealized computer which we are going to examine differs profoundly, in its construction, from real computers. Moreover, even *before* the construction of the first electronic computers, as early as 1936 the mathematician and logician Turing introduced into science the class of machines which we shall describe. In this domain, as in many others, fiction preceded reality.

Nevertheless, even from the conceptual point of view, a Turing machine is much less unrealistic than it might seem at first glance. True, it has a potentially infinite memory: but when an electronic computer has a sufficient number of tape drives and interchangeable disk stacks available, we have practically the same situation. Also, a Turing machine reads only one symbol at a time: but this symbol can have a complicated meaning. Finally, just like the central processing unit of a real computer, a Turing machine has only a finite number of internal states or configurations. At any given moment its behavior depends on the state it is in and on what information it is receiving. Except for the convention that the information input is idealized as the reading of a *single* atomic symbol, its behavior is that of a real computer.

4.2.1. Informal Description

A Turing machine is made up of:

1. A *central processing unit* which can be in one of a certain number of *internal states* which correspond to the possible configurations of the elements of an electronic computer (the memory cells, the circuits, etc.);

2. A *tape* on which, initially, the data to be processed are written and on which the intermediate computations are later written when the machine is calculating.

The writing is carried out using the letters of an alphabet; the tape is divided into squares in each of which only one symbol appears; and finally, when the computer is writing new symbols, it is supposed to have an infinite amount of tape available.

3. A *read-write head*, which allows for communication between the central processing unit and the tape. The read-write head can work on just one square at a time, and can

replace the symbol read from the square by a new symbol;

move the tape left or right when the need arises.

The machine works in the following way: in a situation which is determined by the internal state and the symbol read from the tape, the machine will continue by changing its state and by acting upon the tape. Transition rules determine the behavior of the machine: they specify that, in a certain situation, the machine continues in a certain way.

Following M. Davis[1], we shall now make more precise these general notions of how a Turing machine works.

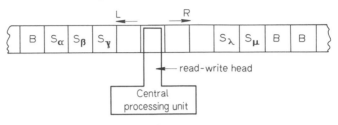

Fig. 4-1

4.2.2. Exact Description

The symbols which the machine reads and writes on the tape are written as follows: $S_0, S_1, ..., S_n$. They constitute the *alphabet* of the machine. S_0 is interpreted as a blank; it appears in the empty squares and therefore plays a special rôle. It will also be written B or #. Replacing S_i by S_0 is equivalent to erasing S_i. S_1 will be often designated by "1" (one) or by "|" (stick).

The internal states are written: $q_1, q_2, q_3, ...$; a given machine has a finite number of such states. The symbols R and L mean that the tape is moved one square to the right or to the left, respectively.

We now give some definitions.

(1) *An expression* is a finite string on the base set: $S_0, S_1, ...; q_1, q_2, ...;$ R, L.

(2) *A quadruple* in an expression having one of the following three forms:

$$q_i \quad S_j \quad S_k \quad q_l,$$
$$q_i \quad S_j \quad R \quad q_l,$$
$$q_i \quad S_j \quad L \quad q_l.$$

(3) A Turing machine is a finite set of quadruples none of which have the same first two symbols.

Operation. With these definitions, the operation of such a machine can be interpreted in the following precise manner:

1. The initial pair of a quadruple constitutes the *situation* of the machine: the machine is in the state q_i and reads the symbol S_j.

---
[1] Davis, M. *Computability and Unsolvability*, New York, McGraw-Hill, 1958.

2. The move from a given situation $q_i S_j$ is determined by the final pair of the unique quadruple corresponding to that situation. This move belongs to one of the following three types:

Type $S_k q_l$: the machine replaces S_j by S_k and switches from state q_i to state q_l.

Type $R q_l$: the machine moves the tape one square to the right and switches from state q_i to state q_l.

Type $L q_l$: the machine moves the tape one square to the left and switches from state q_i to state q_l.

The condition imposed on the set of quadruples of a machine, namely that no two quadruples have the same first two symbols, means that in a given situation there is at most *one* move possible. We shall call such a machine "*deterministic*". A machine which is not so constrained, and which may be faced with several possible moves, will be called "non-deterministic". We now add the following definition:

(4) An expression is called an *instantaneous description* if:

1. it contains no occurrence of L or of R;

2. it contains exactly one occurrence of the type q_i;

3. this q_i is not the rightmost symbol.

Thus, $1 q_3 S_4 B S_2 B B S_1$ and $q_3 B 1$ are instantaneous descriptions, whereas: $L q_1$, $1 S_2$, $q_2 B S_3 q_3 S_1$, $S_1 S_2 q_1$, are not.

Let α be an instantaneous description; we shall call it an instantaneous description of a Turing machine Z if the state q_i which occurs in α is a state of Z and if the other symbols of α are in the alphabet of Z. The instantaneous description describes the behavior of the machine quite precisely. Although the situation of the machine does not take into account the sum total of all the symbols written on the tape, the instantaneous description allows this to be done. With q_i removed, the instantaneous description gives the contents of the tape, and, if S_j is the symbol to the right of q_i in α, then $q_i S_j$ is the situation of Z.

We now give one final definition:

(5) Let α and β be two instantaneous descriptions of a machine Z. Then we write $\alpha \to \beta$ to mean that one of the following cases obtains, where P and Q denote any arbitrary strings of symbols of the alphabet:

$$\exists P, Q: \alpha = P q_i S_j Q \qquad \text{and} \qquad \beta = P q_l S_k Q,$$

$$\exists P, Q: \alpha = P q_i S_j Q \qquad \text{and} \qquad \beta = P S_j q_l Q,$$

$$\exists P, Q: \alpha = P S_k q_i S_j Q \quad \text{and} \quad \beta = P q_l S_k S_j Q.$$

1. The first case formalizes the action of replacing S_j by S_k and switching to the state q_l.

2. The second case formalizes the action of moving the tape one square to the right and switching from state q_i to the state q_l.

3. The third case formalizes the action of moving the tape one square to the left and switching from state q_i to the state q_l.

The following are immediate consequences of the definition (5) (for deterministic machines):

1. $\alpha \rightarrow \beta$ and $\alpha \rightarrow \gamma$ have the consequence $\beta = \gamma$.

2. If Z and Z' are two Turing machines such that every quadruple of Z is a quadruple of Z' (we write in this case $Z \subset Z'$), then $\alpha \rightarrow \beta$ with respect to Z has the consequence $\alpha \rightarrow \beta$ with respect to Z'.

Computation. An instantaneous description α is called *terminal* with respect to a machine Z if there exists no description β such that $\alpha \rightarrow \beta$. By a *computation of some Turing machine* is meant the sequence: α_1, $\alpha_2, \ldots, \alpha_p$ of instantaneous descriptions such that $\alpha_i \rightarrow \alpha_{i+1}$ for $1 \leq i < p$, with α_p terminal. We shall write

$$\alpha_p = \text{Res } Z(\alpha_1),$$

which is to be read: "α_p is the resultant of α_1 for the machine Z".

Initialization. We shall adopt the convention that the machine is to examine a word written in the alphabet $\{S_i\}$; that S_0 represents a blank and that a word is flanked on each side by blanks; that the machine creates as many blanks as it needs for the computation; that one of the states is taken as the initial one; and that the read-write head is positioned at the start in front of the leftmost symbol on the tape.

4.2.3. Examples of Turing Machines

Example 1. The machine Z is defined on the alphabet $\mathfrak{A} = \{S_0, S_1, S_2\}$, and has the internal states q_1, q_2, q_3 — where q_1 represents the initial state. It consists of the following quadruples:

$$
\begin{array}{llll}
q_1 & S_0 & L & q_1, \qquad\qquad (1) \\
q_1 & S_2 & L & q_1, \qquad\qquad (2) \\
q_1 & S_1 & L & q_2, \qquad\qquad (3) \\
q_2 & S_1 & R & q_3, \qquad\qquad (4) \\
q_2 & S_0 & L & q_1, \qquad\qquad (5) \\
q_2 & S_2 & L & q_1, \qquad\qquad (6) \\
q_3 & S_1 & S_2 & q_3. \qquad\qquad (7)
\end{array}
$$

Remarks. 1. If the machine is in the initial state q_1 and reads S_0 or S_2 while operating, it moves the tape left; it is therefore scanning the symbol to the right of S_0 or S_2 and reads it while in the state q_1 [quadruples (1) and (2)].

2. If the machine is in the state q_1 and sees a symbol S_1, it looks to the right of the latter and remembers that it has already seen a symbol S_1: the state q_2 represents the state of "recall of having read S_1" [quadruple (3)].

3. If the machine is in the state of recall and now sees S_0 or S_2, it forgets that it has seen S_1 (return to the state q_1) and shifts the tape to the symbol located immediately to the right of the symbol S_0 or S_2 that it has just examined [quadruples (5) and (6)].

4. If on the other hand, while in the state q_2 the machine sees yet another symbol S_1, it returns to the symbol previously examined (i.e., the S_1 which made it switch to the state q_2) and switches into the state q_3 [quadruple (4)]. It then substitutes S_2 for the first of these two consecutive occurrences of S_1 and switches to the state q_3 [quadruple (7)]. Since it is now in the situation $q_3 S_2$ for which no quadruple exists, it stops.

5. The occurrence of two consecutive symbols S_1 is therefore the only possible way of stopping the machine in its left-to-right scan. If this event does not occur while reading the word presented to it, the machine reaches the end of the word, continues into the blanks on the right and computes indefinitely [quadruple (1)].

With the machine Z in the state q_1, let us give it the word:

$$S_1 \quad S_0 \quad S_2 \quad S_1 \quad S_1 \quad S_0 \quad S_1.$$

We will have the following sequence of instantaneous descriptions:

$$
\begin{array}{llllllll}
q_1 & S_1 & S_0 & S_2 & S_1 & S_1 & S_0 & S_1 & (1), \\
\rightarrow S_1 & q_2 & S_0 & S_2 & S_1 & S_1 & S_0 & S_1 & (2), \\
\rightarrow S_1 & S_0 & q_1 & S_2 & S_1 & S_1 & S_0 & S_1 & (3), \\
\rightarrow S_1 & S_0 & S_2 & q_1 & S_1 & S_1 & S_0 & S_1 & (4), \\
\rightarrow S_1 & S_0 & S_2 & S_1 & q_2 & S_1 & S_0 & S_1 & (5), \\
\rightarrow S_1 & S_0 & S_2 & q_3 & S_1 & S_1 & S_0 & S_1 & (6), \\
\rightarrow S_1 & S_0 & S_2 & q_3 & S_2 & S_1 & S_0 & S_1 & (7) \text{ terminal.}
\end{array}
$$

Let us now give the machine the word: $S_1 S_2 S_3$. In this case, the computation proceeds as follows:

$$
\begin{array}{llllll}
q_1 & S_1 & S_2 & S_2 & & (1), \\
\rightarrow S_1 & q_2 & S_2 & S_2 & & (2), \\
\rightarrow S_1 & S_2 & q_1 & S_2 & & (3), \\
\rightarrow S_1 & S_2 & S_2 & q_1 & S_0 & (4), \\
\rightarrow S_1 & S_2 & S_2 & S_0 & q_1 & S_0 \quad (5)
\end{array}
$$

and so on, indefinitely; the resultant is undefined.

4*

Example 2. *A transcribing machine*

A word is written on the tape in the alphabet $\mathfrak{A} = \{a_1, \ldots, a_n\}$ with blanks # on each side of it. Let $\mathfrak{B} = \{b_1, \ldots, b_n\}$ be another alphabet in one-to-one correspondence with the first: $a_i \leftrightarrow b_i$. The work of the machine T consists in transcribing the given word into the alphabet $\mathfrak{B}$ while keeping a copy of it. In the course of its operation, the machine T uses a marker m. The following are the quadruples that define T.

I. For every index i:

$$q_0, a_i, m, q_i. \tag{1}$$

Reading the rightmost letter a_i while in the initial state q_0, the machine replaces the letter a_i by the marker m, but memorizes a_i by switching to the state q_i.

$$q_i, m, R, q_i. \tag{2}$$

Seeing the marker m while in the state q_i (which memorized the reading of a_i), T moves the tape right, remaining in the state q_i.

$$q_i, \#, a_i, q_i^i. \tag{3}$$

When T is in the state q_i (memorization of a_i) and finds a blank, it writes a_i in place of the blank and switches to the state q_i^i: "I've recopied the a_i that I read".

$$q_i^i, m, L, q_i^i. \tag{4}$$

When T reads the marker, it moves the tape left.

II. For every pair of indices (i, j).

$$q_1, a_j, L, q_i. \tag{1}$$

$$q_i^i, a_j, L, q_i^i. \tag{2}$$

$$q_i^i, b_j, L, q_i^i. \tag{3}$$

When T has recopied a_i and is in the state q_i^i, whatever letter it may read, it moves the tape left and remains in the state q_i^i.

$$q_i^i, \#, b_i, r. \tag{4}$$

As soon as T finds a blank, it transcribes a_i by writing b_i. It then switches to the backtrack state r.

III. For every index j.

$$r, b_j, R, r. \tag{1}$$

$$r, a_j, R, r. \tag{2}$$

Whatever letter T may read while in the backtrack state, it remains in that state and moves the tape to the right.

$$r, m, \#, r. \tag{3}$$

T doesn't stop moving the tape right until it finds the marker that had been left in place of the a_i which was read and transcribed as b_i. The marker is erased, and the machine remains in the backtrack state.

$$r, \#, L, q_0. \tag{4}$$

Upon seeing the blank which has just been substituted for the marker, T moves the tape left in order to scan the next symbol and switches back to the initial state q_0. When T has finished the transcription, it will be in the state q_0 scanning some letter b_j. Since the situation (q_0, b_j) does not correspond to any of the quadruples, the machine stops.

Both words are now written on the tape, separated by a blank.

4.3. "Numerical" Turing Machines

4.3.1. Computation of Functions

Very general types of algorithms can be carried out with the Turing machines described in § 4.2.2. The two preceding examples defined two "non-numerical" algorithms. In point of fact, there is no fundamental difference between numerical and non-numerical, so far as Turing machines are concerned[1]. When manipulating symbols, it is possible to give them a numerical interpretation, or not to do so; if one wishes to calculate with numbers, then all sorts of representations may be used.

In order to handle non-negative integers, we shall use an abstract alphabet of two letters: $\mathfrak{A} = \{S_0, S_1\}$. S_0 will correspond to a blank, written B; S_1 will correspond to a stick, written |. Every non-negative integer n will be represented by a sequence of $n + 1$ sticks. This convention allows the number zero, written as one stick, to be distinguished from the blank used as a separator. The representation of n will be written as $\bar{n}$; for example

$$\bar{0} = |, \qquad \bar{1} = ||, \qquad \bar{4} = |||||.$$

The k-tuple $(n_1, n_2, \ldots, n_k)$ will be represented by: $\bar{n}_1 \, B \, \bar{n}_2 \, B \ldots B \, \bar{n}_k$. Given an expression M, i.e., a finite string on the base set:

$$\{B, |; q_1, q_2 \ldots; R, L\},$$

we shall write as $\langle M \rangle$ the number of sticks it contains.

---

[1] Insofar as electronic computers are concerned, however, this distinction is of rather considerable practical importance. The convenience of a machine in a given field is a function of the number of built-in operations it has: arithmetical operations in the field of numerical computation, and Boolean operations, substitution operations, etc., in the field of non-numerical computation.

4.3.2. The Concept of a Computable Function

Let Z be a Turing machine and $q_1, \ldots$ its states. With each n-tuple $(m_1, \ldots, m_n)$ of non-negative integers we shall associate the instantaneous description: $\alpha_1 = q_1 \, \overline{m}_1 \, B \, \overline{m}_2 \ldots B \, \overline{m}_n$. If for the machine Z there exists a computation starting from α_1 and ending with the terminal description α_p: $\alpha_1 \to \alpha_2 \cdots \to \alpha_p$, then the integer $\langle \alpha_p \rangle$ is a function which depends on the machine Z and the initial n-tuple; we shall write

$$\langle \alpha_p \rangle = \Psi_Z^{(n)}(m_1, \ldots, m_n).$$

If there exists no computation beginning with α_1, i.e., there exists no finite integer p such that α_p is a terminal description, then the function $\Psi_Z^{(n)}$ is undefined for the n-tuple in question.

Starting from a machine Z we have ended up with a function whose values are non-negative integers; this function is defined on N^n or possibly on a subset of N^n (a partially defined function). Conversely, let us begin with functions defined on N^n or on a subset of N^n.

Definition. A function f defined on a subset of N^n is said to be *partially computable* if there exists a Turing machine Z such that

$$f(x_1, \ldots, x_n) = \Psi_Z^{(n)}(x_1, \ldots, x_n)$$

for every n-tuple to which there corresponds a value of f. A function is said to be *computable* if it is defined on N^n and is partially computable.

4.3.3. Example of a Computable Function

The function $f(x, y) = x + y$ defined on pairs of non-negative integers is a "computable" function, in the usual sense of the word. We shall show that it is computable according to Turing's definition. To this end, we construct a machine Z defined on the alphabet $\{B, |\}$ such that

$$x + y = A_Z^{(2)}(x, y).$$

The simplest idea would be to write on the tape the representations of $\bar{x}$ and $\bar{y}$ separated by a blank and require the machine to furnish $x + y$. Recall that $x + y = \langle \bar{x} \rangle + \langle \bar{y} \rangle - 2$. The reader can easily verify that the following machine Z is a solution to the problem.

$q_1 \mid B q_2$	(1)	Erase the first stick of the first representation;
$q_2 \, B \, L \, q_3$	(2)	Move the tape up to the first stick of the second
$q_3 \mid L \, q_3$	(3)	representation;
$q_3 \, B \, L \, q_4$	(4)	
$q_4 \mid B q_4$	(5)	Erase the first stick of the second representation.

The machine stops because the situation $q_4 \, B$ does not appear in any quadruple, and at that point the tape contains $x + y$ sticks.

4.3.4. Example of a Partially Computable Function

From our point of view, the function $g(x, y) = x \dot- y$ is defined only on the subset $x \geq y$; we shall show that it is partially computable according to Turing's definition.

To this end we shall construct a Turing machine which carries out subtraction. The representations $\bar{x}$ and $\bar{y}$ are written on the tape to the left and to the right, respectively, of the blank square which separates them. The machine will work by successively canceling one stick on the extreme left of $\bar{x}$ and one on the extreme right of $\bar{y}$. The following are the quadruples:

$q_1 \mid B q_1$ (1) Erase the stick to the left of $\bar{x}$;

$q_1 B L q_2$ (2) Move the tape one square left;

$q_2 \mid L q_2$ (3) Keep moving past $\bar{x}$;

$q_2 B L q_3$ (4) At the separating blank, switch to the state q_3 and begin on $\bar{y}$;

$q_3 \mid L q_3$ (5) Move past $\bar{y}$;

$q_3 B R q_4$ (6) Upon reaching the blank square to the right of $\bar{y}$, the machine switches to the state q_4 and returns to the rightmost stick of $\bar{y}$;

$q_4 \mid B q_4$ (7) Erase this rightmost stick;

$q_4 B R q_5$ (8) Move the tape one square right and shift to the "interrogation" state.

Whether the computation will now continue or terminate depends on the results of certain tests.

$q_5 \mid R q_6$ (9) If the square being scanned contains a stick, the computation continues; otherwise, since the situation $q_5 B$ is not the head of any quadruple, the computation stops;

$q_6 \mid R q_6$ (10) Move the tape up to the separating blank, remaining in the state q_6;

$q_6 B R q_7$ (11) Meeting the separating blank causes the machine to switch to the state q_7; it is now to the right of $\bar{x}$;

$q_7 \mid R q_8$ (12) If there is still a stick left in $\bar{x}$, the computation continues;

$q_7 B R q_7$ (13) But if there are no more ($x < y$), then the tape will be moved to the right indefinitely;

$q_8 \mid R q_8$ (14) Move to the extreme left of what remains of $\bar{x}$;

$q_8 B L q_1$ (15) Position the machine at the head of what remains of $\bar{x}$ in order to begin the next cycle.

The function $x \dot- y$, which is partially computable, can be easily and trivially extended to become a computable function (cf. exercise 8 below). It must not be concluded from this that every partially computable function necessarily yields a computable function by some trivial extension.

4.4. Exercises

1. Construct a Turing machine which recopies and inserts a blank between two consecutive letters.

2. Construct a Turing machine which inserts a marker at each end of the word written on the tape.

3. Construct a Turing machine which writes the mirror image of a given word.

4. We define a Turing machine with a set of quintuples:

$$(q_i, S_j, S_k, q_e, \delta_m).$$

If the machine, when in the state q_i, reads the letter S_j, it writes S_k, switches to the state q_e and shifts the tape by the amount δ_m. The possibilities are: -1, Move left; 0, Don't move; $+1$, Move right. Recast the theory of Turing machines and the computations of this chapter using such a modified machine.

5. Construct a Turing machine which calculates the successor function: $S(x) = x + 1$.

6. Write out the computations for the subtractions $3 - 2$ and $2 - 3$.

7. Construct a Turing machine which computes the i-th projection function:

$$U_i^{(n)}(x_1, x_2, \ldots, x_n) = x_i; \quad 1 \leq i \leq n.$$

8. Construct a Turing machine for computing the function $x \div y$ which is defined by:

$$x \div y = x - y \qquad \text{if } x \geq y,$$
$$x \div y = 0 \qquad \text{if } x < y.$$

One may just simplify the machine for ordinary subtraction.

9. Construct a machine which computes the function defined in 8. and encloses the result between two markers.

10. Construct a machine for computing the product: $(x + 1)(y + 1)$. Then modify the machine in such a way as to enclose the result between two markers.

Chapter V

Computability — Decidability

5.0. Résumé of the Chapter

Several concepts related to computability and solvability, which are indispensable for their application to grammars, will be explained in this chapter. The detailed steps of many of the proofs have been left as exercises both for the sake of brevity and for a clearer presentation of the ideas involved.

5.1. The Computation of Functions

The simple example of subtraction shows us that the computation of functions rapidly leads to very complex Turing machines. In order to avoid having to construct such complicated machines directly, we shall introduce techniques of composition of some elementary and standardized machines, much in the way that elementary instructions are used to form subroutines when programming for computers.

5.1.1. Linking and Standardization

The following techniques will be employed:

Separation of States. When constructing a machine with the help of other machines that have already been written, the states of the compound machine must be distinguished from those of its component machines (each of which have, for example, a state q_1). To this end we shall use the following convention:

If Z is a Turing machine, then $Z^{(n)}$ denotes a similar machine each of whose states are obtained from those of Z by increasing the subscripts by n. (The operation that shifts Z to $Z^{(n)}$ is quite analogous to that of loading a subroutine into an electronic computer in such a way that its first instruction is located at the address n).

The Standard Machine. It is convenient if the results obtained by one machine ("outputs") can be used as the data ("input") to another machine. One way of standardizing the linking of the machines consists in introducing a *final* state.

We have already agreed that every machine will begin its computation in the state q_1; in much the same way we shall agree that a machine ends all its computations in a certain state q_θ. To this end, we define θ, for a given Turing machine Z, to be the largest subscript used in indexing its internal states; furthermore, none of the situations of Z contains the state q_θ. A machine having such a configuration becomes a *standard* machine.

Erasure. It will be remembered that the result given by a machine is the number of sticks written on the tape at the end of its computation. But the machine's alphabet may contain more symbols than just the blank and the stick. In order that this result may be used as input, it is useful to group the sticks together and erase all the other symbols.

Marking. When a machine is scanning its input (for example, the result of some preceding machine) we must prevent it from exploring the tape indefinitely. To this end, we transform every standard machine Z into another standard machine Z' which carries out the same computations but which also encloses them between a left and right marker. The construction of such a machine was proposed in some of the exercises at the end of Chapter IV, for particular cases. Exercise 5.1.2 below treats the general case.

Storage. Since the component machines of a compound machine will not necessarily be linked together linearly, it is sometimes necessary to store intermediate results during a computation. Such a storage can also be accomplished with markers. More precisely, if the machine Z associates the result $(r_1, \ldots, r_j)$ with the input $(d_1, \ldots, d_i)$, it is possible to construct a machine Z_1 which associates the result $(p_1, \ldots, p_k, r_1, \ldots, r_j)$ with the input $(p_1, \ldots, p_k, d_1, \ldots, d_i)$.

In particular, it may be the initial input which must be stored. In this case it will be convenient to recopy it somewhere (for example, using the transcribing machine) and then to store it using the machine Z_1 described below.

5.1.2. Exercise. Marking Machine

Let Z be a standard machine with alphabet $\{S_0 (\text{or } B), S_1 (\text{or } |), S_2, \ldots\}$, and states $q_1, q_2, \ldots, q_\theta$. We shall now construct a machine Z' which computes as Z does but which encloses its computations between a left marker λ and a right marker ρ (if either of these symbols is in the alphabet of Z, it goes without saying that we will choose other ones).

a) Define a machine Z_1 which reads the initial input, tests each end of the input for the presence of a double blank, prints the markers λ and ρ, and then positions itself on the left in front of λ. Five states suffice to define Z_1.

b) Construct a machine Z_2 by adding 5 to each of the subscripts of the states of Z, and by adding quadruples to it in such a way that Z_2 moves $\lambda(\rho)$ if necessary one square left (right) and then returns to the main computation.

c) Construct a machine Z_3 which standardizes Z_2.

d) Construct a machine Z_4 which erases all the symbols except the sticks, consolidates the sticks into one block and then adds one additional stick (so that the result may be taken as a number).

5.1.3. Exercise

a) Construct a Turing machine which codes the alphabet $\{a, b, c\}$ by means of the alphabet $\{0, 1\}$, following the model described in § 3.4.1.

b) Construct a machine which decodes the preceding code and identifies irregular words.

c) Make one Turing machine from the two preceding machines.

5.2. Operations on Computable Functions

5.2.0.

We return now to those functions which map N^p into N.

5.2.1. Composition

Suppose we are given on the one hand a function of m variables: $f(x_1, \ldots, x_m)$ defined on $D \subset N^m$, and on the other hand m functions of n variables: $g_1(y_1, \ldots, y_n) \ldots g_m(y_1, \ldots, y_n)$, each function g_i defined on a domain $D_i \subset N^n$.

The operation of *composition* associates with these functions a new function h:

$$h(y_1, \ldots, y_n) = f[g_1(y_1, \ldots, y_n), \ldots, g_m(y_1, \ldots, y_n)].$$

The function h is defined on a subset of the intersection of the domains D_i, that subset for which the values of the g_i yield a point of D. The essential result of the operation of composition is the following:

Theorem. *If the functions* f, $g_1, \ldots, g_m$ *are (partially) computable, the function* h *is (partially) computable.*

This proposition can be shown by taking the union of the standard Turing machines which correspond to the functions f, $g_1, \ldots, g_m$. The proof presents no difficulty and is left as an exercise. An immediate corollary of this theorem is that the class of (partially) computable functions is closed under the operation of composition.

5.2.2. Minimalization

The operation of *minimalization* associates with each function $f(y, x_1, \ldots, x_n)$, defined everywhere on N^{n+1} (N. B.) the function $h(x_1, \ldots, x_n)$, whose value for a given n-tuple is the least value of y, if one exists, such that $f(y, x_1, \ldots, x_n) = 0$. The function h may be defined only on a subset of N^n. A function $f(y, x_1, \ldots, x_n)$ is called *regular* (for y) if the function $h(x_1, \ldots, x_n)$ obtained by minimalization is defined everywhere.

The essential result concerning minimalization is the following theorem:

Theorem. *If the function* $f(y, x_1, \ldots, x_n)$ *is computable, then the function* h *obtained by minimalization is partially computable. Moreover, if the function* f *is regular, then the function* h *is computable.*

This proposition can be proven by constructing a Turing machine which successively computes $f(0, x_1, \ldots, x_n)$, $f(1, x_1, \ldots, x_n)$ until the value 0 is obtained for f (if one were never to obtain the value 0, the machine would compute indefinitely).

5.2.3. Exercises

1. Prove the theorem concerning the composition of functions.

2. Minimalization:

a) Construct a standard machine T having three states q_1, q_2, q_3 which associates $(0, x_1, \ldots, x_n)$ with the input $(x_1, \ldots, x_n)$.

b) Let $f(y, x_1, \ldots, x_n)$ be a (partially) computable function. Show that there exists a standard machine U which associates the representation of $[f(y, x_1, \ldots, x_n), y, x_1, \ldots, x_n]$ with the input $y, x_1, \ldots, x_n$. Increase the subscripts of the states of U in order to link it with T.

c) Construct a machine V which reduces the representation of $f(y, x_1, \ldots, x_n) = r$ by one stick so that the contents of the tape can be taken into consideration; link V to U.

d) Connect another machine W which adds a stick to $\bar{y}$ thus changing it to $y + 1$, if $r \neq 0$.

e) Connect a standard machine Y which, for $r = 0$, erases the tape and sets its contents equal to y.

f) Verify that the machine consisting of the union of T, U, V, W, Y satisfies the required conditions.

3. It will be remembered that the functions $(x + 1)(y + 1)$, on the one hand, and $x \div y$ on the other, are computable; these results were given as exercises. (The function $x \div y$ is obtained by a trivial extension of the function $x \dot- y$, i. e., by giving $x \dot- y$ the value $x - y$ or zero, according to whether $x \dot- y$ is defined or not.)

From these results (and from the projection functions) show that the function x y is computable.

4. Show that the functions x^h are computable for $h \in N$.

5.2.4. Modified Turing Machines

Various extensions of Turing machines can be imagined, for example:

1. The addition to a machine Z of a set A and of quadruples $S_i \, q_j \, q_k \, q_l$ which indicate that, if the machine is in the situation (S_i, q_j) and has the instantaneous description α, then the machine switches to the state q_k or q_l according as the contents $\langle \alpha \rangle$ of the instantaneous description belong to A or not. This extension, which has been treated by Davis, does not increase the computational power of Turing machines.

2. The addition of specialized components: input tape, output tape, tapes for the intermediate results, more complex instructions. It is relatively simple, in general, to show that these more complex machines are equivalent to simple Turing machines.

5.3. Gödel's Techniques

5.3.0.

We have already pointed out that, insofar as Turing machines are concerned, the distinction between "numerical" and "non-numerical", which is of practical importance, is not especially relevant. During the 30's, the mathematician and logician Gödel used a code based on the natural numbers for the names of certain metamathematical objects in order to prove, in connection with the problem of the foundations of arithmetic, the famous theorem which now bears his name.

Gödel's techniques make it possible to use numbers for what is essentially non-numerical; programmers who have had occasion to compute the addresses of instructions will understand this immediately.

We have a base set, an alphabet, and we shall manipulate finite strings of occurrences of symbols. With every finite string, which is a non-numerical entity, we are going to associate an arithmetic integer — its *Gödel number* — such that the following properties obtain:

1. There exists a Turing machine which, for every string on its tape, furnishes as its result the desired number.

2. There exists a Turing machine which, for any number written on its tape, gives one of two answers:

either: "there is no string which corresponds to this number";

or: "the string corresponding to this number is ...".

Thus, the number associated with a string characterizes it; the number is its proper name and, since it is a number, computations can be made with it[1]. In the same way, we may number sequences of strings.

5.3.1. One Procedure (Among Others)

Turing machines involve expressions which contain:

the symbols S and q with various subscripts;

the symbols L and R.

For numbering the subscripts we shall use a binary system having the numbers z (zero) and u (one); the subscripts will be written on the line:

$$S_0 \quad \text{becomes} \quad S \; z,$$
$$S_1 \quad \text{becomes} \quad S \; u,$$
$$S_2 \quad \text{becomes} \quad S \; u \; z,$$
$$S_3 \quad \text{becomes} \quad S \; u \; u,$$
$$q_5 \quad \text{becomes} \quad q \; u \; z \; u.$$

---

[1] To make computations does not mean "to make stupid computations". The computations in question will be adapted to the nature of the objects that are manipulated (just as in programming you don't compute the cosine of an address!).

If we need sequences of strings, we will use the separator "!". Then we have the symbols {S, q, z, u, L, R, !}; with the empty string we associate the number 0.

With the single letter strings we associate, respectively

$$S, \quad q, \quad z, \quad u, \quad L, \quad R, \quad !$$
$$1, \quad 2, \quad 3, \quad 4, \quad 5, \quad 6, \quad 7.$$

With each arbitrary string we associate the octal number which corresponds to it canonically.

Example. The quadruple $q_3 S_5 S_0 q_4$ is written: q u u S u z u S z q u z z, to which there corresponds the octal number: 2 4 4 1 4 3 4 1 3 2 4 3 3.

Given a string, the determination of its number is mechanical, and can therefore be carried out by a Turing machine. Conversely, to 0 there corresponds the empty string. To every octal number without the number 0 there corresponds just one string (or just one sequence of strings). To every octal number having one number 0 (at least) there corresponds no string or sequence of strings.

5.3.2. The Gödel Number of a Turing Machine

A Turing machine is a set of quadruples $Q_1, Q_2, \ldots, Q_n$. With each quadruple we associate its Gödel number:

$$gn(Q_1), gn(Q_2), \ldots, gn(Q_n).$$

We then order these numbers from the smallest to the largest; it is not even necessary to separate them with 7's, since the q's and the S serve as markers. In this way, every Turing machine is assigned a Gödel number. Since the procedure is mechanizable, it can be executed by a Turing machine G_1 (it is not trivial to remark that G_1 can compute, among others, its own number). Conversely, there exists a Turing machine G_2 which, given as input an octal number, will answer:

either "this number is not the Gödel number of any machine";
or "this number is the Gödel number of a machine whose quadruples are the following ...".

Note that if one submits its own Gödel number to G_2, it also supplies an answer.

5.3.3. Exercise: an "Historical" Code

In his first papers, Gödel used the following procedure. Given the string

$$M = {}^{\backprime}\gamma_1 \gamma_2 \cdots \gamma_n{}^{\prime},$$

which is to be coded. The code is to take into account that the symbol γ_k occupies the k-th place in the expression; hence *both* the symbols *and* their places must be coded.

1. The symbols are coded by mapping them bijectively onto the odd integers greater than 1 in the following way:

$$\text{Symbols } \gamma_i: \quad L \ \ R \ \ S_0 \ \ q_1 \ \ S_1 \ \ q_2 \ \ S_2 \ \ q_3 \ \ \dots.$$
$$\text{Numbers } a_i: \quad 3 \ \ 5 \ \ 7 \ \ 9 \ \ \ 11 \ \ 13 \ \ 15 \ \ 17 \ \dots.$$

2. The positions of the symbols are coded by mapping them bijectively onto the set of primes ordered by increasing magnitude:

$$\text{Position:} \quad 1 \ 2 \ 3 \ 4 \ \ 5 \ \dots \ k \ \ \dots.$$
$$\text{Prime:} \quad 2 \ 3 \ 5 \ 7 \ 11 \ \dots \ p_k \ \dots.$$

3. To the string '$\gamma_1 \, \gamma_2 \dots \gamma_n$' there corresponds the normalized factorization:

$$2^{a_1} \times 3^{a_2} \times 5^{a_3} \times \dots \times p_k^{a_k} \times \dots \times p_n^{a_n},$$

hence a positive integer which we write as $gn(M)$: the Gödel number of M. Conversely, the number $gn(M)$ so obtained can be decomposed into a normalized factorization in just one way, and only the string M corresponds to it. We complete the coding by setting the integer 1 to be the Gödel number of the empty string.

Sequences of Strings. In the same way, a sequence of strings $M_1, M_2, \dots, M_j, \dots, M_q$ can be coded by means of the number

$$2^{gn(M_1)} \times 3^{gn(M_2)} \times \dots \times p_j^{gn(M_j)} \times \dots \times p_q^{gn(M_q)}.$$

a) Code the quadruple $(q_1 | R \, q_2)$.

b) Decode $2^{17} \, 3^{11} \, 5^7 \, 7^{11}$.

c) Code the sequence $\varphi = (q_1 | R \, q_2, q_3 | B \, q_1)$.

d) Show that coding the γ_i by the *odd* integers a_i allows one to decide whether a Gödel number is the Gödel number of a string or of a sequence of strings. Show that $gn(\varphi) = gn(\psi)$ implies $\varphi = \psi$. To do this, decompose $gn(\varphi)$ into $2^m \cdot (2q+1)$, and then distinguish the cases according to the parity of m.

5.4. Recursive Sets and Recursively Denumerable Sets

5.4.0. The Functions $Q_z^p(\mathfrak{X})$

Given any integer z, two mutually exclusive cases are possible, and only these two:

1. Either there is no Turing machine whose Gödel number is z;

2. Or there is one, and it is unique.

However, by its very definition, we say that a function $f(\mathfrak{X})$, where

$$\mathfrak{X} \in N^p \xrightarrow{\ f\ } f(\mathfrak{X}) \in N$$

is partially computable to mean that it is *the* function which a certain Turing machine calculates (when this is possible) from the input $\mathfrak{X}$. In other words, with every partially computable function $f(\mathfrak{X})$ we can associate the Gödel number z of the Turing machine which computes this function (there may be several machines which compute the same function).

We now define the function $Q_z^p(\mathfrak{X})$ in the following way. Given a non-negative integer z and an input $\mathfrak{X} \in N^p$:

1. If z is the Gödel number of a machine Z which computes the partially computable function $f(\mathfrak{X})$, then $Q_z^p(\mathfrak{X})$ is the same as $f(\mathfrak{X})$.

2. If z is not the Gödel number of any machine, then $Q_z^p(\mathfrak{X})$ is equal to 0. Then it is clear that the sequence: $Q_0^p(\mathfrak{X}), Q_1^p(\mathfrak{X}), \ldots, Q_n^p(\mathfrak{X}), \ldots$ enumerates, with possible repetitions, the set of partially computable functions of p arguments. The following remark will be useful later: we then also know how to enumerate the domains of definition of partially computable functions.

5.4.1. The Nature of the Functions $Q_z^p(\mathfrak{X})$

A function Q_z^p is is clearly a function of $p+1$ arguments which takes its arguments in N^{p+1} and its values in N. Given z and $\mathfrak{X}$, it must first be determined, in order to calculate the value of Q_z^p, whether z is the Gödel number of a Turing machine. This is a decoding problem with answers *yes* or *no* which can be given to the Turing machine G_2 (§ 5.3.2). If the answer is *no*, $Q_z^p = 0$; if the answer is *yes*, $\mathfrak{X}$ is given as input to the machine Z whose quadruples "analyze" z. Adding G_2 to Z, we then obtain a Turing machine which computes $Q_z^p(\mathfrak{X})$.

Theorem. *The functions $Q_z^p(\mathfrak{X})$ are partially computable functions.*

A Turing machine which computes the function $Q_z^p(\mathfrak{X})$ is called *universal*: by writing the appropriate number z on its tape we enable it to compute the partially computable function which corresponds to this number.

5.4.2. Vocabulary

A definition of *recursive functions* is to be found in a note at the end of this chapter. For the moment, we wish only to clarify a problem of nomenclature. It will be shown that the class of computable functions and the class of recursive functions are identical, so that the two adjectives "recursive" and "computable" are in principle synonymous. Nevertheless, there are cases where the custom is to say "recursive", and the other adjective is not used. We shall conform to this usage.

5.4.3. Definitions

We shall often have occasion to use the characteristic function of a set. Let $E \subset N$. The characteristic function of E, written C_E, is defined by

$$C_E(x) = \begin{cases} 1, & \text{if } x \in E, \\ 0, & \text{if } x \notin E. \end{cases}$$

The characteristic function of a set $E \subset N^p$ is defined in an analogous way.

Recursive Set. We say that a set is recursive if its characteristic function is *computable* (cf. the note on vocabulary in § 5.4.2). Saying that a set is recursive is equivalent to saying that there exists a Turing machine which, when presented with the input $\mathfrak{X}$, gives in every case an answer which is either 1 or 0.

Recursively Denumerable Sets. A set is said to be *recursively denumerable* if it is the domain of definition of (at least) one partially computable function. We know theoretically how to enumerate the partially computable functions of an integral variable, of two integral variables, etc., so that we also know, in principle, how to enumerate the recursively denumerable sets: $\mathfrak{N}_0, \mathfrak{N}_1, \ldots, \mathfrak{N}_i$.

5.4.4. The Connection between the Two Concepts

Theorem. *A set is recursive if and only if both the set and its complement are recursively denumerable.*

1. Let us suppose the set R to be recursive. There exists a Turing machine which computes its characteristic function, which is a computable function. From this Turing machine we can construct two others. One of these corresponds to the partially computable function

$$f(\mathfrak{X}) = \begin{cases} 1 & \text{if } \mathfrak{X} \in R \\ \text{undefined} & \text{if } \mathfrak{X} \notin R, \end{cases}$$

$$\bar{f}(\mathfrak{X}) = \begin{cases} 0 & \text{if } \mathfrak{X} \in \bar{R} \\ \text{undefined} & \text{if } \mathfrak{X} \notin \bar{R}. \end{cases}$$

It then follows that both R and $\bar{R}$ are recursively denumerable.

2. Suppose that R and $\bar{R}$ are recursively denumerable. They are then domains of definition of the partially computable functions $f(\mathfrak{X})$ and $\bar{f}(\mathfrak{X})$ which are associated with the machines Z and $\bar{Z}$, respectively. If $\mathfrak{X}$ is given, we submit it to both Z and $\bar{Z}$: one of the machines gives a result, the other does not.

If it is Z which gives a result, then we have $C_R(\mathfrak{X}) = 1$; if it is $\bar{Z}$, then we have $C_R(\mathfrak{X}) = 0$. The pair Z, $\bar{Z}$ is equivalent to a unique Turing machine. Therefore the function C_R is computable and R (as well as $\bar{R}$) is recursive.

5.4.5. Non-Equivalence of the Two Concepts

This theorem leaves open the question of whether there exist recursively denumerable sets which are *not recursive*. We shall prove the existence of such sets by using a "diagonal procedure".

Consider the set of Turing machines associated with the functions of an argument; let us submit as input to each machine its own Gödel number. Then there are two possible outcomes: either the machine Z, computing with input $z = gn(Z)$, stops and gives a result (in which case we call it *self-applying*), or else it doesn't stop.

The function under study here is none other than $Q_z^1(z)$, and it is clearly a partially computable function. It would be possible to construct a Turing machine which computes it by "tinkering around" with the universal machine that computes $Q_z^1(x)$. The set G of Gödel numbers which correspond to self-applying machines is therefore recursively denumerable.

Suppose it were recursive; this amounts to the supposition that its complement $\overline{G}$ is also recursively denumerable. G would then be attached to some Turing machine of Gödel number λ and would carry this number λ in the enumeration of the recursively denumerable sets:

$$\overline{G} = \mathfrak{N}_\lambda.$$

If x is an arithmetic integer we then have:

$$x \in \overline{G} \iff x \in \mathfrak{N}_\lambda.$$

But, by virtue of the definition itself, we have:

$$x \in \overline{G} \iff x \notin \mathfrak{N}_x,$$

hence:

$$x \in \mathfrak{N}_\lambda \iff x \notin \mathfrak{N}_x.$$

If we take $x = \lambda$, we obtain:

$$\lambda \in \mathfrak{N}_\lambda \iff \lambda \notin \mathfrak{N}_\lambda.$$

This contradiction proves that G is not recursive.

5.4.6. The Halting Problem for Turing Machines

When we submit an input to a Turing machine, there are only two possible results, and these are mutually exclusive:

The machine finally stops; it gives an answer.

The machine computes indefinitely.

We can then pose the following problem: does there exist a Turing machine T whose input is in the form of couples, and which, when given as input the couple

$$[z = gn(Z); X],$$

answers:

either "Yes, the machine Z whose Gödel number is z, will give an answer when computing with input X";

or "No; useless to submit the input X to Z, for Z will never stop".

Suppose that such a Turing machine T exists. Let E be a recursively denumerable set which is not recursive: *we know that such sets exist!* E is the range of a partially defined function f_{z_α} which is computed by the machine Z_α. Let x be any integer. Then T allows the following kind of answer to be given:

"Yes, we have $x \in E$, and Z_α will stop".

"No, we have $x \in \bar{E}$, and Z_α will not stop".

Then E would be recursive, which is contrary to the hypothesis. Consequently:

Theorem. *The halting problem for a Turing machine is undecidable.*

5.5 Further Remarks

5.5.1. Real Computers

We have called *universal* a machine U which computes the function $Q_z^p(\mathfrak{X})$. If we give this machine the input $(z, \mathfrak{X})$, it will yield as its result the one which a machine Z, such that $g\,n(Z) = z$, would have yielded when given $\mathfrak{X}$ as input. The analogy of the universal Turing machine U with electronic computers now becomes clear. U is the counterpart of the computer, and z is a particular program which is loaded into the computer together with the input upon which the program z must compute.

The halting problem also takes on a concrete meaning: given a program P and the inputs δ upon which it is supposed to calculate, does there exist a general program G which will tell us whether P, computing on δ, will stop or not? The answer is that G does not exist; in particular, there is no hope of writing a program some day which is capable of detecting all the programming errors which result in an infinite computation.

5.5.2. "Philosophical" Digression

The results concerning undecidability do not authorize us to engage in any philosophical speculation on the limitations of the powers of man as compared with those of the machine. It is a question here of proofs, within a mathematical theory, of the non-existence of certain objects, just as in arithmetic it can be proven that there is no rational number whose square is 2.

If the discovery of irrational numbers posed some metaphysical problems for the ancient Greeks, it is because this discovery upset a "naive" explanation of the world, an explanation based upon integral relations. The concept of undecidability upsets nothing; it merely allows us to recognize that some problems are poorly posed. What to do about this depends on the nature of each problem. It is sometimes convenient to take into consideration particular cases for which the problem is decidable and can therefore be studied mathematically. In other situations, one might be interested in a practical study of the problem, a study which is nevertheless of a general character; in such a case, one "makes do", or, in more noble language, one uses *heuristics*. An example of such a situation is the search for rules which will detect programming errors — only partially, of course, but quite usefully — that lead to loops; or again, the search for classes of computations for which there may exist a general error-detection procedure.

5.5.3. Note on Recursive Functions

Recursive functions, which have such an important rôle in mathematical logic, can be characterized in many ways. The definition which we shall give here (following M. Davis) is that of J. Robinson. Its connection with a similar definition based on Turing machines is easily seen.

Definition. A function is said to be *partially recursive* if it can be obtained by a finite number of applications of composition and minimalization beginning with the basic functions:

(1) $S(x) = x + 1$, the successor function;

(2) $U_i^n(x_1, \ldots, x_n) = x_i$, $1 \leq i \leq n$, the projection function;

(3) $x + y$, the addition function;

(4) $x \div y$, the subtraction function with trivial extension;

(5) $x\,y$, the product function.

A partially recursive function is recursive if the operations which define it are applied only to regular functions.

The essential results for these functions are the following:

Theorem. *If a function is (partially) recursive it is (partially) computable.*

This proposition can be proven with the help of elementary and standardized Turing machines. The proof presents no great difficulty, and is left as an exercise.

The converse is also true.

Theorem. *If a function is (partially) computable it is (partially) recursive.*

We shall give only some very brief indications of the method to be used to prove this last theorem. To begin with, it is necessary to introduce the concept of predicates.

Definition. By n-ary predicate is meant a function which has its arguments on a set of n-tuples and its values on the set {*True, False*}.

Example. $P(x, y) \equiv (x + y = 3)$ has the value *False* for (1, 1), the value *True* for (1, 2) and the value *False* for (4, y), for every y.

The characteristic function of an n-ary predicate is the characteristic function of the set on which the predicate takes the value *True* (on the *extension* of the predicate). A predicate is said to be computable if its characteristic function is computable.

A predicate $P(x_1, \ldots, x_n)$ is called *semi-computable* if there exists a partially computable function $f(x_1, \ldots, x_n)$ whose domain of definition is the set on which P takes the value *True*. The associated function f is not defined on the complementary set where P takes the value *False*.

It is clear that every computable predicate is semi-computable. Its characteristic function C, always defined, has the value 0 (N.B.!) on the extension of the predicate (and 1 outside of it). We can define f as, for example:

$$f = \min_y [C + y = 0].$$

Then we have the following theorem:

Theorem. *The predicate* $R(x_1, \ldots, x_n)$ *is computable if and only if the predicates* R *and* $\neg R$ *are semi-computable.*

Turing Predicates. Given a non-numerical predicate bearing on the definitions related to a Turing machine and which is made up of negation $\neg$, the connectives $\vee$ and $\wedge$, and of bounded quantifiers, Gödel's numbering technique makes it possible to translate it into a predicate containing numerical arguments.

Examples. The predicates:

QUAD(x):   True if x is the Gödel number of a quadruple, false otherwise;

TM(x):   True if x is a Gödel number of a Turing machine described by a set of quadruples, false otherwise;

MOVE(x, y, z): True if x and y are the Gödel numbers of two instantaneous descriptions (α) and (β) and if $(\alpha) \to (\beta)$ holds for the Turing machine with Gödel number z, false otherwise;

U(y):   If y is the Gödel number of a sequence of expressions $M_1, M_2, \ldots, M_n$, then $U(y) = \langle M_n \rangle$.

By compounding such predicates, we obtain from simple predicates more complex ones which are all computable; in this way we construct by successive stages the predicate $T_n(z, x_1, \ldots, x_n, y)$ where z is a Gödel number of a machine Z, and y is the Gödel number of the computation $(x_1, \ldots, x_n)$ of Z.

We can therefore effectively associate a predicate T_n with every computable function and with every argument of that function. In order to obtain its characteristic function we need use only the techniques for constructing recursive functions. This is the way to prove the result mentioned above, namely, that every computable function is recursive.

5.5.4. Computability and Recursiveness

These theorems prove the equivalence of computability and recursiveness. The concept of computability is due to Turing, that of recursiveness to Kleene. Although they were defined independently, both these concepts are concerned with the same problem of formalizing the intuitive concept of computability. It is a rather remarkable fact that a certain number of definitions introduced independently of each other (Gödel, Church, Post, Markov) for this purpose are all equivalent to each other and to the two discussed here. Church's famous thesis draws a philosophical conclusion from this equivalence, asserting that these different concepts all formalize the intuitive notion of computability correctly and that this latter notion cannot be extended. Until now, experience has confirmed Church's thesis.

From a practical point of view, it is more interesting to restrict the notion of computability in order to adapt it to the presently available computing machines, and this line of research is being pursued in many computation centers.

5.5.5. Exercises

1. Give a detailed proof that recursiveness implies computability.

2. Prove that the following functions are recursive by showing how to obtain them from the basic functions:

a) The null function: $\forall x \, N(x) = 0$.

b) The function $\delta(x)$ which is zero for all x except for $x = 0$ for which $\delta(0) = 1$.

c) The square root which is a whole number.

d) The quotient which is a whole number and the remainder which is a whole number.

3. Show that if R and S are recursive sets, then the sets $R \cup S$, $R \cap S$ and $\bar{R}$ are also recursive.

4. Show that if P and Q are recursive predicates, then the predicates $P \vee Q$, $P \wedge Q$, and $\neg P$ are also recursive.

5. Show that the following predicates are computable (introduce the characteristic functions):

a) $x = y$.

b) $x < y$.

c) $x \mid y$ (x divides y).

d) $Prime(x)$ (x is prime).

Chapter VI

Combinatorial Systems and Turing Machines; Undecidable Problems

6.1. Systems and Turing Machines

6.1.0.

We have presented two of the mathematical entities which were specifically created for formalizing the intuitive notion of computability, namely:

Turing machines;

Combinatorial Systems;

and we have also pointed out that the concept of a Turing machine is equivalent to that of a recursive function. We shall now show that it is also equivalent to the concept of a combinatorial system.

6.1.1. Computations of a Turing Machine and Semi-Thue Systems

Let Z be a Turing machine and let the quadruples which define it be divided into three types:

$$q_i \, S_j \, S_k \, q_l \tag{1}$$

$$q_i \, S_j \, R \, q_l \tag{2}$$

$$q_i \, S_j \, L \, q_l. \tag{3}$$

Recall that S_1 is the stick "|" and that the positive integer m is represented by $m+1$ consecutive sticks, in other words, $m = |^{m+1}$.

If we communicate to Z its input m in the form $\overline{m}$, Z begins its computation on m in the instantaneous description $q_1 \, \overline{m}$, and either there exists or there does not exist a result for this computation. Let us write P_Z for the set of non-negative integers for which the computation gives a result; we are not interested, moreover, in this result itself, but simply in its existence. We shall suppose, as always, that we may possibly have modified Z so that it encloses its computations between two markers h.

With each pair (Z, m) we associate a semi-Thue system $(ST)_1$ with axiom h $q_1 \, \overline{m}$ h. We choose the productions of the system in such a way that certain theorems of $(ST)_1$ correspond to the instantaneous descriptions of Z, whereas other theorems will allow us to associate a terminal instantaneous description with the theorem h r h whose meaning is: "Z can be applied to the input m, and there exists a result for this computation".

Formal construction of $(ST)_1$.

(a) With each quadruple of Z of type $q_i \, S_j \, S_k \, q_l$ we associate the production schema

$$P \, q_i \, S_j \, Q \to P \, q_l \, S_k \, Q,$$

whose effect is to make Z switch from the instantaneous description
$P \, q_i \, S_j \, Q$ to the one which results from this by the application of the
quadruple in question.

(b) With each quadruple of type $q_i \, S_j \, R \, q_l$ we associate all the productions

$$P \, S_k \, q_i \, S_j \, Q \rightarrow P \, q_l \, S_k \, S_j \, Q$$

(there are as many as there are S_k) whose effect again consists in making Z
switch from the instantaneous description $P \, S_k \, q_i \, S_j \, Q$ to the one which
results from the application of the quadruple in question.

(c) With each quadruple of type $q_i \, S_j \, L \, q_l$ we associate the production

$$P \, q_i \, S_j \, Q \rightarrow P \, S_j \, q_l \, Q$$

whose effect can be described exactly as we have already done in (a)
and (b).

The productions defined up to this point correspond to those situations of Z for which a quadruple applies. Consider now all the other
situations, those for which the machine stops and which therefore appear
only in the terminal descriptions. Our intention is to replace the result
of a computation by the unique answer $h \, r \, h$ (existence of a result). In
order to do this we introduce other productions which are applicable
only to those theorems of $(ST)_1$ associated with the terminal instantaneous descriptions. These are:

(d) $P \, q_i \, S_j \, Q \rightarrow P \, q \, S_j \, Q$

for all pairs (q_i, S_j) which are not situations of Z. These productions
introduce the marker q.

(e) $P \, q \, S_j \, Q \rightarrow P \, q \, Q.$

These productions erase symbols written to the right of the marker q.

(f) $P \, q \, h \, Q \rightarrow P \, r \, h \, Q.$

These productions introduce the marker r upon reaching the marker
h on the right.

(g) $P \, S_j \, r \, Q \rightarrow P \, r \, Q.$

These productions erase symbols to the left of r, with the exception
of h.

We are now in a position to state and prove the essential theorem of
this section.

Theorem. *The Turing machine Z is applicable to the input* m *if and only
if* $h \, r \, h$ *is a theorem of the semi-Thue system* $(ST)_1$ *associated with Z by
the preceding construction.*

Using Frege's symbol "⊢" whose meaning will be clear immediately
from the context, this theorem (or more exactly, this meta-theorem) can
be written:

$$m \in P_Z \Leftrightarrow \underset{(ST_1)}{\vdash} h \, r \, h.$$

1) *From left to right.* $m \in P_Z$ means that there exists a computation beginning in the state q_1 with input m. In other words, there exists a finite sequence of instantaneous descriptions $\alpha_1, \alpha_2, \ldots, \alpha_n$ where $\alpha_1 = h\,q_1\,m\,h$, α_n is terminal, and $\alpha_i \to \alpha_{i+1}$, $1 \leq i < n$.

We therefore have $\vdash_{(ST_1)} \alpha_n$, and the situation which appears in α_n appears in no other quadruple of Z. But then the production (d) $P\,q_i\,S_j\,Q \to P\,q\,S_j\,Q$ is applicable, followed by the erasure productions (f) and (g) until $h\,r\,h$ is obtained.

2) *From right to left.* From an examination of the productions (d), (e), (f) and (g), it is apparent that every proof that culminates in $h\,r\,h$ must necessarily contain a theorem $h\,P_0\,q\,Q_0\,h$ and that there exists in $(ST)_1$ a demonstration $M_1, M_2, \ldots, M_n$ of $h\,P_0\,q\,Q_0\,h$.

We therefore have $M_1 = h\,q_1\,\overline{m}\,h$, $M_n = h\,P_0\,q\,Q_0\,h$ and $M_i \to M_{i+1}$, $1 \leq i < n$. There exists an integer s such that $s < n$, every M_i contains a q_{α_i} and M_s is a terminal instantaneous description of Z. Hence, $m \in P_Z$.

Remarks on the structure of the system $(ST)_1$. It will be noticed that $(ST)_1$ depends on the integer m only by its axiom $h\,q_1\,\overline{m}\,h$; the productions and the alphabet, on the contrary, do not depend on m. The proof that $(ST)_1$ is monogenic is left as an exercise.

When m ranges over the set of non-negative integers, we obtain a family of semi-Thue systems of the type $(ST)_1$. By means of this family the *unique* theorem $h\,r\,h$ is associated with the subset of integers m to which Z applies. This situation suggests inverting the procedure and constructing a system which, starting from the *axiom* $h\,r\,h$, yields as terminal theorems the integers to which Z applies.

6.1.2. Turing Machines and Semi-Thue Systems

Let us therefore consider the system $(ST)_2$ which is obtained from the systems $(ST)_1$ in the following way:

1. The axiom of $(ST)_2$ is $h\,r\,h$.

2. The productions of $(ST)_2$ are the inverses of the productions common to all the $(ST)_1$.

Our study of $(ST)_1$ shows that this is equivalent to saying: "$h\,q_1\,\overline{m}\,h$ is for Z an initial instantaneous description which has a resultant" or: "$h\,q_1\,\overline{m}\,h$ is a theorem of $(ST)_2$". In view of this we can state a theorem.

Theorem. *A Turing machine Z is applicable to the input m if and only if* $h\,q_1\,\overline{m}\,h$ *is a theorem of the semi-Thue system* $(ST)_2$ *obtained by "inverting" the systems* $(ST)_1$ *associated with the pairs* (Z, m).

Remark. It is possible to complete $(ST)_2$ by the semi-Thue productions which allow h and q_1 to be erased. The system $(ST)_3$ thus obtained allows us to write more elegantly:

$$m \in P_Z \underset{(ST)_3}{\Leftrightarrow} \vdash m.$$

6.1.3. Turing Machines and Thue Systems

In the preceding section, we associated a semi-Thue system with a machine Z; we shall now associate a Thue system with it.

Consider then the system (T) defined on the same alphabet as previously used, and for which

1. The axiom is h r h;
2. The productions are those of $(ST)_1$ and $(ST)_2$ combined.

This is clearly a Thue system since the productions of $(ST)_2$ are the inverses of those of $(ST)_1$. We shall prove that the set of theorems of (T) coincides with the set of theorems of $(ST)_2$.

Every theorem of $(ST)_2$ can be shown to be a theorem of (T) by construction: the system $(ST)_2$ starts from the same axiom and makes use of a subset of the productions of T. The converse will have to be examined more carefully.

We shall write $R_1, R_2, ..., R_t$ for the productions of $(ST)_2$ and $S_1, S_2, ..., S_t$ for their inverses, respectively, i.e., for the productions of $(ST)_1$. The reader will note that the introduction of the S_i allows a proof to be lengthened "unnecessarily", by taking a step backwards and then forwards again. For example:

$$M (by \; R_1) \to N (by \; R_2) \to P$$

can be lengthened into

$$M (by \; R_1) \to N (by \; S_1) \to M, \quad etc.$$

The proof is equivalent to showing that (T) does not contain more theorems than $(ST)_2$, but proofs that may possibly be longer.

Given then a proof of a word M in (T), let us begin by removing all the unnecessary steps obtained by repetition. The proof becomes:

$$h \, r \, h = M_1, M_2, ..., M_p = M.$$

It is possible that this new proof will no longer make use of any other productions but those of $(ST)_2$, in which case the theorem is proven.

Let us therefore suppose that for a certain subscript j, where $1 \leq j < p$, there appears for the *first* time a production of type S which allows M_j to be rewritten as M_{j+1}. Can M_j be the axiom h r h? We have seen, in connection with $(ST)_1$, that this system culminates in h r h; hence no inverse production in $(ST)_2$ can possibly yield h r h. It follows that M_j is a consequence of M_{j-1} with respect to some R_1; in other words, M_{j-1} is deduced from M_j by the application of a rule of type S.

But then M_j has the consequences M_{j+1} and M_{j-1} with respect to the productions S, and these consequences are different since every repetition has been eliminated from the proof of M. This result contradicts the monogenicity of $(ST)_1$.   Q.E.D.

Theorem. *The set of theorems of the Thue system* (T) *coincides with the set of theorems of the semi-Thue system* $(ST)_2$.

In brief, we have shown that the productions which were added to $(ST)_2$ in order to obtain (T) produce no new theorems but only variants in the proofs.

6.1.4. Résumé of Results Thus Far

In these last few chapters we have proven a certain number of theorems of equivalence. We now add to these the following result (whose proof is left as an exercise), namely, that with every Thue system we can associate a Post system having the same theorems. The situation is summarized in Fig. 6-1:

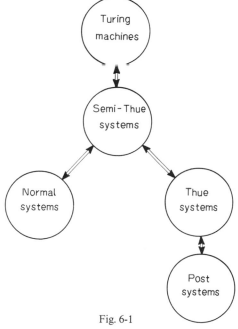

Fig. 6-1

Every set generated by a system can be generated by any one of the others and an equivalent system can be effectively constructed from the given system. From the equivalences between Turing machines and formal systems already proven it follows that:

Theorem. *Every recursively denumerable set can be generated by a semi-Thue, Thue, normal, or Post system (indifferently).*

6.1.5. Exercises

1. Show that the system $(ST)_1$ is monogenic.

2. Show that in a Thue system the set of proofs can be reduced, without changing the set of theorems, in such a way that the reduced proofs contain no repeated steps.

6.2. Undecidable Problems

6.2.1. Consequences of the Halting Problem

We have studied the following problem: does there exist a general algorithm (a Turing machine) which will always give a yes or no answer to the question whether a Turing machine with a specified input will yield a result? The answer to this *general* problem is no. (Note: in particular cases it is possible to give an affirmative answer to this problem as restricted to the particular case).

The construction of the systems $(ST)_2$ and (T) associated with a machine S makes the set of theorems of $(ST)_2$ and (T) correspond to the set of arguments of the machine. Upon choosing for Z a machine whose halting problem is undecidable, we then obtain associated semi-Thue and Thue systems whose decision problem is recursively undecidable. In the case of a system, the decision problem consists in knowing whether a word written in the alphabet of the system is a theorem of the system or not. By constructing the normal system and the Post system associated with the semi-Thue and the Thue systems, respectively, we obtain for each category a system whose decision problem is undecidable.

6.2.2. The Word Problem

Let us now return to the word problem which we stated in Chapter I. Given a quotient monoid defined by n Thue relations: $P_1 \sim Q_1, \ldots, P_n \sim Q_n$, we asked whether it was possible to decide upon the equivalence or non-equivalence of two words A and B.

Consider first the Thue system having A as its axiom, and $P_1 \leftrightarrow Q_1, \ldots,$ $P_n \leftrightarrow Q_n$ as its productions. Deciding whether B is equivalent to the word A, or deciding whether B is a theorem of the Thue system are two equivalent problems.

Consider now the undecidable Thue system which we have constructed and associate with it the monoid obtained by forming a Thue relation from each pair of Thue productions: it is clear that we have obtained a monoid for which the word problem is recursively undecidable.

6.2.3. Post's Correspondence Problem

Consider the following English words:

$M_1 = $ "on"   Preposition indicating position of contact.

$N_1 = $ "ion"   An electrified particle.

$M_2 = $ "rebel"   To oppose authority; to be insubordinate.

$N_2 = $ "re"   The second tone of the diatonic scale.

$M_3 = $ "li"   Chinese unit of measure.

$N_3 = $ "bell"   A hollow metallic vessel that rings when struck.

Then the word $M = $ "rebellion" can be decomposed in two ways: rebel/li/on and re/bell/ion. Thus M gives rise to a double orthographic decomposition: $M = M_2 M_3 M_1 = N_2 N_3 N_1$, based upon the triples (M_1, M_2, M_3) and (N_1, N_2, N_3). Furthermore, if the word M_i appears in the j-th place in the first decomposition, then the coupled word N_i must also appear in the j-th place in the second decomposition.

The Problem of Double Decomposition. Given two n-tuples of words, written in the alphabet $\mathfrak{A}$, which are coupled by their subscripts: $(G_1, \ldots, G_n)$ and $(H_1, \ldots, H_n)$, we can ask whether there exists a finite index sequence $i_1, i_2, \ldots, i_k$, such that we obtain a double decomposition:

$$G_{i_1} G_{i_2} \ldots G_{i_k} = H_{i_1} H_{i_2} \ldots H_{i_k}, \qquad \text{where } i_j \in \{1, 2, \ldots, n\}.$$

To this *particular* question one may be able to answer positively (by offering some example, perhaps) or negatively (by pointing out an impossibility, as would happen if every G_i were longer than the coupled H_i).

Post's Problem. Post posed another problem, more general than the one mentioned above, namely: "Does there exist a general algorithm which, given two arbitrary n-tuples, can decide whether or not there exists an index sequence which yields a double decomposition?". We shall now give the general outlines of a proof which will allow the reader to show that this problem is undecidable.

Sketch of a Proof. Given two particular n-tuples on the alphabet $\mathfrak{A}$: $(G_1, \ldots, G_n)$ and $(H_1, \ldots, H_n)$, we define the normal system (N) containing no empty word. The axiom is a non-empty word $A \in \mathfrak{A}^*$, and the set of productions are $G_i P \to P H_i$, $1 \leq i \leq n$.

Let us examine the way (N) produces its theorems. The axiom is A; suppose we can write this word as $A = G' P'$, where G' is one of the G_i. Then a possible consequence of this is $A = G' P' \to P' H'$, where H' designates the H_i paired with G_i. Suppose that $P' H'$ in turn can be rewritten $P' H' = G'' P''$, where G'' designates still another G_i. We then have $G'' P'' \to P'' H''$, etc.

A proof in (N), then, proceeds as shown in Fig. 6-2 (where the relation of consequence is indicated by the arrow pointing down):

(0) $A = G' P'$

           $\downarrow$

(1) $P' H' = G'' P''$

              $\downarrow$

(2) $P'' H'' = G''' P'''$

. . . .

                               $\downarrow$

(k − 1) $P^{(k-1)} H^{(k-1)} = G^{(k)} P^{(k)}$

                                   $\downarrow$

(k) $P^{(k)} H^{(k)} = B.$

Fig. 6-2

From this, there follows immediately the following:

(0 *bis*) $A H' = G' P' H'$ $= G' G'' P''$

(1 *bis*) $A H' H''$ $= G' G'' P'' H'' = G' G'' G''' P'''$

. . . .

(k − 2 *bis*) $A H' H'' \dots H^{(k-1)}$ $= G' G'' \dots G^{(k-1)} P^{(k-1)} H^{(k-1)}$

                                            $= G' G'' \dots G^{(k-1)} G^{(k)} P^{(k)}$

(k − 1 *bis*) $A H' H'' \dots H^{(k-1)} H^{(k)} = G' G'' \dots G^{(k-1)} G^{(k)} P^{(k)} H^{(k)}$

                                            $= G' G'' \dots G^{(k-1)} G^{(k)} B$

Fig. 6-3

Since the H_i and the G_i are not empty, but the P_i may be, we have the following kinds of inequalities:

Degree of $A H'$ ≥ Degree of $G' G''$,

Degree of $A H' H'' ≥$ Degree of $G' G'' G'''$, etc.

The essential result so far is then clearly the following:

Proposition. If B is a theorem of (N) there exists an index sequence yielding the "pseudo-Post" equality:

$$A H' H'' \dots H^{(k)} = G' G'' \dots G^{(k)} B,$$

and the inequalities:

$$\text{Degree of } A H' \dots H^{(j)} \geq \text{Degree of } G' \dots G^{(j)}.$$

Conversely, starting from such an equality and its associated inequalities, it is possible to reconstruct the P_i and a proof of B (the proof is left as an exercise).

Thus, we observe that the problem of whether a given word belongs to the system (N) is equivalent to a "pseudo-Post" problem. In order to obtain Post's problem, the parasitic inequalities must be eliminated, as well as the words A and B. It is actually possible (see the exercises) to construct a normal system derived from (N) for which the word problem is equivalent to Post's problem, from which follows the undecidability of the latter.

Post's problem, in turn, will be useful in proving undecidability theorems pertaining to certain formal grammars.

An Interpretation of Post's Problem. Let $\mathfrak{A}$ and $\mathfrak{B}$ be two alphabets (possibly identical). Consider the mapping of a free monoid $\mathfrak{A}^*$ in (or on) the monoid $\mathfrak{B}^*$ compatible with concatenation. Such a mapping is a homomorphism of the monoid, and is defined by the images of the single-letter words.

Given now two such homomorphisms φ and ψ, we may ask whether there exists a word M of $\mathfrak{A}$ which has the same image under φ and ψ: $\varphi(M) = \psi(M)$. This problem is known as the problem of the diagonalization of two homomorphisms of free monoids: we see that it is equivalent to Post's problem.

6.2.4. Summary of Undecidable Problems

We have constructed an entity with an undecidable problem (a Turing machine) and have obtained other results with the help of equivalence theorems. Fig. 6-4 below summarizes the sequence of ideas involved.

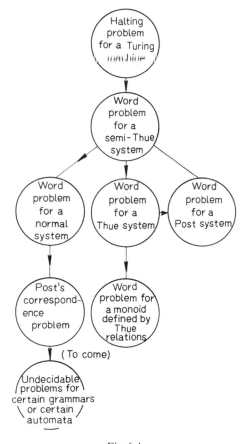

Fig. 6-4

6.2.5. Exercises

1. Give some special cases where Post's correspondence problem can be solved, either by producing an index sequence which answers the question, or by proving that no such sequence exists.

2. Elimination of the parasitic conditions in the "pseudo-Post" problem.

a) We have already proven that with every system we can associate an equivalent system, by means of a code, whose alphabet contains only two letters, a and b. We shall suppose that (N) has already been reduced in this way.

With the system (N) we associate the anti-normal system (AN) whose axiom and productions are the mirror images of those of (N). From (AN) we proceed to the system (ANl), whose alphabet contains the marker h and which adds to each word of (AN) the marker h on the right. Finally, we construct a *normal* system (NC) which contains all the words of (ANl) plus all those which can be obtained from these by cyclical permutations.

$$\text{Alphabet:} \quad \{a, b, h\};$$

(NC) Axiom: $\tilde{A}\,h;$

$$\text{Productions:} \{\tilde{G}_i\,h\,P \rightarrow P\,h\,\tilde{H}_i \,|\, 1 \leq i \leq n\}$$
$$\text{and} \quad a\,P \rightarrow P\,a, \ b\,P \rightarrow P\,b, \ h\,P \rightarrow P\,h.$$

The productions of (NC) are of the form:

$$\{K_i\,P \rightarrow P\,\overline{K}_i \,|\, 1 \leq i \leq n+3\}.$$

Compare the word problem and the pseudo-Post problem for this system (NC) and show that the inequalities are now superfluous (they are satisfied in the case of equality). Use the number of occurrences of the marker h.

b) We can now eliminate the words A and B, or more precisely, $\tilde{A}\,h$ and $\tilde{B}\,h$. To this end, we start with the pseudo-Post equality and code the elements in such a way that we obtain an equality independent of A and B (the Post equality); we can then show that this latter equality is true only when the pseudo-Post equality is also true.

We introduce $n+5$ couples $(F_i, \overline{F}_i)$:

if $\qquad K_i = x_1\,x_2 \ldots x_p, \qquad F_i = x_1\,k\,x_2\,k \ldots x_p\,k;$

if $\qquad \overline{K}_i = y_1\,y_2 \ldots y_p, \qquad \overline{F}_i = k\,y_1\,k\,y_2 \ldots k\,y_p,$

where $x_j, y_j \in \{a, b, h\}$ and k designates a new letter. With the sequence $\tilde{A}\,h = x_1\,x_2 \ldots x_j$, we associate the couple

$$(F_{n+4}, \overline{F}_{n+4}) = (k\,k;\ k\,k\,x_2 \ldots k\,x_j);$$

with the sequence $\tilde{B}\,h = y_1\,y_2 \ldots y_j$ we associate the couple:

$$(F_{n+5}, \overline{F}_{n+5}) = (y_1\,k\,y_2\,k \ldots y_j\,k\,k,\ k\,k).$$

With this coding the proposition can be proven by analyzing each case and using a *reductio ad absurdum* based on the arrangement of the occurrences of k.

PART II
Some Important Classes of Languages

Chapter VII
Context-Free Languages.
Presentation. Preliminaries.

7.1. Grammar and Description

7.1.0.

In the course of the introductory chapters we have presented a language as a part of a free monoid generated by the letters of an alphabet (the words of a vocabulary) and a grammar as an algorithm which allows the words (the sentences) of a language to be enumerated. We also underlined the interest of an algorithm which, given a word (a sentence), would decide whether it belongs to the language or not.

The details concerning algorithms which were given afterwards will now enable us to formulate a certain number of general results about grammars and languages.

7.1.1. Grammars and Turing Machines

A grammar has been considered as an algorithm and the concept of an algorithm has been related to the concept of a Turing machine (or of a combinatorial system). With the exception of some variations in the presentation, we can than define the most general grammar in terms of a Turing machine (or of a combinatorial system). To say that the grammar G of a language L defined on a vocabulary V is an enumerating algorithm is equivalent to saying that there exists a Turing machine Z_G which associates a sentence φ_1 with the number 1, a sentence φ_2 with the number 2, ..., and a sentence φ_n with every integer n. The machine Z_G produces the recursively denumerable set: $\{\varphi_1, \varphi_2, ..., \varphi_n, ...\}$.

It is possible to present the same algorithm (or a related one) in the form of a recognition test. A sentence φ is submitted to the machine; if this sentence belongs to the language the machine should stop after a finite number of operations. Hence:

1. If the machine stops, φ belongs to the language;
2. If a stop has not yet been noted, then nothing can be concluded.

However, it is impossible, within the class of languages that are recursively denumerable, and nothing more, to give a recognition algorithm that will answer *yes* or *no*.

Classes of Grammars. The extreme generality of the definitions which we have just discussed does not allow us to describe many specific features of real languages — whether natural or artificial — and their grammars. It is therefore necessary to adopt a more precise point of view. According as the criteria which we introduce are more or less restrictive, we obtain classes of grammars, arranged in a hierarchy of inclusion. To these different classes there correspond classes of automata which are more specialized than Turing machines (or classes of combinatorial systems).

It is possible to define all these different classes from the outset, but in view of the pedagogical aim of this work it seems preferable to begin our study with a class occupying a middle position in the hierarchy. This is a class which is encountered rather naturally as soon as one concerns oneself with syntax and which we shall now present from a heuristic point of view.

7.1.2. A Structure in General Use

We shall take English sentences as our examples. We shall also take it for granted that we know whether a sequence of English words constitutes a sentence or not, and we shall make use of the concepts of parsing which we learned in grade school.

In order to deal with grammar, we shall use names of syntactic categories such as "noun", "verb", "noun phrase", etc. It goes without saying that if the word "noun" is a noun, the word "verb" is not a verb; we must distinguish between a category and the word (or possibly the sequence of words) which is used to designate it.

In quite the same way in formal grammars, the vocabulary *per se* of the language — which we shall call the terminal vocabulary — is to be distinguished from the auxiliary vocabulary which is used to state and manipulate the rules.

Sentence Structure. A sentence generally contains one (or several) subject(s), one (or several) verb(s), and one (or more) object(s) or predicate(s). The sentence (1) "Fido barks" has the simple structure (I) 'Noun Verb'. Often, however, the subject is accompanied by various modifiers and is then the kernel of a noun phrase. Thus, the sentence (2) "The hungry dog barks" has the structure (II) 'Noun phrase Verb'. By analogous extensions we obtain such sentences as (3) "The hungry dog barks plaintively at the caravan" which can be structured as (III) 'Noun phrase Verb phrase Preposition Noun phrase'.

Let us now introduce some abbreviations, which the reader will understand quite readily, such as S for sentence, NP for noun phrase, etc. Then we can state rules of the type: S → 'NP VP Prep NP', i.e., "One possible way to obtain a sentence is to take a noun phrase, followed by a verb phrase, followed by a preposition and a noun phrase". At a lower level we will have rules like: NP → 'Art Adj N', VP → 'V Adv'.

Tree Structure. A convenient way of representing the syntactic structure of a sentence consists in using parentheses which are labelled by the names of the syntactic categories. For the sentence (3) above we will have:

$$\left[{}_{S}\left[{}_{NP}\left[{}_{Art}\text{The}\right]\left[{}_{Adj}\text{hungry}\right]\left[{}_{N}\text{dog}\right]\right]\left[{}_{VP}\left[{}_{V}\text{barks}\right]\left[{}_{Adv}\text{plaintively}\right]\right]\left[{}_{Prep.}\text{at}\right]\left[{}_{NP}\left[{}_{Art}\text{the}\right]\right.\right.$$

$$\left.\left.\left[{}_{N}\text{caravan}\right]\right]\right]$$

Fig. 7-1

An equivalent method is to use a tree with labelled nodes. The transition from one representation to the other can be done quite mechanically.

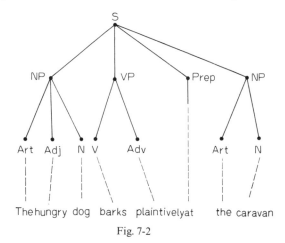

Fig. 7-2

The choice of a tree to represent the structure of a sentence is somewhat arbitrary and we might certainly have used a more general type of graph, for example a graph with cycles. Empirical reasons dictated the choice of a tree. Trees are simple graphs, and although certain phenomena are not represented (like restrictions between non-contiguous elements), they are quite satisfactory for a first approximation: their simplicity is not bought at too great a price.

In the field of programming languages the situation is roughly the same: a program can be analyzed as a series of strings belonging to various syntactic categories.

Return to Grammars. Tree structures will play an important rôle in syntactic description and we shall require of grammars not only that they enumerate sentences but also that they associate one or more structures with each sentence according as it is ambiguous or not. It will therefore be important to study algorithms which, given a sentence, will decide whether it belongs to the language and assign it the corresponding tree (or trees). In the next section of this chapter we shall give some *a priori* definitions in which the reader will recognize the concepts which we have introduced here intuitively.

7.1.3. Exercises

1. Formulate the rules in such a way that the sentence of Fig. 7-2 can be represented by a binary tree.

2. What happens if we introduce such a rule as "NP → Art NP"?

7.2. Definitions; Decidable Properties

7.2.0.

We are going to define an extremely important class of grammars and languages, a class so important that many workers discovered it starting from apparently quite different points of view. Chomsky first gave a thorough characterization of this class of languages, which he also named "context-free"; this is how they are now referred to in the literature. In fact, it is the grammar rules of these languages which are formulated independently of any context, whence their name which was first appled to the grammars and then to the languages.

We shall use the abbreviations CF-languages and CF-grammars for context-free languages and context-free grammars.

7.2.1. Definitions
A CF-grammar is defined by:

1. A finite terminal vocabulary V_T.
2. A finite auxiliary vocabulary V_A.
3. An axiom $S \in V_A$.
4. A finite number of context-free rules of the form $A \to \varphi$, where

$$A \in V_A \quad \text{and} \quad \varphi \in \{V_A \cup V_T\}^*.$$

The combinatorial system which corresponds to a CF-grammar is thus a semi-Thue system, but of a special form. This system contains non-terminal theorems and possibly also terminal theorems. We term CF-language the set of terminal theorems of the associated semi-Thue system, or, in other terms, the set of sentences generated by the CF-grammar on the terminal vocabulary.

In this case, we usually speak of a *derivation* rather than a proof.

Examples. 1. Let the grammar be defined by $V_A = \{S\}$; $V_T = \{a, b, c\}$;

$$G_m: \begin{vmatrix} S \to a\,S\,a \\ S \to b\,S\,b \\ S \to \quad c \end{vmatrix}.$$

One possible derivation of this grammar is then:

$$S \to a\,S\,a \to a\,a\,S\,a\,a \to a\,a\,b\,S\,b\,a\,a \to a\,a\,b\,c\,b\,a\,a$$

which is written

$$S \Rightarrow a\,a\,b\,c\,b\,a\,a.$$

More generally, the notation $\varphi \Rightarrow \psi$ means that there exists a derivation starting from φ and ending with ψ.

It is immediately apparent that the general form of the sentences generated by the grammar G_m has the structure $x\,c\,\tilde{x}$ where x represents an arbitrary sequence of a and b, and $\tilde{x}$ is the mirror image of x. We abbreviate these facts by using the following notation:

$$L_m = L(G_m) = \{x\,c\,\tilde{x} \mid x \in \{a, b\}^*\}.$$

2. Given the grammar: $V_A = \{S, A\}$; $V_T = \{a, b\}$;

$$G_0: \begin{vmatrix} S \to a\,A \\ A \to A\,b \end{vmatrix}.$$

It is clear that the derivations continue indefinitely without ever reaching a terminal sentence: G_0 generates the empty language.

Classification of the Rules. A CF-grammar thus generates non-terminal sentences and a (possibly empty) set of terminal sentences which constitute the language $L(G)$. We shall call penultimate a non-terminal sentence which is capable of yielding a terminal sentence by the application of just one rule (the last step in the derivation). A penultimate contains one non-terminal symbol and only one.

A necessary condition for the language $L(G)$ not to be empty is that there exist one or more rules, called *terminal*, of the form:

$$A \to \tau; \quad A \in V_A; \quad \tau \in V_T^*.$$

All other rules are called non-terminal.

Example. The grammar G_m contains two non-terminal rules $S \to a\,S\,a$ and $S \to b\,S\,b$; it contains the unique terminal rule $S \to c$.

The grammar G_0 contains no terminal rule.

7.2.2. Correspondence between Grammars and Languages

To every CF-grammar there corresponds a CF-language which may be empty. It should be noted that the correspondence is not injective: several grammars may generate the same language.

Example. An example is given by the grammar: $V_A = \{S, A\}$; $V_T = \{a, b, c\}$;

$$\begin{vmatrix} S \rightarrow & a\,S\,a & (1) \\ S \rightarrow & b\,S\,b & (2) \\ S \rightarrow & c & (3) \\ S \rightarrow a\,b\,S\,b\,a & (4) \\ S \rightarrow & c\,A & (5) \\ S \rightarrow & a\,A & (6) \end{vmatrix}.$$

This grammar generates L_m, just as G_m does, but it differs from G_m:

1. By the addition of the rule (4) which generates certain sentences of L_m "more rapidly".

2. By the addition of the rules (5) and (6) which are unproductive insofar as terminal sentences are concerned.

We shall have more significant examples in what follows.

Given then a grammar, we may at once, without modifying it in any essential way,

1. Prune it, by removing those rules and symbols which produce nothing at the level of terminal sentences.

2. Reorganize its rules, if need be, without any change in the language generated.

Connected Grammar. In order to study a grammar, we can help ourselves by using a graph whose vertices represent the symbols of the auxiliary vocabulary:

$$S = A_1, A_2, \dots, A_p,$$

and the words which appear in the terminal rules:

$$a_1, a_2, \dots, a_q.$$

We draw a directed edge from A_i to A_j (a_k) if there exists a production of the type:

$$A_i \rightarrow \varphi\, A_j\, \psi, \qquad (A_i \rightarrow a_k).$$

If the graph is not connected, then clearly the partial graphs which do not contain the axiom produce nothing. The rules and corresponding symbols may be removed from the grammar. Later, we may adopt another approach, but in any case we may suppose that the grammar has been made connected (i.e., has a connected graph).

About the Empty Word. We are in no way obliged, by any question of principle, to exclude terminal rules of the form: $A \rightarrow E$, where E represents the empty word. However, it turns out to be more convenient, for technical reasons, to eliminate this type of rule. It can be shown (cf. the exercise on this question) that given a CF-grammar which generates a language L containing the empty word, a closely related CF-grammar can be associated with it which generates $L - \{E\}$. In all that follows we shall assume that this reduction has been carried out.

Contraction and Rules. It is clear that if a grammar has a derivation of the kind: $A \Rightarrow \varphi$, where A is non-terminal and φ an arbitrary string, then the language generated is not changed by adding to the grammar the rule: $A \rightarrow \varphi$. We shall say that this rule is obtained by contraction of the derivation.

7.2.3. Non-Empty, Finite, and Infinite Languages

Non-Empty Languages. A necessary and sufficient condition for a CF-grammar to generate a non-empty language is that there exist a derivation of the type $S \Rightarrow \tau$, where τ is a terminal sentence. This is a decidable question, as is shown in the exercise on this problem.

Infinite Languages. Since the terminal vocabulary is finite, a necessary condition for the language $L(G)$ to be infinite is that the length of the terminal sentences be unbounded, hence that the length of the penultimate sentences be unbounded, and finally that the length of the non-terminal sentences also be unbounded. This last condition clearly is not sufficient, since unbounded non-terminal sentences can be found which nevertheless generate only the empty language.

We are therefore led to formulate the problem of infinite languages in the following way:

a) Search for a necessary and sufficient condition for the non-terminal language to be infinite.

b) Search for an additional condition for the terminal language to be infinite.

For point a), let us consider the graph defined in connection with connected grammars. This graph may contain a cycle or loop starting, for example, from A and returning to A. In this case there exists a derivation of the type: $A \Rightarrow \varphi A \psi$. The trivial case $A \Rightarrow A$ corresponds to a simple repetition of A, and we eliminate it by taking: $|\varphi| + |\psi| \neq 0$.

Since the grammar is assumed to be connected, there exists a derivation such that: $S \Rightarrow \alpha A \beta$. The non-terminal language therefore contains an infinite number of sentences of the type: $\alpha \varphi^n A \psi^n \beta$; it is infinite.

Suppose on the other hand that the graph contains no cycle or loop; then the rules: $A_1 \rightarrow \varphi_1$ can no longer contain A_1 on the right. If one of these rules contains A_2, then no rule $A_2 \rightarrow \varphi_2$ can contain either A_1 or A_2 on the right. Thus the non-terminal symbols disappear stepwise after a finite number of operations: the language cannot be infinite.

A necessary and sufficient condition for the non-terminal language to be infinite is that there exist a non-terminal A and a derivation:

$$A \Rightarrow \varphi A \psi, \qquad |\varphi| + |\psi| \neq 0.$$

Remark. If $|\varphi| \cdot |\psi| \neq 0$ also obtains, then A is said to be *self-embedded*.

It can easily be shown that the existence of such a non-terminal language is a decidable question. For point b), a decidable criterion can be found (cf. the exercise on this problem).

Since the three cases of empty, finite and infinite languages cover all the possibilities and are mutually exclusive, the question of finiteness is also decidable.

Theorem. *The question whether a CF-grammar generates an empty, finite or infinite language is decidable.*

7.2.4. Recursiveness

Since CF-grammars have a particular form, we may expect them to generate particular languages. We have taken the precaution to eliminate the rules $A \to E$; under these conditions the length of the strings can only increase (or exceptionally remain the same) at each step of a derivation. To decide whether a given string of non-terminal words belongs to a CF-language or not, it suffices to carry out all the derivations which yield sentences having a length less than or equal to the length of the sentence in question. This procedure will succeed for every sentence and give a *yes* or *no* answer. More concisely:

The CF-languages are recursive.

7.2.5. Example of a Language which is not a CF-Language

In what follows we shall make use of the fact that the language $L = \{a^n b^n c^n\}$ is not a CF-language. Let us now prove this proposition.

Being infinite, L must contain some derivation of the type: $A \Rightarrow \varphi A \psi$, $|\varphi| + |\psi| \neq 0$. It contains non-terminal sentences of the type $\alpha \varphi^n A \psi^n \beta$ for every n. φ, A and ψ must also lead to terminal strings and by contracting the derivations we can add rules of the type $A \to \tau$.

It is easily shown that whatever rules may be chosen, in addition to the sentences $a^n b^n c^n$ other sentences are found whose exponents are not all equal.

Remark. The language $L = \{a^n b^n c^n\}$ is clearly recursive. Consequently: *The class of CF-languages does not exhaust the class of recursive languages.*

7.2.6. Exercises

1. Find a CF-grammar that generates the language: $L_1 = \{a^n b^n c^p\}$, and a CF-grammar that generates the language: $L_2 = \{a^m b^q c^q\}$.

2. Same question for the language $\{x \tilde{x}\}$ on $\{a, b\}$ without a center marker.

3. Show that $\{a^q b^q c^r | p \leq q \leq r\}$ is not a CF-language.

4. Consider the vocabulary $V = V_A \cup V_T$ and production rules of the type $A \to \varphi$, $A \in V_A$. Choose as axiom each element of V_A one after the other. Is it possible for the languages generated to be different? Construct some simple examples. The following is one such example:

$$A \to AC, \qquad B \to Bb,$$
$$B \to BC, \qquad B \to b,$$
$$A \to Aa, \qquad C \to AA.$$
$$A \to a,$$

5. Elimination of the empty word. Let G be a CF-grammar and V_0 the set of $A \in V_A$ such that $A \to E$. Construct the set V_1 which contains V_0 and the $A \in V_A$ such that $A \to \varphi \in V_0^*$; continue in this way.

Study this sequence of sets; give a necessary and sufficient condition for $E \in L(G)$. Starting with G, construct a grammar G' such that $L(G') = L(G) - \{E\}$.

Note that one cannot purely and simply delete the rules $A \to E$. If, in the grammar:

$$G: \quad \begin{vmatrix} S \to aAa \\ A \to E \\ A \to bA \\ A \to c \end{vmatrix}$$

we strike out $A \to E$, it will no longer yield the isolated sentence a a, nor any of the sentences a b^n a. The generation of such sentences must be preserved.

6. Elimination of unproductive rules — the empty language. Let G be a CF-grammar from which the rules $A \to E$ have been eliminated. We write as W_0 the set of A such that $A \in V_A$ and $A \to \tau$, where τ is a terminal sentence. Construct the set W_1 which contains W_0 and the $A \in V_A$ such that $A \to \varphi \in W_0^* - \{E\}$. Continue in this fashion; study the sequence of W_i.

Give a necessary and sufficient condition for $L(G)$ to be empty. Find a procedure for eliminating unproductive rules. Note that in the grammar:

$$G: \quad \begin{vmatrix} S \to BaB \\ B \to Bb \\ B \to b \\ A \to ASA \\ A \to a \end{vmatrix}$$

we obtain

$$W_0 = \{a, b\}$$
$$W_1 = \{a, b, A, B\}$$
$$W_2 = \{a, b, A, B, S\}$$

and yet, if S is the axiom, A remains unproductive since it can never be reached from the axiom S. The situation would be different if a rule $S \rightarrow \varphi A \psi$ were added.

7.3. Closure Properties

7.3.0.

A set is said to be closed with respect to an operation if upon applying this operation to every element, if the operation is unary, or to every pair if the operation is binary, etc., the result is always contained in the set. We shall study the behavior of the CF-languages from this point of view for several simple operations.

7.3.1. Union of Two CF-Languages

Given the two CF-languages: L_1 produced by a grammar G_1 with axiom S_1, and L_2 produced by a grammar G_2 with axiom S_2. By changing the names of the auxiliary symbols if necessary we can arrange that $V_{A_1} \cap V_{A_2} = \emptyset$. Consider now the grammar with the axiom $S \notin V_{A_1} \cup V_{A_2}$ whose rules are the union of the rules of G_1 and G_2 together with $S \rightarrow S_1$ and $S \rightarrow S_2$.

It is clear that we have constructed a CF-grammar and that *the union of two CF-languages is a CF-language.*

7.3.2. Product of Two CF-Languages

Using the same notation, consider the product $L_1 L_2$. In order to define it, we separate the two grammars as was done above and choose as axiom a new symbol S. We then form the union of the rules and add to it $S \rightarrow S_1 S_2$. It is clear that we have constructed a CF-grammar and that: *the product of two CF-languages is a CF-language.*

7.3.3. Star Operation

The product defined above is associative and enables us to define the languages $L^2, L^3, \ldots$, starting with a CF-language L. Consider then the language $L^* - \{E\} = L \cup L^2 \cup L^n \cup \ldots$. Let S be the axiom of the CF-grammar G that defines L. We shall complete G by adding to it the new axiom T (which then replaces S) and the rules: $T \rightarrow ST, T \rightarrow S$. It is clear that the last two rules generate the series $S, S^2, \ldots, S^n, \ldots$ which are themselves heads of derivations leading to $L, L^2, \ldots, L^n, \ldots$. Hence: *the star operation applied to a CF-language defines a CF-language.*

7.3.4. Intersection of Two CF-Languages

1. Given the CF-language $L_0 = \{a^n c a^n\}$ and the CF-language $L_m = \{x c \tilde{x} | x \in \{a, b\}^*\}$ which will be studied in § 8.1.1. Clearly $L_0 \cap L_m = L_0$.

2. Given the two CF-languages: $L_1 = \{a^n\, b^n\, c^p\}$, $L_2 = \{a^m\, b^q\, c^q\}$. Then $L_1 \cap L_2 = \{a^n\, b^n\, c^n\}$ and we have already seen that this language is not a CF-language. From these two examples we see that: *the intersection of two CF-languages may be, but is not necessarily a CF-language.*

7.3.5. Complementation

The language V_T^* is a CF-language because we can generate it with a grammar containing all the rules of the type $S \rightarrow a\, S$, $S \rightarrow S\, a$, $S \rightarrow a$. By the complement L of a language $\bar{L}$ we mean the complement with respect to V_T. We also know that $L_1 \cap L_2 = \overline{\bar{L}_1 \cup \bar{L}_2}$.

If a CF-language remained a CF-language under complementation, it would remain so under intersection as well. Hence:

The complement of a CF-language is not necessarily a CF-language

7.3.6. Mirror Image Operation (Reflection)

The CF-language L having the grammar G: $\{A \rightarrow \varphi\}$ can be associated with the language $\tilde{L}$ having the grammar G: $\{A \rightarrow \tilde{\varphi}\}$ by the mirror image operation. It is clear that:

The application of the mirror image operation to a CF-language yields a CF-language.

7.3.7. Composition

Let L be a CF-language defined on the vocabulary $V_A \cup V_T$, where $V_T = \{a_i | 1 \leq i \leq n\}$, by a grammar G. Furthermore, consider n CF-languages $L_1, \ldots, L_i, \ldots, L_n$ (as many languages as there are terminal words in V_T). We arrange for the intersection of the auxiliary vocabularies, taken two by two, always to be empty, and we name a_i that axiom of the grammar G_i which defines L_i. The union of the grammars G, $G_1, \ldots, G_n$ is a CF-grammar which generates a CF-language obtained from L by *composition.*

The operation of composition performed on a CF-language by means of CF-languages (a suitable number of them) yields another CF-language.

In conclusion, the set of CF-languages is closed under the operations of union, product, star, mirror, and composition.

7.3.8. Exercises

A CF-language is given by a CF-grammar G. Consider all the languages obtained by taking as axiom, one after the other, each of the non-terminal symbols of G. Take the union of these languages; what is the result?

Draw the necessary conclusions as to the role of the axiom in a grammar.

7.4. Classes of CF-Languages

7.4.0.

By further specifying the rules of the obligatory type $A \rightarrow \varphi$, various classes of CF-languages can be defined. These classes of languages, which were introduced for various considerations, do not necessarily have the closure properties of the general class. Certain of their properties can be grasped immediately with the help of the algebraic characterization of the CF-languages, a theory which we shall study later.

Since the CF-grammars do not correspond injectively to the CF-languages, a certain care must be taken in the classification of languages. We shall begin by defining a grammar of class (α) and specifying the properties which its rules must have. We will say that a language L is of class (α) if there exists one grammar (at least) of this type which generates this language. In order to prove, however, that a language *is not* of type (α), it must be shown that all grammars which generate it are not of type (α).

7.4.1. Kleene Languages

In the next chapter, we shall make a detailed study of grammars with non-terminal rules which are all of the type $A \rightarrow a B$; $A, B \in V_A$, $a \in V_T$. These grammars are called "*finite-state* grammars" in the literature (the term *regular* languages is also used). We will call them Kleene grammars, because of the rôle Kleene played in their development, and we shall make use of such abbreviations as K-grammar, K-language.

A K-language is one that can be generated by a K-grammar.

7.4.2. Linear Languages

The non-terminal rules of a *linear* grammar have the form

$$A \rightarrow x B y; \qquad A, B \in V_A; \qquad x, y \in V_T^*.$$

A language is linear if it can be generated by a linear grammar. The K-languages form a subclass of the linear languages.

Another subclass is that of the *minimal linear languages* for which V_A reduces to $\{S\}$ and the set of terminal rules to $S \rightarrow c$, where the symbol c does not appear in any other rule. The language L_m of § 7.2.1 belongs to this last class.

7.4.3. The Meta-Linear Languages

A grammar is said to be *meta-linear* if every φ such that $S \Rightarrow \varphi$ is necessarily of limited degree with respect to V_A. A language is metalinear if there exists a metalinear grammar that generates it.

Example. Given the language defined by $V_A = \{S, T\}$, $V_T = \{a, b, c\}$ and the grammar:

$$G_{2m}: \begin{vmatrix} S \to TT \\ T \to a\,T\,a \\ T \to b\,T\,b \\ T \to c \end{vmatrix}$$

This language is metalinear. It generates the double-mirror-image language $L_{2m} = \{x\,c\,\tilde{x}\,y\,c\,\tilde{y}\}$.

Counter-Example. The grammar

$$\begin{vmatrix} S \to a\,S\,S \\ S \to b \end{vmatrix}$$

is not meta-linear. The language it generates corresponds to the type of formula used in Polish notation in connection with binary operators. It can be shown that no meta-linear grammar can generate it: it is not meta-linear.

7.4.4. Sequential Grammars

A grammar is said to be *sequential* if the non-terminal A disappears definitively once all the rules involving it have been applied, then B disappears once all the rules involving it have been applied, etc. A sequential language is a language that can be generated by a sequential grammar.

Example. The language $L_m = \{x\,c\,\tilde{x}\}$ is trivially sequential, since the non-terminal S can no longer appear once the rule $S \to c$ has been applied. Similarly, L_{2m} (§ 7.4.3) is sequential, since S disappears after the application of $S \to T\,T$ and T after the application of $T \to c$.

On the other hand, the grammar:

$$\begin{vmatrix} S \to a\,d\,T\,d\,a \\ S \to a\,S\,a \\ S \to a\,c\,a \\ T \to b\,d\,S\,d\,b \\ T \to b\,T\,b \end{vmatrix}$$

is not sequential, and it can be shown that it generates a non-sequential language.

7.4.5. Other Classes

In order to describe the syntactic structure of phrases and sentences of natural languages, some authors have defined special classes of grammars.

1. *Normal* grammars have non-terminal rules which are all of the form $A \to B\,C$ and lead to binary trees. In linguistics, these rules answer

the needs of immediate constituent analysis which is based on such binary rules. In these grammars the terminal rules are of the form $A \to a$ and correspond to the *lexicon*.

2. *Predictive* grammars have rules which are all of the form:

$$A \to \varphi = a\,\psi; \quad a \in V_T; \quad \psi \in V_A^*.$$

3. *Dependency* grammars have rules which are all of the form:

$$A \to \varphi = \psi\,a\,\omega; \quad a \in V_T; \quad \varphi, \omega \in V_A^*.$$

7.4.6. Exercises

1. Show that $\{a^m\,b^m\,a^n\,b^n\}$ is not a linear language.

2. What closure properties apply to linear languages?

3. What can be said of the product of a linear language with a K-language?

4. What closure properties apply to the meta-linear languages?

5. Give examples of the intersection of CF-languages belonging to each of the classes that have been defined.

7.5. Exercises

1. Show that the grammar of §7.4.4 generates a non-sequential language.

2. First, show that the language $x\,c\,\tilde{x}\,c\,y\,c\,\tilde{y}$ is not linear. Then, show that $\tilde{x}\,x\,y\,\tilde{y}$ is not linear either. Compare the methods used, and explain why the relatively simple method that works for the first case cannot be extended to the second.

3. Give an example of a CF-language that is not a K-language and that is generated by a mixture of right-linear and left-linear rules, i.e., of the type $A \to a\,B$ and $A \to B\,a$, respectively.

Chapter VIII

Undecidable Properties of CF-Grammars

8.0.

Recall that a property is decidable if there exists a general algorithm that allows us to state either that it is true or that it is false, for all the special cases of it; a property is undecidable if there exists no such algorithm. In order to establish undecidability, it suffices that it be established for a less general class than the class in question.

In the previous chapter, we studied a few decidable properties of CF-grammars: the property of the language generated to be empty, finite or infinite; and the property that a sentence has of belonging to the language or not. We are now going to study a few undecidable properties.

8.1. Problems Related to Intersection

8.1.0.

We have seen that the intersection of two CF-languages can be, but is not necessarily, a CF-language. If it is, it belongs to one of the subclasses which we have defined.

8.1.1. Empty or Non-Empty Intersection

Let us first pose the following problem:

(1) Is it possible to set up a general algorithm which, given two arbitrary CF-languages, will decide whether their intersection is empty or not?

We shall prove that this problem is undecidable; to do this, we shall prove that it is undecidable for a special case.

Let us consider two CF-languages of a special type, defined on the alphabet $\{a, b, c\}$. The first is the mirror language L'_m defined by:

$$G'_m: \begin{vmatrix} S \to a\,S\,a \\ S \to b\,S\,b \\ S \to a\,c\,a \\ S \to b\,c\,b \end{vmatrix}.$$

This language is the same as L_m, with one exception: it does not contain the sentence 'c'.

The second is the language L_n defined by:

$$G_n: \begin{vmatrix} S \to g_i\,S\,h_i; \ 1 \leq i \leq n \\ S \to c \end{vmatrix}$$

where the g_i and h_i are non-empty words defined on the sub-alphabet $\{a, b\}$. The language L_n contains the word 'c', which is precisely why we arranged for L'_m not to contain it: in this way it is impossible to say anything trivial about the intersection.

The question whether the intersection of L'_m with L_n is empty or not is tantamount to the question whether there exists in L_n a mirror sentence $M\,c\,\tilde{M}$. In other words, it is the same as asking whether there exists an index sequence $i_1, i_2, \ldots, i_k$ such that $g_{i_1}\,g_{i_2}\ldots g_{i_k}$ is the mirror image of $h_{i_k}\ldots h_{i_2}\,h_{i_1}$. In the final analysis, this is the same as asking whether there exists an index sequence such that:

$$g_{i_1}\,g_{i_2}\ldots g_{i_k} \text{ and } \tilde{h}_{i_1}\,\tilde{h}_{i_2}\ldots \tilde{h}_{i_k} \text{ are one and the same sentence M.}$$

We recognize here Post's correspondence problem for the couples $(g_1, \tilde{h}_1), \ldots, (g_n, \tilde{h}_n)$ which are in no way special: the problem for L'_m and L_n is undecidable. Since the problem (1) is already undecidable for a special case, it is undecidable in general.

8.1.2. Intersection of CF-Languages (K-Languages)

If the intersection of L_m and L_n contains a sentence such as

$$g_{i_1} g_{i_2} \cdots g_{i_k} \, c \, \tilde{h}_{i_k} \cdots \tilde{h}_{i_2} \tilde{h}_{i_1} = x \, c \, \tilde{x},$$

(corresponding to a solution of Post's problem), then it also contains, for every integer n, the sentences:

$$(g_{i_1} g_{i_2} \cdots g_{i_k})^n \, c \, (\tilde{h}_{i_k} \cdots \tilde{h}_{i_2} \tilde{h}_{i_1})^n.$$

The intersection is thus an *infinite* subset of $\{x \, c \, \tilde{x}\}$, and cannot be a K-language if it is not empty.

But the problem of whether it is empty is undecidable. Since the question whether it is a K-language is already undecidable for a special case, it is undecidable in general. To summarize:

Theorem. *There exist no general algorithms which will decide whether the intersection of two CF-languages is empty or not, or whether the intersection of two CF-languages is a K-language or not.*

This theorem is true even for the exceedingly restricted case of two minimal linear languages, one of which is very specialized.

8.1.3. Intersection and CF-Languages

With the help of a similar technique, but using $L_{2m} = \{x \, c \, \tilde{x} \, c \, y \, c \, \tilde{y}\}$ instead of L_m and the fact that no sub-language of $\{x \, c \, \tilde{x} \, c \, x \, c \, \tilde{x}\}$ is a CF-language, we may prove:

Theorem. *The problem of whether the intersection of two CF-languages is a CF-language is recursively undecidable.*

8.1.4. Complementation

By actually constructing the complements of special CF-languages (so chosen that their complements remain CF-languages) and taking their union (which yields another CF-language), we can further prove:

Theorem. *The problem of whether the complement of a CF-language is empty, infinite, a K-language or a CF-language is recursively undecidable.*

Equivalence. It follows that there cannot exist an algorithm for deciding whether two languages L_1 and L_2 are equivalent. If such an algorithm were available, we could in effect decide whether $L_1 = V_T^*$ since that amounts to knowing whether $\overline{L}_1$ is empty. In the same way, the question whether, for two arbitrary languages L_1 and L_2, $L_1 \subset L_2$ is undecidable.

8.2. Problems Related to Ambiguity

8.2.0.

In § 7.1, we showed how to represent the structure of a sentence by constructing a certain tree. CF-grammars were devised in order to formalize this concept; using the semi-Thue rules $A \to \varphi$ with the special feature that only *one* symbol is to be rewritten, we can represent every derivation by drawing a tree with labelled nodes or by using labelled parentheses. Only the order of rewriting appears nowhere in this representation, but the order is not very significant.

8.2.1. Derivation Trees

For the derivation of the sentence "a a b c b a a' in the grammar:

$$G'_m: \quad \begin{vmatrix} S \to a\,S\,a \\ S \to b\,S\,b \\ S \to c \end{vmatrix}$$

we obtain the tree of Fig. 8-1.

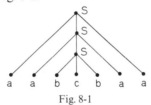

a   a   b   c   b   a   a

Fig. 8-1

This tree is equivalent to the parenthetic expression:

$$[_s a \quad [_s a \quad [_s b \quad [_s c] \quad b] \quad a] \quad a]$$

which can also be generated directly by a modified grammar G''_m. To this end, we introduce two new non-terminal symbols '$[_s$' and '$]$':

$$G''_m: \quad \begin{vmatrix} S \to [_s a\,S\,a] \\ S \to [_s b\,S\,b] \\ S \to [_s c] \end{vmatrix}.$$

The usefulness of the labels is not clearly brought out in this first example since there is only one label. In fact, we have given this example only for comparison with the next one.

7   Gross/Lentin, Formal Grammars

8.2.2. A Normal Grammar Generating L_m

We shall reconsider the same sentence relative to a normal grammar that also generates L_m. Given the normal grammar:

$$V_A = \{S, T, U\}; \quad V_T = \{a, b, c\}; \quad \text{axiom } S;$$

$$G_m: \begin{vmatrix} S \to T\,a \\ T \to a\,S \\ S \to U\,b \\ U \to b\,S \\ S \to c \end{vmatrix}.$$

In this grammar, the sentence 'a a b c b a a' yields the following tree derivation:

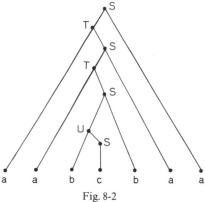

Fig. 8-2

This tree is equivalent to the following parenthetic description:

$$\begin{bmatrix} \begin{bmatrix} {}_a \begin{bmatrix} {}_a \begin{bmatrix} {}_b {}_c \end{bmatrix} \end{bmatrix} {}_b \end{bmatrix} {}_a \end{bmatrix} {}_a \end{bmatrix}.$$

Moreover, it is possible to erase the labels on the right parentheses, since the pairing of the parentheses is determined. Then the expression becomes:

$$\begin{bmatrix} \begin{bmatrix} {}_a \begin{bmatrix} {}_a \begin{bmatrix} {}_b {}_c \end{bmatrix} \end{bmatrix} {}_b \end{bmatrix} {}_a \end{bmatrix} {}_a \end{bmatrix}.$$

In certain cases it is even possible to do without the right parentheses.

8.2.3. Ambiguity

A sentence is said to be *ambiguous with respect to a given grammar* if it can be generated by at least two derivations that correspond to different trees. The number of different trees characterizes the degree of ambiguity of the sentence in the given grammar.

That ambiguity is defined with respect to *a* grammar is understandable, since several different grammars, like G_m and G''_m (in § 8.2.2 and 8.2.1), can generate the same language while at the same time giving different syntactic descriptions of the sentences of this language.

Example. Consider the grammar:

$$(C): \begin{vmatrix} S \to S \times S \\ S \to S + S \\ S \to |S \\ S \to | \end{vmatrix};$$

$$V_T = \{|, \times, +\}; \quad V_A = \{S\}.$$

(C) generates sentences to which a meaning can be assigned. The sticks represent numbers in a "natural" way: *one* by one stick, *two* by two sticks, etc. The symbols have their usual meaning.

Consider then the sentence $\| \times \||| + |$. It can be described by the tree:

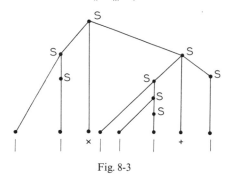

Fig. 8-3

which corresponds to the interpretation $\| \times (\||| + |)$, or 8.

It can also be described by the tree of Fig. 8-4:

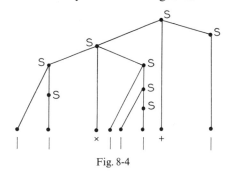

Fig. 8-4

which corresponds to the interpretation $(\| \times \||) + |$, or 7.

7*

Such ambiguities can occur in programming languages and this is remedied either:

1. By attributing to certain operational symbols priority over the others; this procedure is equivalent to ordering the rules of the grammar and imposing an order in the reading of the sentences.

2. Or by introducing additional terminal symbols (like the parentheses above);

3. Or by using Polish notation:

$$(C_p): \begin{vmatrix} S \to \times S\,S \\ S \to + S\,S \\ S \to |\,S \\ S \to |. \end{vmatrix}.$$

In the case of (C_p), the introduction of the period as a marker is necessary in order to separate the symbols for integers; if this were not done, the concatenation of integers would introduce ambiguities.

The following is the Polish notation for the two sentences in question:

$$(1_p): \quad \times \;\|\, . + \;\|\|\, . \,|\, .$$

$$(2_p): \quad + \;\times\; \|\, . \;\|\|\, . \,|\, .$$

Definitions. A language containing ambiguous sentences will be called ambiguous, and the grammar that generates it will also be called ambiguous.

A sentence that can be generated by a grammar according to p different derivation trees has an ambiguity of degree p with respect to that grammar.

8.2.4. Undecidability and Ambiguity

The following question arises: does there exist an algorithm which, given a CF-grammar of any arbitrary kind, can decide whether that grammar is ambiguous or not? We shall show that this problem is undecidable even for the case of linear grammars with three auxiliary symbols.

Consider n couples of words defined on $\{a, b\}$:

$$(g_1, h_1), \ldots, (g_i, h_i), \ldots, (g_n, h_n).$$

Consider also n different markers $d_1, d_2, \ldots, d_n$, and two minimal linear grammars with the central marker c:

$$G_1: \begin{vmatrix} \{S_1 \to d_i\, S_1\, g_i \,|\, 1 \leq i \leq n\} \\ S_1 \to c \end{vmatrix},$$

$$G_2: \begin{vmatrix} \{S_2 \to d_i\, S_2\, h_i \,|\, 1 \leq i \leq n\} \\ S_2 \to c \end{vmatrix}.$$

Neither of these grammars is ambiguous, for the sentences they generate all differ by the order of their markers or by the presence of markers.

The question whether the intersection of the languages $L(G_1)$ and $L(G_2)$ is empty or not is precisely Post's problem, since it is equivalent to proving the existence of the equality:

$$d_{i_1} \ldots d_{i_k} \, c \, g_{i_1} \ldots g_{i_k} = d_{i_1} \ldots d_{i_k} \, c \, h_{i_1} \ldots h_{i_k}.$$

Let us consider then the union of $L(G_1)$ and $L(G_2)$, generated by the following grammar which has the axiom S:

$$G_{1,\,2} : \begin{vmatrix} S \to S_1 \\ S \to S_2 \\ G_1 \\ G_2 \end{vmatrix}.$$

The problem of whether a sentence f is ambiguous amounts to deciding whether it was generated by $S \to S_1 \to (\text{via } G_1) \to f$; and by

$$S \to S_2 \to (\text{via } G_2) \to f;$$

which once again is Post's problem.

The undecidability of the general case is a result of the undecidability for a minimal linear grammer with three auxiliary symbols.

Theorem. *The problem of the ambiguity of CF-languages is undecidable.*

8.2.5. Inherent Ambiguity

Ambiguity has been defined with respect to a given grammar. Consider the grammar:

$$G_a : \begin{vmatrix} S \to a \, S \, a \\ S \to b \, S \, b \\ S \to a \, a \, S \, a \, a \\ S \to c \end{vmatrix}.$$

Every sentence containing two consecutive a's is ambiguous in G_a: it can be obtained by applying the first rule twice or the third rule once. The grammar G_m (§ 8.2.2), on the other hand, generates the same language and is not ambiguous. We shall say that the language L_m is not ambiguous with respect to the *class of minimal linear grammars*.

Then the following question arises: do there exist languages all of whose grammars (taken in a certain class) are ambiguous? Parikh has shown that every CF-grammar that generates the language

$$L_{i\,a} = \{a^p \, b^q \, c^r \,|\, p = q \quad \text{or} \quad q = r\}$$

is ambiguous. Intuitively, we see that L_{i_a} is the union of two CF-languages: $\{a^p\, b^m\, c^m\}$ and $\{a^n\, b^n\, c^q\}$, and the sentences '$a^n\, b^n\, c^n$' are generated twice.

8.3. Ambiguities of CF-Languages

8.3.0.

The aim of this section is to fill out the sketchy presentation of ambiguity that has been given thus far. Section 8.3.1 deals with the characterization of ambiguous words in a certain CF-language, and Section 8.3.2 with inherent ambiguity (cf. § 8.2.3).

8.3.1. Ambiguity of the Double-Mirror-Image Language (without Markers)

8.3.1.1. *The Problem*

Given the double mirror language L^2 on the terminal alphabet $\mathfrak{A}$; L^2 is defined by the grammar having the axiom S, a non-terminal T and rules:

$$(G) \quad \left| \begin{array}{c} S \rightarrow TT \\ (\forall\, a \in \mathfrak{A})\, S \rightarrow a\,T\,a \quad \text{and} \quad S \rightarrow a\,a \end{array} \right|.$$

We will show that L^2 contains ambiguous words and will characterize them. In the course of the proof we shall use the following lemma (Lyndon and Schützenberger):

Lemma. *If A, B, and C are words that belong to a free monoid $\mathfrak{A}^*$, then the hypothesis $AB = BC$ and $|A| \neq 0$ implies that there exists a non-negative integer α and two words U and V of $\mathfrak{A}^*$ such that:*

$$A = UV, \quad B = (UV)^\alpha U, \quad C = VU.$$

Proof. $AB = BC$ implies that $AAB = ABC = BCC$, and more generally: $(\forall\, \lambda \in \mathfrak{N})\, A^\lambda B = BC^\lambda$. Since A is not empty, the degree of A^λ approaches infinity as λ approaches infinity; it follows that the degree of A^λ for some λ must exceed that of B. Then there exists a non-negative integer α and a word U which is either empty or is a proper head of A, with $B = A^\alpha U$. Returning to the hypothesis, we have $AA^\alpha U = A^\alpha UC$, whence $AU = UC$. Taking $A = UV$, we obtain $UVU = UC$, $VU = C$.
Finally,

$$AB = UV(UV)^\alpha U = (UV)^\alpha UVU = BC.$$

8.3.1.2. *Computation of the Ambiguous Words*

Let $A \in L^2$ be an ambiguous word; it gives rise to the equality

$$A = W\tilde{W}X\tilde{X} = Y\tilde{Y}Z\tilde{Z}. \tag{1}$$

We shall write the degree of a word by the corresponding lower-case letter. We can take $w < y$, hence there exist two words M and N such that:

$$Y\tilde{Y} = W\tilde{W}M, \quad m \neq 0, \tag{2}$$

$$Y = WN \qquad n \neq 0. \tag{3}$$

From (2) and (3) we deduce $W N \tilde{N} \tilde{W} = W \tilde{W} M$, whence $N \tilde{N} \tilde{W} = \tilde{W} M$, or, by taking the mirror image:

$$\tilde{M} W = W N \tilde{N}. \tag{4}$$

The lemma applies, and yields:

$$\tilde{M} = U V, \tag{5}$$

$$W = (U V)^x U, \tag{6}$$

$$N \tilde{N} = V U. \tag{7}$$

$\widetilde{N \tilde{N}}$ is an even palindrome, which implies that $V U$ also is. However, $\widetilde{V U} = \tilde{U} \tilde{V}$, whence the condition

$$V U = \tilde{U} \tilde{V} \tag{8}$$

This condition does not imply that M is a palindrome.

The construction of $\tilde{M}$ is easy: we take a palindromic word, factorize it as $V U$, and then invert U and V.

a) For $u = v$, $\tilde{M}$ is of the form $U \tilde{U}$.

b) For $u < v$, $V U = \tilde{U} B U$, where B is a palindrome, and we have: $\tilde{M} = U V = U \tilde{U} B$, with $\tilde{B} = B$.

c) For $u > v$, $V U = V C \tilde{V}$, where C is a palindrome, and we have: $\tilde{M} = U V = C \tilde{V} V$, with $\tilde{C} = C$.

For every Z, the word $A = Y \tilde{Y} Z \tilde{Z} = W \tilde{W} M Z \tilde{Z} = W N \tilde{N} \tilde{W} Z \tilde{Z}$ has the double mirror factorization $(W N \cdot \tilde{N} \tilde{W})(Z \cdot \tilde{Z})$. It remains only to prove the factorization $(W \cdot \tilde{W})(X \cdot \tilde{X})$. Let us examine case b) which also includes a).

We have $\tilde{M} = U V = U \tilde{U} B$ and $M = B U \tilde{U}$, hence $X \tilde{X} = B U \tilde{U} Z \tilde{Z}$. The factorization is possible if the necessary and sufficient condition that $B = Z \tilde{Z}$ is satisfied. We will thus obtain words with at least a double factorization (a degree of ambiguity equal to or greater than 2) by taking B as a palindrome of even degree and its first and second 'halves' as Z and $\tilde{Z}$.

For case c), we have $\tilde{M} = U V = C \tilde{V} V$, hence $X \tilde{X} = \tilde{V} V C Z \tilde{Z}$. The word is a palindrome if the necessary and sufficient condition that $Z = V$ is satisfied.

The degree of ambiguity increases, of course, if we take special cases of B (or C) and U (or V).

Example. $V = b a c c$; $U = a b$; $N = b a c$;

$$a b b a c c = \tilde{M} = U V,$$

$$M = c c a b b a = B U \tilde{U}; \quad B = c c.$$

The word $(W N \tilde{N} \tilde{W})(Z \tilde{Z})$, with $W = (a b b a c c)^3 a b$ has a second factorization:

$$[(a b b a c c)^3 a b \cdot b a (c c a b b a)^3] [(c c a b \cdot b a c c)].$$

8.3.2. Inherent Ambiguity

8.3.2.1. *Study of the Language:* $L_1 = \{a^m c a^n \mid m \geq n \geq 0\}$.

Recall that a linear grammar is minimal if the only non-terminal is the axiom and the only terminal rule is $S \to c$, where c appears only in this rule. We shall prove that every minimal linear grammar that generates L_1 is ambiguous.

By definition every minimal linear grammar of L_1 has the form:

$$\left| \begin{array}{l} \{S \to a^{p_i} S a^{q_i} \mid 1 \leq i \leq N\} \\ S \to c \end{array} \right. .$$

We must have $p_i \geq q_i$, otherwise the grammar would generate the words $a^m c a^n$ with $m < n$. The rules, then, are of the following three types:

$$S \to a^{p_k} S, \qquad p_k > 0$$
$$S \to a^{p_j} S a^{q_j}, \qquad p_j \geq q_j > 0$$
$$S \to c.$$

Since these rules must generate the words $a c$ and $a c a$ in particular, every minimal linear grammar necessarily contains the rules: $S \to a S$, $S \to a S a$. Conversely, it is clear that these rules, together with $S \to c$, suffice to generate L_1. Let us examine the behavior of a grammar containing such rules.

Suppose we want to generate the word $a^m c a^n$; we apply the rule $S \to a S$ λ times and the rule $S \to a S a$ μ times. Then we must have $\lambda + \mu = m$ and $\mu = n$. The derivation tree depends on the order followed in applying the rules. There are as many orders of application possible as there are ways of choosing n numbers from $m + n$ numbers, i.e., C_m^n.

The degree of ambiguity of $a^m c a^n$ is C_m^n.

Example. For $a^4 c a^2$ we have the following $C_4^2 = 6$ derivations:

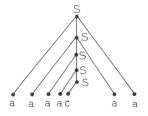 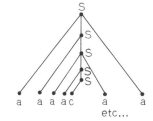

etc...

Fig. 8-5

Note that L_1 is not inherently ambiguous with respect to the class of linear CF-grammars. Indeed, the grammar G_L below generates L_1 non-ambiguously:

$$G_L \begin{vmatrix} S \to a\,S\,a \\ S \to a\,T \\ T \to a\,T \\ T \to c \\ S \to c \end{vmatrix}.$$

This property is due to the fact that G_L is sequential. We note here the important fact that *the concept of inherent ambiguity is relative to the class in question.*

8.3.2.2. *A sufficient condition for the non-ambiguity of a minimal linear grammar*

Let $\mathfrak{A}^*$ be the free monoid generated by $\mathfrak{A} = \{x_1, \ldots, x_n\}$ and $\mathfrak{B}^*$ the free monoid generated by $\mathfrak{B} = \{a, b, \ldots, l\}$. Consider the mapping of $\mathfrak{A}^*$ into (and possibly onto) $\mathfrak{B}^*$ which is obtained by replacing every letter x_i of a word of $\mathfrak{A}^*$ by a given word f_i of $\mathfrak{B}^*$. This mapping is said to be a code if the words of $\mathfrak{B}^*$ obtained as images can have only one inter-pretation.

Example. $\mathfrak{A} = \{1, 2, 0\}, \qquad \mathfrak{B} = \{a, b\}$

$$\begin{cases} 1 \to b\,a \\ 2 \to b\,a\,a \\ 0 \to b \end{cases} \quad \text{is a code}$$

$$\begin{cases} 1 \to a \\ 2 \to a\,a \\ 0 \to b \end{cases} \quad \text{is not a code}$$

$$1\,1 \to a\,a \quad \text{and} \quad 2 \to a\,a.$$

Given this definition, it is clear that the minimal linear grammar

$$\begin{vmatrix} \{S \to f_i\,S\,g_i \mid 1 \leq i \leq N\} \\ S \to c \end{vmatrix}$$

is unambiguous if the sufficient condition that at least one of the mappings $\{i \to f_i;\ i \to g_i \mid 1 \leq i \leq N\}$ be a code is satisfied. By the very definition we can in effect reconstruct the derivation of a word in a unique way.

Note that this sufficient condition is not necessary. Even if none of the mappings is a code, it may happen that we can use them to reconstruct every derivation.

Example. Given the grammar:

$$\begin{vmatrix} S \rightarrow a\,a\,S\,a \\ S \rightarrow b\,b\,S\,b \\ S \rightarrow a\,S\,b\,b \\ S \rightarrow b\,S\,a\,a \\ S \rightarrow c \end{vmatrix}.$$

The set $\{a\,a, b\,b, a, b\}$ of the f_i is the same as that of the g_i and does not yield a code. Nevertheless, the language generated is not ambiguous. It suffices to examine the first and last letters of a word in order to discover the first rule that was applied; we iterate this process and reconstruct the derivation.

Chapter IX

Push-Down Automata

9.0.

In the first section of chapter VII we explained that the class of recursively denumerable languages is associated with the class of Turing machines but that in order to deal with real languages, it would be necessary to restrict our point of view and introduce some additional hypotheses. In this way, the CF-languages are associated not with the most general class of combinatorial systems (which is equivalent to the class of Turing machines), but with a rather special class of semi-Thue systems. In a similar fashion there exists a class of automata which are specific to the CF-languages. We shall show that this is the class of push-down automata.

Actually, we shall have to give up the deterministic nature which we have ascribed to automata up to now, and starting with this chapter the word automaton will be used as an abbreviation for "a not necessarily deterministic automaton". For more exact descriptions and for the proofs of the equivalence between CF-languages and languages described by push-down automata, we refer the reader to the bibliography.

9.1. An Automaton that Accepts the Sentences of a CF-Language

9.1.0

The automaton about to be described formalizes in a reasonable way the concept of "push-down" or "stack", which is well-known to programmers.

9.1.1. Physical Description

The automaton contains:

1. An input tape (E) divided into squares and potentially infinite in both directions.

2. A memory tape (M) which is bounded on one side (by convention, on the left) but potentially infinite on the other side. The tape (M) is divided into squares.

3. A computing unit (A) with two operating heads: one to read the input tape, the other to read the memory tape, and to erase and write on it. Each of these heads can move the tape in a way that will be specified below.

The Input Tape. Before operation, one symbol per square can be written on this tape, using the input vocabulary: $V_E = \{a_1, a_2, \ldots, a_p\}$. For convenience, we add to this vocabulary a neutral word e having a special status and we have:

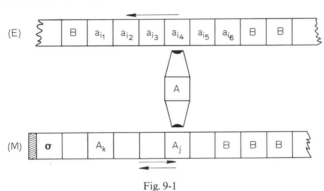

Fig. 9-1

The symbol "e" is not to be confused with the blank square which is indicated as B. The sentences, which are enclosed between blanks, are written on (E) by means of V_E. Let us agree to write from left to right.

The Memory Tape. The automaton writes on this tape using the vocabulary: $V_M = \{A_1, A_2, \ldots, A_q\}$ which may include V_E. We add the neutral word e to this base vocabulary and a distinguished symbol σ which is not to be written by the automaton in the course of computation. In this way we define:

$$\overline{V}_M = \{e\} \cup V_M \cup \{\sigma\}.$$

The Computing Unit. The computing unit can be in one of a finite number of internal states $S_0, S_1, \ldots, S_i, \ldots, S_j, \ldots, S_n$.

9.1.2. Operation

To describe the operation of the automaton, we begin with the following definitions:

1. The *degree* λ is an integer defined with respect to the vocabulary V_M by the relations: $\lambda(\sigma)=-1$; $\lambda(e)=0$; $\lambda(\varphi)=$ the number of words contained in φ if $\varphi \in V_M^*$.

2. A *physical situation* of the automaton is a triple (a_i, S_j, A_k), where a_i is the symbol, written on (E), which is being scanned by the first head; S_j is the internal state of the automaton; and A_k is the symbol, written on (M), which is being scanned by the second operating head.

3. A *situation* of the automaton is either the triple of a physical situation or a triple obtained by replacing the a_i or A_k (or both) of a physical situation by e. It is here that we see the non-deterministic nature of the automaton appear: in a given physical situation, it can "shut the eye" that was looking at a_i or the one that was looking at A_k. It then "sees" the neutral word.

If the automaton is in the physical situation (a_i, S_j, A_k), then it is at the same time in the four situations:

$$\Sigma_1 = (a_i, S_j, A_k)$$
$$\Sigma_2 = (e, \ S_j, A_k)$$
$$\Sigma_3 = (a_i, S_j, e)$$
$$\Sigma_4 = (e, \ S_j, e).$$

4. An *instruction* is a quintuple of the form: $\Sigma \rightarrow (S_m, x)$, where Σ is a situation, S_m a state, and x is either e, σ, or a string of words of V_M.

5. An *abstract* (push-down) *automaton* is a finite set of rules of the type: $\Sigma_i \rightarrow (S_{m_i}, x_i)$. Since the automaton is not deterministic, there is no reason why there cannot be several instructions starting from the same situation.

We can now describe a computation of the automaton in detail.

The Computation. The input to the computation is a string of words of V_E, which has already been written on the input tape, with blanks on each side:

Fig. 9-2

At the beginning of the computation, the computing unit is in the initial state S_0, and the first read-head is scanning the leftmost symbol of the given string. σ has been written in the first square (on the left) of tape (M) and the second read-head is scanning this square. The computation begins from the physical situation (a_{i_1}, S_0, σ) and continues in the following way.

Suppose the automaton has arrived at a situation Σ. If there is no rule that applies to Σ, the automaton blocks. If there are one or more rules that apply to Σ, the automaton necessarily chooses one of them. Let $\Sigma \rightarrow (S_m, x)$ be the rule chosen. As a result of this rule:

1. The computing unit switches to the state S_m.

2. According as the first symbol of the situation is an e or is a_i, the read-head either doesn't move the tape (E) or else moves it so that it can see the symbol to the right of a_i.

3. According to what x is, the second head acts upon the tape (M) in in the following way:

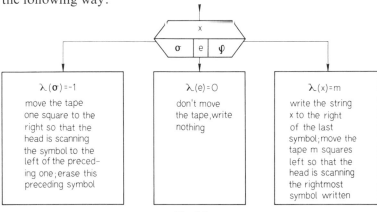

Fig. 9-3

Accepted String. A string is said to be *accepted* by the automaton if the computation finishes in the situation (B, S_0, B). A string is *acceptable* if there exists a computation which begins in the situation and under the conditions described above and finishes in the situation (B, S_0, B).

Since the automaton is not deterministic, it is possible for an acceptable sentence not to be accepted in the course of a particular computation. The set of sentences which are acceptable for a given automaton is a language, and the automaton is said to *accept* the language.

Before speaking of the class of languages which are acceptable for the class of push-down automata, we shall examine two examples.

9.1.3. Automaton Accepting the Language L_m

Consider the language: $L_m = \{x \, c \, \tilde{x} \mid x \in \{a, b\}^*\}$. Can a push-down automaton be constructed which will accept the language L_m?

The presence of the central marker c makes the task simpler. It will suffice to recopy the proposed sentence until arriving at c, after which this sentence x will be read *backwards* and compared word by word with the second half x̃ of the proposed sentence. If the attempt succeeds, everything is erased. Thus, if the sentence proposed is correct, the tape (M) is empty at the end; otherwise the automaton blocks without having emptied its memory.

We must therefore provide for an initial state S_0, a read state S_1, and an erase state S_e. We obtain the following rules:

1. $(a, S_0, \sigma) \rightarrow (S_1, a)$ ⎱ recopy the first word of the sentence onto (M)
2. $(b, S_0, \sigma) \rightarrow (S_1, b)$ ⎰ and switch to the state S_1 (read state).

3. $(a, S_1, a) \rightarrow (S_1, a)$
4. $(a, S_1, b) \rightarrow (S_1, a)$ recopy the words of the sentence onto (M) one by one, remaining in the state S_1; when the
5. $(b, S_1, a) \rightarrow (S_1, b)$ part of the sentence x has been read, (M)
6. $(b, S_1, b) \rightarrow (S_1, b)$ contains x.

7. $(c, S_1, a) \rightarrow (S_e, e)$ ⎱ when the "middle point" c is read, switch to
8. $(c, S_1, b) \rightarrow (S_e, e)$ ⎰ the state S_e (erase state); no action on (M).

9. $(a, S_e, a) \rightarrow (S_e, \sigma)$ ⎱ comparison of the second half of the sentence with the memory (M), and erasure when
10. $(b, S_e, b) \rightarrow (S_e, \sigma)$ ⎰ there is agreement.

11. $(B, S_e, \sigma) \rightarrow (S_0, \sigma)$ erasure of the marker σ of (M).

Example. Consider the sentence a b a c a b a. The succession of configurations of the push-down automaton is the following:

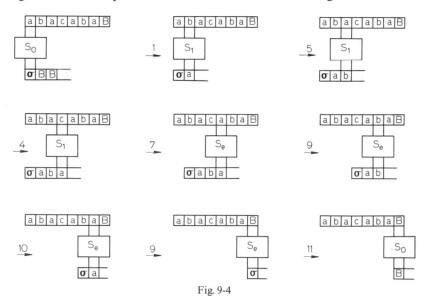

Fig. 9-4

Note that the automaton that has been constructed is deterministic: there is no need to make use of situations of the type (e, S, ...).

9.1.4. Automaton Accepting the Language L_n

We consider now the language $L_n = \{x\, \tilde{x} \mid x \in \{a, b\}^*\}$, which differs from the preceding one by the absence of the central marker. Let us apply the same procedure for examining sentences. Since reading now continues without going backwards and there is no longer anything to indicate the center, the automaton is necessarily non-deterministic. A move to the erase state must be provided for at each position.

An incorrect sentence will surely not be accepted; let a correct sentence be proposed. If the move to the erase state is effected in the middle, the sentence will be accepted; otherwise the automaton will block or will finish reading without having emptied its memory.

We leave it to the reader to write the rules of this automaton.

9.2. Language-Generating Automata

Up to now we have considered
   1. a physical apparatus (tapes and computing unit),
   2. a set of rules of the form: $\Sigma \rightarrow (S_m, x)$,
which define what we have termed an abstract automaton.

We then interpreted these rules using the physical apparatus and obtained a physical automaton which examines the sentences proposed to it and — at least in one of its modes of operation — *accepts* the sentences of the language and rejects all others. But another interpretation can be given to the set of rules which constitute the abstract automaton, an interpretation in which the physical automaton, modified, *generates* the sentences of the same language.

The generating automaton has internal states which are the counterparts of those of the recognition automaton (we shall take them to be the same). It has the same memory tape (M), but it writes on (E) instead of reading it. To the instruction $(a_i, S_j, A_k) \rightarrow (S_m, x)$ of the recognition automaton, there corresponds the instruction $(S_j, A_k) \rightarrow (a_i, S_m, x)$ of the generating automaton (and vice-versa). Physically, this instruction means the following: with the generating automaton in the situation (S_j, A_k), it *writes* a_i on tape (E) and switches to the state S_m; for the rest, it uses (M) in the same way as the recognition automaton. At the outset, we assume it to be in the state S_0 with the word σ written on the extreme left of (M).

The generating automaton is determined by only a part of the situation that determines the action of the recognition automaton, but it is clear that every correct computation of the recognition automaton can be translated into a correct computation of the generating automaton, and vice-versa. The modified automaton generates the language accepted by the first automaton. It produces a correct sentence when, starting from the initial conditions, it returns to the state S_0 with the tape (M) empty.

Example. Let us examine again the rules of the automaton which accepted $L_m = \{x \, c \, \tilde{x}\}$. Here is the new interpretation of the rules:

1. and 2.: Write the same symbol on (E) and (M), switch to the state S_1.

3 − 6.: Write the same symbol on (E) and (M), remain in the state S_1.

7. and 8.: Write the central marker on (E), switch to the state S_e.

9. and 10.: Write on (E) the symbol read from (M) and move (M) backwards.

11.: Having reached the initial σ, erase it, switch to the state S_0 and write a blank on (E).

We leave the detailed description of how the automaton generates the sentence 'a b a c a b a' as an exercise for the reader.

The sentence-generating automaton is not deterministic even when the analogous recognition automaton has this property. Such was the case in the preceding example. Several "reduced" situations, like (S_1, a), (S_1, b), can give rise to various productions: this freedom of choice allows the automaton to construct the first part of a sentence "at random". During the construction of the second part of the sentence, its behavior is deterministic.

Conclusion. If we consider in the abstract the collection consisting of a vocabulary V_E, another vocabulary V_M and a set of rules: $\{\Sigma_i \rightarrow (S_{m_i}, x_i)\}$ then it is immaterial whether we say that the abstract automaton defined by this collection accepts or generates a language.

9.3. The Class of Languages Accepted (Generated) by the Class of Push-Down Automata

9.3.0.

We have given two examples where, starting from a CF-grammar G, a push-down automaton was constructed that accepted (generated) the language L(G). We shall now generalize this result.

9.3.1. Automaton Accepting a CF-Language

$$V_A = \{A_i \, | \, 1 \leq i \leq m\}; \quad V_T = \{a_j \, | \, 1 \leq j \leq n\}$$

$$\text{axiom: } S = A_1;$$

$$G: \quad \begin{vmatrix} A_i \rightarrow \omega_{i, 1}, \ldots, A_i \rightarrow \omega_{i, k_i} \\ 1 \leq i \leq m \end{vmatrix}.$$

We now construct a push-down automaton. The input vocabulary, $\overline{V_E}$, consists of V_T plus e; the memory vocabulary, $\overline{V_M}$, consists of $V_T \cup V_A$ together with e and σ; there is an initial state [0], a "pre-syntactic" state [1] and as many "syntactic" states [A_i] as there are auxiliary words A_i.

The list of instructions contains:

1. An initial instruction: (e, [0], σ) → ([1], S).

2. Instructions which switch to a syntactic state: (e, [1], A_i) → ([A_i], σ), as many as there are syntactic states (or auxiliary words).

3. Production (or analysis) instructions: (e, [A_i], e) → ([1], ω_{i, k_i}), as many as there are rules of the CF-grammar.

4. Read (or write) instructions (a$_j$, [1], a$_j$) → ([1], σ), as many as there are terminal words.

5. A terminal instruction: (e, [1], σ) → ([0], σ).

Operation During Generation. Starting from the correct initial conditions, the automaton switches to the pre-syntactic state, writes the name of the axiom and erases it after having committed it to memory, i.e., after having switched to the corresponding syntactic state. In this state, it chooses the right side of some rule $S \to \omega_{1, k}$, writes it on the memory tape, positions itself on the last word it has written, and returns to the pre-syntactic state [1].

More generally, if the automaton reads the left side of some rule on its memory tape, it erases it, switches to the corresponding syntactic state, writes the corresponding production, and, switching back to the pre-syntactic state, examines the last word it has written. If, on the other hand, the automaton reads a terminal, it writes it on the input tape and then erases it.

The procedure ends when the automaton finds the extreme left σ after a last write. Clearly, this operation is equivalent to making derivations according to the CF-grammar and recopying the terminals which result (in the reverse order, however).

Operation During Recognition. A bit less intuitively perhaps, this type of operation is guaranteed by the ambivalence of push-down automata.

Remark. This automaton is strongly non-deterministic; note, however, that there is no rule (e, [1], e) → ([A_i], σ). The switch to any syntactic state is motivated.

Example. Let us compare this general procedure, for the case of L_m, with the more specific procedure studied in § 9.1.3. The CF-grammar is:

$$|S \to a\,S\,a, \quad S \to b\,S\,b, \quad S \to c| \quad \text{with} \quad V_A = \{S\}, \quad \text{and} \quad V_T = \{a, b, c\}.$$

Since there is only one auxiliary symbol, the axiom S, there will be only one syntactic state. We obtain the following rules:

1. $(e, [0], \sigma) \rightarrow ([1], S)$.

2. $(e, [1], S) \rightarrow ([S], \sigma)$.

3. $(e, [S], e) \rightarrow \begin{cases} ([1], a\ S\ a) \\ ([1], b\ S\ b) \\ ([1], c). \end{cases}$

4. $\left. \begin{array}{l} (a, [1], a) \\ (b, [1], b) \\ (c, [1], c) \end{array} \right\} \rightarrow ([1], \sigma)$.

5. $(e, [1], \sigma) \rightarrow ([0], \sigma)$.

These rules are fewer in number than those given in §9.1.3 which were deterministic for the recognition of a given sentence. The reader will profit from a study of how these new rules are derived from the old.

9.3.2. Grammar Generating the Language Accepted by an Automaton

The construction of a CF-grammar that generates the language accepted by a push-down automaton is possible, but more delicate. It requires a prior normalization of the rules of the automaton. We shall accept this result without proof and state the theorem:

9.3.3. Theorem

The class of languages accepted (generated) by push-down automata is identical with the class of CF-languages.

9.3.4. Exercises

1. Using the generalized procedure of §9.3.1, construct an automaton that accepts the sentences of the "Polish" language:

$$\left| \begin{array}{l} S \rightarrow C\ S\ S \\ S \rightarrow \neg S \\ S \rightarrow V \\ V \rightarrow V' \\ V \rightarrow p \end{array} \right| .$$

2. Construct an automaton that accepts the language:

$$\left| \begin{array}{l} S \rightarrow T\ T \\ T \rightarrow T\ a \\ T \rightarrow b\ T \\ T \rightarrow c \end{array} \right| .$$

3. The language $L = \{a^p\, b^q\, c^r \mid p+q \geq r\}$ is a CF-language. Give a CF-grammar of it. Find what class it belongs to. Construct a deterministic push-down automaton that accepts this language.

4. *Problem.* In what follows, we shall study several properties of the prefixed notation still called "Polish" notation. For simplicity, every binary operator is written as a, and every operand as b.

We shall consider the "Polish" grammar G_p defined by the axiom S, the terminal letters a and b, and the rules: $S \to a\, S\, S$, $S \to b$. G_p generates a set P of terminal or non-terminal words and a terminal language L (hence $L \subset P$).

1. Given a word X defined on the alphabet $\{S, a, b\}$ we shall write: $\alpha(X)$ for the degree of X with respect to the letter a; $\beta(X)$ for the degree of X with respect to the set of letters b and S; and $\gamma(X)$ for the rank of X, i.e., for the function $\gamma(X) = \alpha(X) - \beta(X)$.

Examples. $\qquad X = a\, b^3\, a^2\, S^4, \quad \alpha(X) = 3,$

$$\beta(X) = 7, \quad \gamma(X) = -4.$$

$$Y = a\, b\, a^2\, b^2\, a\, b^3, \quad \alpha(Y) = 4,$$

$$\beta(Y) = 6, \quad \gamma(Y) = -2.$$

1.1. Prove the implication:

$$X \in P \;\Rightarrow\; \gamma(X) = -1.$$

1.2. We decompose a word X into a left factor (head) H and a right factor (tail) T which are both non-empty. Prove the implications:

$$X = H\,T \quad \text{and} \quad X \in P \;\Rightarrow\; \gamma(H) \geq 0,$$

$$X = H\,T \quad \text{and} \quad X \in P \;\Rightarrow\; \gamma(T) \leq -1.$$

1.3. Conversely, show that if for every proper head of X we have $\gamma(H) \geq 0$ and if $\gamma(X) = -1$, then $X \in P$.

1.4. Using the result of 1.3, construct a deterministic push-down automaton M that accepts the language L.

1.5. A push-down automaton is said to be without control if all of its instructions are of the form $(a, S_i, e) \to (S_j, x)$. Can M be without control? What then is (would be) the rôle of the memory tape?

2. In this section we shall take into consideration the structure that G_p gives to L.

2.1. Show how the derivation tree of a word of L can be determined (either by successive groupings or by successive scans).

Application. The tree of a^3 b a b² a b a b² a b². Show that G_p is not ambiguous.

2.2. Suppose we wanted to construct an automaton T having an input tape, a scratch tape and an output tape, and such that for the input $f \in L$ it supplies the word $T(f)$, which is the translation of f into a parenthesized structure: a b b yields (b a b), a a b b b yields ((b a b) a b), etc. Study whether such a construction is possible, and if it is, construct the automaton T.

3.1. Write p_i for the integers greater than 1, and k for a fixed integer. Show that for a given k there exists an infinite number of words of L of the form $a^{p_1} b^{p_1} a^{p_2} b^{p_2} \ldots a^{p_k} b^{p_k}$ b.

3.2. Using this result, show that the language L cannot be generated by a meta-linear grammar.

Note: This question is independent of the preceding ones.

9.4. Survey of the Applications of CF-Languages

9.4.0.

We have said that the CF-languages are those accepted (generated) by push-down automata, and we have also remarked on the importance of push-down techniques in programming. This first insight into the relationship between CF-languages and programming is the starting point of our brief survey of the applications of CF-languages in programming and automatic information processing.

9.4.1. Examples of Applications

The importance of CF-languages probably arises from the fact that:

1. they allow the recursive embedding of strings;

2. the procedures for the generation of these languages are very intuitive;

3. the algorithms for sentence recognition are simple.

They were discovered independently by various workers in the field of formalized syntax. We shall cite the principal variants.

Backus normal form, a notational variant for the rules of CF-grammars:

$$\langle A \rangle ::= \langle B \rangle \langle C \rangle | n \langle D \rangle$$

which can be written
$$A \to B C \quad A, B, C, D \in V_A$$
$$A \to n D \quad n \in V_T.$$

In linguistics: the immediate constituent models of Wells and Harris, and the categorial grammars of Bar-Hillel; the equivalence of these with CF-grammars has been proven.

In automatic translation: almost all of the grammars constructed have been shown to be CF-grammars.

Most programming languages are such that they can be given a syntactic description in terms of CF-grammars.

9.4.2. ALGOL

In addition to arithmetic expressions, ALGOL contains other means of self-embedding; among these we may point out the following:

a) the existence of derivations

$$\langle \text{unlabelled compound} \rangle \Rightarrow (\text{BEGIN})^n \langle \text{unlabelled compound} \rangle (\text{END})^n.$$

It is therefore syntactically correct for a program to start with n BEGIN and to end with n END.

b) conditional expressions where, between every IF and THEN, another IF ... THEN may be embedded; this corresponds to derivations of the type:

$$\langle \text{if clause} \rangle \Rightarrow (\text{IF } \varphi_0)^n \langle \text{if clause} \rangle (\varphi_1 \text{ THEN } \varphi_2)^n$$

where φ_0, φ_1, and φ_2 are given by the rules and may have various configurations.

9.4.3.

Fortran has been written in Backus normal form, i.e., in the form of a CF-language. Certain restrictions could not be formalized in Backus normal form.

9.4.4. Lisp (McCarthy)

We shall present a CF-grammar for all the S-functions which are the base of the LISP system. It is easily verified that the grammar we shall give corresponds to the rules of definition. We give the rules for enumerating the S-representations which are the fundamental list structures of LISP; we shall not take into account operators like LAMBDA, LABEL, QUOTE, which are closely tied to the programming of the system. We shall take:

$$V_T = \{A, \ldots, Z, 0, 1, \ldots 9, (,), , \}$$

$V_A = \{C_a \text{ (character)}, S_a \text{ (atomic symbol)}, S_e \text{ (S-expression)},$
$P_r \text{ (predicate)}, E_c \text{ (conditional expression)}, P_a \text{ (couple)},$
$S_f \text{ (S-function)}, S_r \text{ (S-representation)}\}.$

The rules are:

$$S_r \rightarrow \begin{Bmatrix} S_f \\ P_r \\ S_e \end{Bmatrix} \qquad\qquad P_r \rightarrow \begin{Bmatrix} (ATOM, S_e) \\ (EQ, S_e, S_e) \\ E_c \end{Bmatrix}$$

$$S_f \rightarrow \begin{Bmatrix} E_c \\ (CAR\ S_r) \\ (CDR\ S_r) \\ (CONS, S_r, S_r) \end{Bmatrix} \qquad \begin{aligned} S_e &\rightarrow \begin{Bmatrix} (S_e \cdot S_e) \\ S_a \end{Bmatrix} \\ S_a &\rightarrow \begin{Bmatrix} C_a\ S_a \\ C_a \end{Bmatrix} \end{aligned}$$

$$P_a \rightarrow \begin{Bmatrix} (P_r, S_r) \\ (P_r, S_r), P_a \end{Bmatrix} \qquad C_a \rightarrow \begin{Bmatrix} A \\ \vdots \\ Z \\ 0 \\ 1 \\ \vdots \\ 9 \end{Bmatrix}.$$

$$E_c \rightarrow (COND, P_a)$$

The self-embedding properties are evident from the rules; in particular, they allow recursive definitions of lists.

9.4.5.

The undecidability theorems which we have already quoted have certain practical consequences which have already been noted by various authors.

The undecidability of the equivalence of two grammars means that there exists no general procedure which, given two grammars, can decide whether they generate the same set of sentences or not. One may expect that the comparison of families of languages as closely related as the different versions of Fortran or the variants of ALGOL may be difficult to carry out. In each particular case, procedures, or rather, heuristics, will have to be found which will give only approximate answers. These same remarks hold for the problem of ambiguity in a language.

Chapter X

Kleene Languages and Finite Automata

10.0.

Defined and studied by Kleene in connection with a simple model of the neuron, regular languages (also called finite-state languages) have been applied to the field of circuit construction and have given rise to numerous results there. These languages were also encountered in another form by Markov, who also recognized their linguistic application. More recently, Shannon has taken up these questions again from the same probabilistic viewpoint as Markov. He applied them to natural languages and defined a special class of automata: the finite automata.

10.1. The K-Grammars

10.1.0.

We shall study here those of the general properties of Kleene languages which involve only "logical" concepts, and will not deal with probabilistic applications. We shall give several definitions, or variants of definitions, and prove their equivalence. Although the K-languages are special cases of CF-languages, it is more interesting and instructive to establish their properties independently.

10.1.1. Definition

Kleene grammars, or K-grammars, which define the K-languages on the alphabet $V = V_A \cup V_T$ with $V_A = \{A_i | 1 \leq i \leq n\}$, where A_1 is the axiom, and $V_T = \{a_j | 0 \leq j \leq m\}$, have rules of the form:

$$(r) \quad A_i \to a_j A_k \quad \text{or else} \quad (l) \quad A_i \to A_k a_j.$$

Each grammar contains a finite number of rules (r) or (l), where the *or* is exclusive; furthermore, there are the dictionary or terminal rules: $A_i \to a_j$, where the arrow means "is rewritten as".

Example. $V = \{P, Q\} \cup \{a, b\}$, axiom P

$$(Gr): \quad \begin{vmatrix} P \to a\,P \\ P \to a\,Q \\ Q \to b\,Q \\ Q \to b \end{vmatrix}.$$

This grammar enumerates the language consisting of a string of a's followed by a string of b's: $\{a^m b^n | n, m \geq 0\}$. The same language can be described by the grammar (Gl):

$$(Gl): \quad \begin{vmatrix} P \to P\,b \\ P \to Q\,b \\ Q \to Q\,a \\ Q \to a \end{vmatrix}.$$

With the help of the grammar (Gr) we can derive the sentence $a^3 b^2$:

$$P \to a\,P \to a\,a\,P \to a\,a\,a\,Q \to a\,a\,a\,b\,Q \to a\,a\,a\,b\,b.$$

Remark. The finite languages are K-languages; a set of N sentences $\{f_1, f_2, \ldots, f_N\}$ can be described by a grammar G having only terminal rules:

$$(G) = \{P \to f_i \mid 1 \leqq i \leqq n\}.$$

10.1.2. Grammatical Descriptions

Like the CF-grammars, the K-grammars enumerate tree structures.

Example. For the sentence a a a b b, derived by (Gr), we have the tree structure:

Fig. 10-1

This structure can be parenthesized as:

$$(a\,(\,a\,(\,a\,(\,b\,(\,b\,)\,)\,)\,)\,).$$
$$\text{P} \quad \text{P} \quad \text{P} \quad \text{Q} \quad \text{Q}$$

A structure like the following:

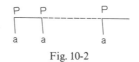

Fig. 10-2

is called right recursive. If we had used (Gl) to derive a a a b b, we would have obtained the tree structure:

Q Q Q P P

a a a b b

or: (((((a)a)a)b)b)
PPQQQ

Fig. 10-3

which is called left recursive.

10.1.3. Application to COMIT

COMIT is an example of a programming language that can be described by means of a K-grammar. It contains instructions like:

$$\text{NAME 1} \quad \Sigma\ \text{SYMB} = \Sigma\ \text{SYMB}' / / \text{INST}, \ldots \quad \text{NAME 2}.$$
$$\qquad\quad \text{left side} \qquad\qquad\qquad \text{right side}$$

NAME 1 is the name of the rule; Σ SYMB and Σ SYMB$'$ are arbitrary strings of words or numbers separated by $+$ signs.

Example. $1 + CUP + \$ + GLASS + 2$.

A COMIT rule is performed from left to right only.

a) Σ SYMB refers to certain strings in the memory of the computer which for COMIT is structured as a single string.

b) Σ SYMB$'$ carries out certain operations on the symbols referred to by Σ SYMB; Σ SYMB are the operands, and Σ SYMB$'$ the operations.

c) INST is a series of instructions to be carried out on the result of the operations effected by Σ SYMB$'$.

d) NAME 2 is the name of the next rule that is to be executed.

The number of elements that may appear in Σ SYMB and Σ SYMB$'$ is limited only by the size of the computer used, but certain restrictions may be established between Σ SYMB and Σ SYMB$'$. In order to have a K-language, the operations of Σ SYMB$'$ must be defined independently of the operands. If, during compilation, a check is desired on whether the operations of Σ SYMB$'$ actually have operands defined in the ΣSYMB, restrictions between the left and right sides of a rule are introduced and these restrictions may be embedded to an unlimited depth. In this case, the COMIT language is nothing more than a K-language.

10.2. The Finite Automata

10.2.0.

Just as push-down automata have been associated with the CF-languages, so we shall associate with the K-grammars rather special machines which are the finite automata.

10.2.1. Description

A finite automaton can take on only a finite number of states $S = \{S_j\}$; it has a reading head that scans a tape divided into squares each of which contains an element of a vocabulary $V = \{a_i | 0 \leq i \leq n\}$, where a_0 is the symbol for the neutral element.

One of the states of the machine, $S_0 \in \{S_j\}$ is distinguished and is called the initial state.

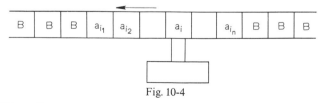

Fig. 10-4

10.2.2. Operation

Intuitively, we may imagine the operation of the machine as follows: a string $\alpha \in V^*$ will be written on the tape; we may take the squares on each side of α to be filled by the symbol B. The automaton begins in the state S_0, the reading head set to scan the leftmost symbol of α. The automaton switches state and moves the tape one square left. These transitions are brought about by rules (μ) of the form: $(a_i, S_j) \to (S_k)$ which are finite in number and where (a_i, S_j) is the situation of the automaton and S_k the state it switches to in the next move.

If the automaton is in a situation (a_{i_1}, S_{j_1}) for which there are no rules (μ), it is blocked. If, after the "computation", the automaton is in the situation (B, S_0), it is said to have accepted (α). The languages accepted by this class of automata are the K-languages.

Example. The automaton accepting the language

$$\{a^m\, b^n \,|\, n, m > 0\}$$

$$(a, S_0) \to S_1$$
$$(a, S_1) \to S_1$$
$$(b, S_1) \to S_2$$
$$(b, S_2) \to S_2$$
$$(B, S_2) \to S_0.$$

10.2.3. Variants

There exist in the literature a certain number of variants of this definition which are purely notational. The principal ones are:

the neutral element can be taken as a marker, or it can also be eliminated;

instead of returning to the initial state S_0 at the end of a computation, the automaton may end up in a final state S_f, or in one of the possible final states of the machine: $\{S_f\} \subset \{S_j\}$;

instead of defining the transitions of the automaton by the rules (μ), a table of transitions or a transition function is defined on the model of:

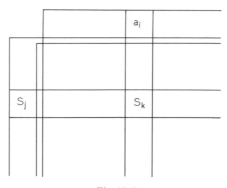

Fig. 10-5

Example. Considering once more the language $a^m b^n$ already mentioned above, we obtain the table:

	a	b	B
S_0	S_1		
S_1	S_1	S_2	
S_2		S_2	S_0

Fig. 10-6

We shall write the transition function as $M(a_i, S_j)$; it is defined on a subset of $V \times S$ and takes its values in (possibly on) S. When the automaton is not deterministic, M takes its values in the set of subsets of S.

W shall extend M to the domain $V^* \times S$ in the following way:

Let $\varphi \in V^*$, $\varphi = \varphi_1 a_i$;   we set $M(\varphi, S_j) = M(\varphi_1, M(a_i, S_j))$.

10.2.4. Representation by Graph

With each automaton we can associate a graph in the following way: with each state we associate a vertex, and with each transition rule $(a_i, S_j) \rightarrow S_k$ we associate a directed edge going from S_j to S_k and labelled a_i.

Example. In our example we have:

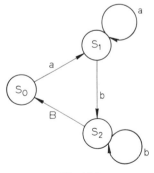

Fig. 10-7

In the same way, we can associate a graph with each grammar by taking the non-terminal symbols as the vertices and the non-terminal rules as the directed edges. For the terminal rules, we associate a directed edge pointing towards a special symbol R.

Example. For the example presently being used, we have:

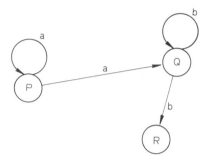

Fig. 10-8

From inspection of the graph of the automaton it is clear that its functioning in the generation or the recognition of sentences is the same. It suffices to give a different interpretation to the edges:

a) *Generation:* when switching from the state S_j to the state S_k, the automaton *writes* a_i on the tape (which is empty to begin with) and moves the tape one square left.

b) *Recognition:* in order to switch from state S_j to state S_k the automaton must *read* a_i on the tape and move it one square left.

The similarities between the rules of grammars and the rules of automata and between the figures almost suffices to prove the equivalence of these definitions. The equivalence becomes evident if we adopt the following conventions:

the rules of the grammars will all be of the form $A_i \to a_j A_k$, and the terminal rules will be written $A_i \to a_j R$, where R is a special symbol: $R \notin V_A$ and A_1 is the axiom.

With this grammar we can associate the following automaton:

the alphabet will be V_T,

the states will be the symbols of $V_A \cup \{R\}$,

the initial state will be A_1, and the final state R,

the transition rules will be $(a_j, A_i) \to A_k$ for each rule of the grammar $A_i \to a_j A_k$.

Every word generated by the grammar is accepted by the automaton. In the same way, starting from an automaton, an equivalent grammar can be constructed just as straightforwardly.

10.3. Other Classes of Finite Automata

10.3.1. Non-Deterministic Automata

Given an automaton A defined by its states S (including initial states $\{S_0\}$ and final states $\{S_f\}$) and its transition function $M(a_i, S_j)$ defined on $V \times S$ having values in S. If, for every couple (a_i, S_j), $M(a_i, S_j)$ has at most one value, the automaton is called deterministic; if several transitions are possible, it is called non-deterministic and $M(a_i, S_j)$ then takes its values in the set of subsets of S: $\mathfrak{P}(S)$.

Let us consider the finite automaton B which is constructed from A in the following way: the set of states is the set of subsets of S, say, T; the set of initial states is $\{T_0\} = \{S_0\}$, and $\{T_f\}$ is the set of subsets of S that contain one S_f, at least; the transition function $M(a_i, T_j)$ is the set of $M(a_i, S_j)$ such that $S_j \in T_j$. The automaton B is deterministic; in fact, we see that it is equivalent to A.

This result shows that with every non-deterministic automaton we can associate an equivalent deterministic automaton. *A priori*, we might imagine that these more general automata would enable us to define other languages than the K-languages, but this is not so.

10.3.2. Automata with Bidirectional Tape Movement

Another generalization of the concept of finite-state automata consists in allowing arbitrary tape movement instead of only unidirectional movement, as has been the case so far. Thus, in the course of examining a letter of a square on the tape, the automaton might go backwards, look at another letter, then go forward again, etc., up to the leftmost symbol of the word under analysis.

More formally, the transition function would determine the tape movement. It would be defined on the product set $S \times \{L, R\}$: S is the set of states, and L and R mean that the tape is to be moved one square left or right, respectively.

It can be shown that this generalization does not change the class of languages that are accepted, which are still the K-languages; i.e., with every bidirectional automaton we can associate an ordinary automaton that is equivalent to it.

10.3.3. K-Limited Automata

Kleene defined a restricted class of automata made up of automata whose state is determined uniquely by the last k symbols of the word that are accepted, where k is given in advance. It can be decided whether a word belongs to the language generated by the automaton by examining just the last k letters of the word.

An example of a finite automaton that is not k-limited for any k is the following:

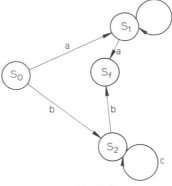

Fig. 10-9

This concept has been used in certain studies of natural languages, studies of words of k letters for example. A matrix is taken whose rows correspond to the strings of k letters of the language in question, and whose columns correspond to the letters of this language. The probability that the letter corresponding to a column follow the k letters that correspond to a row is inserted at the intersection of that row and column. The production of a word by a k-limited automaton which has this matrix representation is carried out in the following way. When the automaton is in the state which corresponds to the rightmost string of k letters of the word: $a_{i_1} a_{i_2} \ldots a_{i_k}$, it generates a letter a_1 as a function of these k letters and is then in the state that corresponds to the string: $a_{i_2} a_{i_3} \ldots a_{i_k} a_1$.

10.4. Closure Properties. Kleene's Structural Characterization

10.4.0.

We shall prove that the class of K-languages forms a Boolean algebra.

10.4.1. Union

Same proof as for the CF-languages.

10.4.2. Complementation

Consider a K-grammar (G) on $V_T = \{a_i\}$ having the axiom A_0 and the rules $A_i \to a_j A_k$, with $a_0 = E \in V_T$, $V_A = \{A_j | 0 \leq j \leq n\}$. We shall associate with it a K-grammar $(\overline{G})$ defined on $V_T = \{a_i\}$, $\overline{V}_A = \{B_j | 0 \leq j \leq n+1\}$, having axiom B_0 and generating the complement of $L(G)$ with respect to V_T^*:

(1) With every rule $A_j \to a_i A_k (i \neq 0)$ we associate $B_j \to a_i B_k$.

(2) With every triple (A_j, a_i, A_k) $(i \neq 0)$ such that there is no rule $A_j \to a_i A_k$ in (G) we associate the rule $B_j \to a_i B_{n+1}$.

($\overline{G}$) has the further rules:

(3) $B_{n+1} \to a_0 B_0$, $B_{n+1} \to a_j B_{n+1}$ for $j \geq 1$.

(4) $B_j \to B_0$ when there is no rule $A_j \to A_0$ in G.

Rules (1) and (4) exclude L(G) from $\overline{L(G)}$ by 'extending' the sentences of L(G). The rules of (2) allow strings that are not in L(G) to be generated. The rules of (3) allow arbitrary sequences to be generated, starting from the symbol B_{n+1}.

It follows from this that the intersection of two K-languages is a K-language.

10.4.3.

Using the same method as for the CF-languages, it can be shown that the product of two K-languages is a K-language, and that the operations $\sim$ and $*$, applied to a K-language, generate a K-language.

These results are strengthened by the following theorem.

Kleene's Theorem. *The class of K-languages is the smallest class of languages that contains the finite languages and is closed under the operations of union, product and $*$.*

10.4.4. Decision Procedures

A certain number of questions which were raised in connection with Turing machines and push-down automata are also pertinent to finite automata. Here, they are decidable: there exist algorithms for deciding whether or not

a finite automaton accepts a non-empty language;

a finite automaton accepts an infinite language;

two finite automata are equivalent.

10.4.5. Kleene's Structural Characterization

Kleene's theorem allows a simple recursive definition of the K-languages to be given; furthermore, this definition is related to the graphs of automata or of grammars.

Given a vocabulary V, we shall first define the *representing expressions* of strings of V*:

1) a finite string of V* is a representing expression;

2) if X_1 and X_2 are representing expressions, then $X_1 X_2$ is a representing expression;

3) if the X_i: $1 \leq i \leq n$ are representing expressions, then $(X_{i_1}, \ldots, X_{i_m})^*$ is a representing expression, $i_k \in \{1, \ldots, n\}$.

These expressions represent sets of strings of V* in the following way:

1) a finite string of V* represents this same string of V*;

2) if X_1 represents the set of strings Σ_1 and X_2 represents Σ_2, then $X_1 X_2$ represents the set of all the strings $\varphi_1 \varphi_2$ such that $\varphi_1 \in \Sigma_1$ and $\varphi_2 \in \Sigma_2$;

3) if the X_i: $1 \leq i \leq n$ represent the sets of strings Σ_i: $1 \leq i \leq n$, then $(X_{i_1}, \ldots, X_{i_m})^*$ represents the set of strings $\varphi_{i_1} \varphi_{i_2} \ldots \varphi_{i_m}$ such that $\varphi_{i_k} \in \Sigma_{i_k}$ $i_k \in \{1, 2, \ldots, n\}$.

In this last case, we may have $m > n$, and we may also have repetition of an arbitrary number of φ_i taken in the Σ_i; the order in which the φ_i are concatenated does not matter.

Every K-language can be described by a set of representing expressions.

Example.

a b represents the language made up of the unique word a b.
(a)* represents the language $\{a^n | n \geq 0\}$.
(a)* (b)* represents the language $\{a^p b^q | p, q \geq 0\}$.
(a, b)* represents the monoid defined on $\{a, b\}$.

Graphs may conveniently be associated with these expressions in the following way:

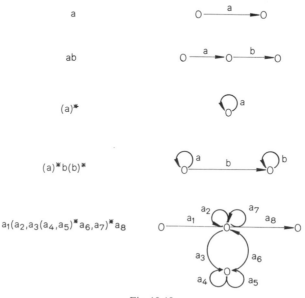

Fig. 10-10

Starting from these graphs, we can shift systematically to the graphs of automata and of grammars, and vice-versa; i.e., the definitions of the K-languages by representing expressions and by finite automata are equivalent.

10.5. K-Languages and CF-Languages

10.5.1. Self-Embedding

The restricted nature of the K-languages is due to the fact that a K-language can always be generated by a grammar containing no self-embedded auxiliary symbol, whereas the grammars of certain CF-languages are all self-embedded.

Consider the language $L = \{a^n b^n \mid n > 0\}$ generated by the CF-grammar

$$\begin{vmatrix} S \to a\,S\,b \\ S \to a\,b \end{vmatrix}.$$

We shall prove that it cannot be generated by a K-grammar.

L being infinite, the K-grammar must necessarily have a derivation of the type $A_i \Rightarrow x\,A_i$. Since x can only be of the form a^p, the grammar must contain such derivations as:

$$A_i \Rightarrow y\,A_j \quad y = a^q\,b^r \quad q, r \geq 0,$$
$$A_j \Rightarrow z\,A_j \quad z = b^m.$$

Then this grammar generates the words $a^p\,b^q$ with $p \neq q$.

A K-language can be generated by a self-embedded grammar, and we may ask whether, given a CF-grammar, it can be decided whether it generates a K-language or not. The answer to this question is no; this follows from a problem related to the determination of the nature of the intersection of two CF-languages.

10.6. One-Sided Finite Transducers

10.6.1. Example

Let $\mathfrak{A}$ be a finite automaton. If we furnish it with an output tape on which some symbol of an output alphabet $V_S = \{b_i\}$ will be written at each step, we obtain a new automaton $\mathfrak{T}$ that belongs to the class of *one-sided finite transducers*.

The operation of $\mathfrak{T}$ is specified by rules of the type: $(a_i, S_j) \to (S_k, b_l)$; when the transducer $\mathfrak{T}$ has accepted a pattern by the intermediary of the finite automaton $\mathfrak{A}$ that is a part of the transducer, it also furnishes a "translation" into $\{b_i\}^*$. This word is the transduction image of f by $\mathfrak{T}$ and is written as $\mathfrak{T}(f)$.

9 Gross/Lentin, Formal Grammars

The automaton $\mathfrak{T}$ can be represented by a diagram whose nodes correspond to the states. For every rule of the type $(a_i, S_j) \to (S_k, b_l)$, an arrow labelled (a_i, b_l) is directed from S_i to S_j. In this representation, it is clear that the set of transductions of the words accepted by $\mathfrak{T}$ is also a K-language.

Furthermore, by interchanging a_i and b_l in the rules: $(b_l, S_j) \to (S_k, a_i)$ the transducer $\mathfrak{T}^{-1}$, the inverse of $\mathfrak{T}$, is formed. The inverse transducer has a diagram derived from that of $\mathfrak{T}$ by labelling the arrows (b, a) instead of (a, b).

10.6.2. General Definition

More generally, a one-sided finite transducer is an automaton $\mathfrak{T}$ which is defined by the following data:

1. an input alphabet $V_I = \{a_1, \ldots\}$ and an output alphabet $V_0 = \{b_1, \ldots\}$ containing at least two letters each;
2. a finite set of states $\Sigma = \{S_0, \ldots\}$;
3. a transfer mapping: $\Sigma \times V_I \to \Sigma$;
4. an output mapping: $\Sigma \times V_I \to V_0^*$.

The transducer starts in a state considered to be initial, say S_0; it reads the first symbol of a word $f = a_{i_1} a_{i_2} \ldots a_{i_n}$, switches to the state corresponding to the pair (S_0, a_{i_1}), and writes the symbol (or the string) corresponding to this same pair. Then it reads the symbol a_{i_2}, etc.

The transducer is termed one-sided because the transduction is accomplished by a single left-to-right read. The transducer blocks if it arrives at a situation not provided for in the rules; but if it finishes reading then it furnishes the transduction at the same time.

10.6.3. Transduction of a CF-Language

Let us consider now a CF-grammar G and a one-sided finite transducer $\mathfrak{T}$. We should like to determine the nature of the language $\mathfrak{T}(\Lambda)$ transduced by $\mathfrak{T}$ from $\Lambda = L(G)$.

We note at once that $\mathfrak{T}$ accepts the intersection of Λ with the maximal K-language that it accepts. If this intersection is empty, we have $\mathfrak{T}(\Lambda) = e$ (the transducer we are considering does not give as output a non-empty string for an empty input). For the case where the intersection does not reduce to the empty word, we shall prove that $\mathfrak{T}(\Lambda)$ is a CF-language and we shall give a CF-grammar for it, G'.

Let $V_A = \{A_i | 0 \leq i \leq n\}$ be the auxiliary vocabulary of G, where A_0 is the axiom, and let $V_T = \{a_j\}$, $\{S_k\}$ be the set of states of the transducer $\mathfrak{T}$, where S_0 is the initial state and $\{S_f\}$ the final states.

The rules of G' are defined as follows. The axiom is a new symbol A'_0; the other non-terminals are triples of the form (S_i, α, S_j), where S_i and S_j

are states of $\mathfrak{T}$ and α is a terminal or non-terminal symbol used by G. Furthermore:

1. $A'_0 \to (S_0, A_0, S_i)$ is a rule, for all i.

2. If $A_m \to \alpha_1 \ldots \alpha_h$ is a rule of G, then for all i, j, $\beta_1, \ldots, \beta_{h-1}$, G' contains the rules: $(S_i, A_m, S_j) \to (S_i, \alpha_1, S_{\beta_1})(S_{\beta_1}, \alpha_2, S_{\beta_2}) \ldots (S_{\beta_{h-1}}, \alpha_h, S_j)$.

3. If $(a_j, S_p) \to (S_q, b_l)$ is a rule of $\mathfrak{T}$, then G' contains the rule:

$$(S_f, a_j, S_q) \to b_l.$$

4. Finally, in order to be sure that the non-terminals really appear on the left side of the rules, we adopt the convention that G' contains the rules $(S_i, a, S_j) \to (S_i, a, S_j)$ a for all a, i, and j not covered by 3.

Let L be the K-language accepted by $\mathfrak{T}$.

Λ) $f \in L$ and $f \in \Lambda \Rightarrow \mathfrak{T}(f) \in L(G')$.

Let $f = a_{i_1} \ldots a_{i_k}$. $f \in \Lambda$ implies the existence of a computation of transduction $(a_{i_1}, S_0) \to (S_{n_1}, b_{i_1}), \ldots (S_{n_{k-2}}, a_{i_k}) \to (S_f, b_{i_k})$, hence $\mathfrak{T}(f) = b_{i_1} b_{i_2} \ldots b_{i_k}$. $f \in L$ implies the existence of a derivation $A_0 \Rightarrow f$,

$$A_0 \Rightarrow a_{i_1} \ldots a_{i_k},$$

hence of the derivation

$$A'_0 = (S_0, A_0, S_f) \Rightarrow (S_0, a_{i_1}, S_{n_1})(S_{n_1}, a_{i_2}, S_{n_2}) \ldots (S_{n_{k-1}}, a_{i_k}, S_f).$$

Then by the rules 4) we have $A'_0 \Rightarrow b_{i_1} b_{i_2} \ldots b_{i_k} = \mathfrak{T}(f)$, from which it follows that $\mathfrak{T}(f) \in L(G')$.

B) $g \in L(G') \Rightarrow \mathfrak{T}^{-1}(g) \in L \cap \Lambda$.

If $g = b_{i_1} \ldots b_{i_k}$ then $\mathfrak{T}^{-1}(g) = a_{i_1} \ldots a_{i_k}$. We also have

$$A'_0 = (S_0, A_0, S_f) \Rightarrow g = b_{i_1} b_{i_2} \ldots b_{i_k}.$$

Each b_α is the result of a rule $(S_i, a_\alpha, S_j) \to b_\alpha$ with the condition $(a_\alpha, S_i) \to (S_j, b_\alpha)$. Hence $\mathfrak{T}^{-1}(g) \in \Lambda$, which proves our result.

In the special case where the transducer does no more than recopy the input sentence: $(a_i, S_j) \to (S_k, a_i)$, we have the result:

Theorem. *The intersection of a CF-language and a K-language is a CF-language.*

These results, which have been proven by means of very restricted transducers (one-to-one correspondence between the input and output letters), are valid in general. We shall note only that the result is valid for the languages of Schützenberger:

Theorem of Jungen Schützenberger. *The intersection of an algebraic language and a rational language is an algebraic language.*

Exercise. Show that with every K-language defined on V one can associate a graph such that each vertex is the initial vertex of exactly card (V) edges each of which is labelled by a different element of V.

Chapter XI

Languages Defined by Systems of Equations

11.1. Functions whose Arguments and Values are Languages

11.1.0. Operations

In connection with languages, we defined a certain number of operations, among them:

1. Set union $L \cup M$, a commutative and associative operation;

2. Multiplication LM, which consisted in forming the cartesian product and then concatenating the components in each pair: $LM = \{x\,y \,|\, x \in L, y \in M\}$. This operation is not commutative, but it is associative, as is word concatenation, from which it is derived.

It will be noted that multiplication is distributive with respect to union: $L(L_1 \cup L_2) = LL_1 \cup LL_2$. Since we have defined these operations as operating on the class of languages, we are now able to introduce the concepts of variables, formal expressions and functions.

11.1.1. Variables and Expressions

When we consider a family of languages: $\{L_1, L_2, \ldots, \}$ we shall always suppose that they are defined on the same terminal vocabulary V_T and that there exists a single auxiliary vocabulary V_A that can describe all the grammars.

By language, we always mean a well-defined set of terminal sentences.

Language Variables. We now consider *language variables*, i.e., variables $\mathfrak{L}, \mathfrak{M}, \mathfrak{N}$ which can take their values on a family of languages.

Example. We are working with the class of CF-languages and we introduce the variable $\mathfrak{L}$. A "linguistic" value that can be attributed to $\mathfrak{L}$ might be, for example:

$$\mathfrak{L} = L_m = \{x\,c\,\tilde{x} \,|\, x \in \{a, b\}^*\}.$$

Formal expressions. Using the *constants* t, a, ..., which are fixed terminal sentences, the variables $\mathfrak{L}, \mathfrak{M}, \mathfrak{N}, \ldots$, and the operation signs, we can write formal expressions like:

$$t \mathfrak{L}; \quad t \mathfrak{L} \cup a; \quad \mathfrak{L} a \mathfrak{M} \cup a \mathfrak{L} t; \ldots$$

which take on a definite "linguistic" value if definite "linguistic" values are attributed to the variables.

Examples. 1. The alphabet is {a, e, i, o, u, g, n, s, t}. The constant t is the terminal sequence 'a b'; we shall examine the expression t $\mathfrak{L}$. Let us give the variable the value: L = {stain, use, negation}, which is a finite language made up of three terminal strings. Then the expression t $\mathfrak{L}$ takes on the "linguistic" value: L' = {abstain, abuse, abnegation} which is another finite language made up of three strings.

2. Let us attribute to $\mathfrak{L}$ the value L_m, where $L_m = \{x c \tilde{x} \mid x \in \{a, b\}^*\}$. Then the expression t $\mathfrak{L}$ has as its value the language

$$\{a b c, \ a b a c a, \ a b b c b, \ a b a b c b a, \ldots\},$$

which is obtained by prefixing all the strings of L_m with ab.

Expressions of the first kind. A formal expression is said to be an expression of the *first kind* if, starting from terminal constants and language variables, only the operations of set union and product are used to form it. The order of its monomials does not matter.

Example. In the notation of the preceding examples, the expression a b $\mathfrak{L} \cup a \mathfrak{M} \cup \mathfrak{M}$ b a $\mathfrak{L}$, is an expression of the first kind, with two variables $\mathfrak{L}$ and $\mathfrak{M}$, made up of three monomials.

11.1.2. Functions and Equations

It is clear that giving an expression is equivalent to giving a certain *function*. If every variable describes a family of languages, the values taken on by the expression describe a well-determined family of languages. We define a mapping of the set of arguments onto the set of values taken on, or a function which has its arguments on a family of languages and its values on (or, by extension, in) a family of languages.

We stress again that, for the moment at least, when we attribute a "linguistic" value L to a language variable $\mathfrak{L}$, L is a language considered strictly from the point of view of set theory. In particular, the sentences of L are not accompanied by any description.

Example. The alphabet is {a, b, c} and we shall take the class of linear languages as the domain of the arguments. Then the expression: $\mathfrak{L} \mathfrak{M} \mathfrak{L} \cup \mathfrak{M}$ a $\mathfrak{M}$ defines on this domain a function with "linguistic" values.

Equations. We shall use the classic notation of the theory of functions, namely: $y = f(\mathfrak{L}, \mathfrak{M}, \ldots)$ in writing the functions just defined.

If we consider certain values of y, $\mathfrak{L}$, ... as known and the others as unknown, then we obtain *equations* whose unknowns are languages; we intend to solve such equations. Conversely, given a language, we can try to construct some interesting equations of which this language is a solution.

We shall first study these new concepts for a special case.

11.1.3. Equations Related to the Mirror Language L_m

Let us consider the language L_m on the terminal alphabet $\{a, b, c\}$ defined by the grammar:

$$\begin{vmatrix} S \to a\,S\,a \\ S \to b\,S\,b \\ S \to \quad c \end{vmatrix}$$

and let us examine the function defined by the expression $a\,\mathfrak{L}\,a$.

If we attribute the value L_m to $\mathfrak{L}$, the function has as its value the language $a\,L_m\,a$; this last is a sub-language of L_m, containing all the strings that begin (and end) with a, and only those strings.

Consider now the expression $a\,\mathfrak{L}\,a \cup b\,\mathfrak{L}\,b$; for $\mathfrak{L} = L_m$, the function defined by this expression has as its value the language obtained by removing just the word c from L_m. Then it is clear that:

$$L_m = a\,L_m\,a \cup b\,L_m\,b \cup c.$$

The language L_m therefore is *a* solution of the equation:

$$\mathfrak{L} = a\,\mathfrak{L}\,a \cup b\,\mathfrak{L}\,b \cup c.$$

11.1.4. Solution of the Equation Obtained

But we may also ask whether the language L_m (on the vocabulary $\{a, b, c\}$) is the only solution of the preceding equation. Let us then try to solve this equation, which we shall write as $\mathfrak{L} = f(\mathfrak{L})$.

In view of the meaning of the right side, it is clear that every solution L necessarily contains the single-letter word c, hence contains the language $L_1 = \{c\}$. Containing L_1, every solution necessarily contains

$$L_2 = a\,L_1\,a \cup b\,L_1\,b \cup c = \{a\,c\,a,\ b\,c\,b,\ c\}.$$

Containing L_2, every solution necessarily contains

$$\begin{aligned} L_3 &= a\,L_2\,a \cup b\,L_2\,b \cup c \\ &= a\,\{a\,c\,a,\ b\,c\,b,\ c\}\,a \cup b\,\{a\,c\,a,\ b\,c\,b,\ c\}\,b \cup c \\ &= \{a\,a\,c\,a\,a,\ a\,b\,c\,b\,a,\ b\,a\,c\,a\,b,\ b\,b\,c\,b\,b,\ a\,c\,a,\ b\,c\,b,\ c\}. \end{aligned}$$

More generally, we see that L necessarily contains the sets:

$$L_1 = \{c\}, \quad L_2 = f(L_1), \dots, L_n = f(L_{n-1}), \dots$$

obtained by a recursive procedure, and that each of these sets contains the preceding.

The sequences obtained at any given step are not changed by any succeeding step. Under these conditions, it can be proven rigorously (and understood intuitively) that the sequence of sets L_n is a perfect definition of a set which is the *inductive limit* of the sequence and which we shall write as $\lim_{n \to \infty} L_n$.

It is clear that this limit is nothing else but the mirror language L_m with which we began, so that this language turns out to be the *minimal* solution of the equation. From the point of view we have adopted, it is correct to call it the *solution*.

Notational Variants. In order to solve the preceding equation of the type $\mathfrak{L} = f(\mathfrak{L})$, we took L_1 as $\{c\}$; the constant c can be obtained by assuming that there exists a set ω which is an annihilator[1] for concatenation. Setting $L_0 = \omega$, we obtain:

$$f(L_0) = \{a \, \omega \, a \cup b \, \omega \, b \cup c\} = c = L_1,$$

which regularizes the writing of the recursive process.

11.1.5. Derivational History

We mentioned at the beginning of this chapter that the multiplication of languages, like the concatenation of words, is an associative operation. Given three languages L_1, L_2, L_3, we have $(L_1 L_2) L_3 = L_1 (L_2 L_3)$ and the parentheses may be dispensed with. However, it is clear that if we keep the parentheses or any symbols used in their place, we also keep a record of the history of the words obtained.

Suppose that the languages L_1, L_2, and L_3 are each given by an enumeration of their strings:

$$L_1 = \{x_1, x_2, \dots, x_i, \dots\}$$
$$L_2 = \{y_1, y_2, \dots, y_j, \dots\}$$
$$L_3 = \{z_1, z_2, \dots, z_k, \dots\}.$$

If we first take $L_1 L_2$ and then $(L_1 L_2) L_3$, the language obtained contains $x_i \, y_j \, z_k$ whose structural history is $((x_i \, y_j) \, z_k)$. On the other hand, if we first take $(L_2 L_3)$ and then $L_1 (L_2 L_3)$, the language thus obtained contains

---

[1] This "annihilator" ω is not to be confused with the empty word which is neutral for concatenation.

the same sequence with the structure $(x_i(y_j z_k))$. In the same way, the language $a\,L_1$ contains the sequence $a\,x_i$ with the structure $(a)(x_i)$.

When solving the equation $\mathfrak{L}=f(\mathfrak{L})$, we shall keep track of the structure of the solution which depends on the sequence of steps appearing in that solution.

Example of a Structured Solution. We solve the following equation in the way just described:

$$\mathfrak{L}_0=\omega$$
$$\mathfrak{L}_1=\{a\,\omega\,a\cup b\,\omega\,b\cup c\}=\{(c)\}$$
$$\mathfrak{L}_2=\{a\,(c)\,a\cup b\,(c)\,b\cup c\}$$
$$\qquad=\{(a\,(c)\,a),(b\,(c)\,b),(c)\}$$
$$\mathfrak{L}_3=\{a\,\{(a\,(c)\,a),(b\,(c)\,b),(c)\}\,a,\,b\,\{(a\,(c)\,a),(b\,(c)\,b),(c)\},(c)\}$$
$$\qquad=\{(a\,(a\,(c)\,a)\,a),(a\,(b\,(c)\,b)\,a),(b\,(a\,(c)\,a)\,b),$$
$$\qquad\quad(b\,(b\,(c)\,b)\,a),(a\,(c)\,a),(b\,(c)\,b),(c)\},\quad\text{etc.}$$

Using parentheses to set off each word as soon as it is formed, and making use of the distributivity of the multiplication of languages with respect to set union, we bring out the structural history of the language L_m.

In this example we recognize this structural history as identical to the one ascribed to the strings of L_m by the CF-grammar used to define L_m, namely: $S\to a\,S\,a$, $S\to b\,S\,b$, $S\to c$. At the level of $\mathfrak{L}_3$, for example, we find the descriptions:

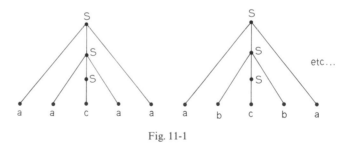

Fig. 11-1

The absence of a label is in accord with the fact that there is only one non-terminal symbol.

But the interest of a structural history is clearly even greater in the case of ambiguous grammars. The preceding grammar was not ambiguous; we shall now experiment on the grammar which describes the expressions obtained by means of a binary operator.

11.1.6. Example with an Ambiguous Grammar

Consider the CF-grammar $V_A = \{S\}$; $V_T = \{a, b\}$; $|S \rightarrow S\,a\,S,\ S \rightarrow b|$. Aside from the derivation $S \rightarrow b$, every other derivation begins with:

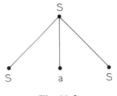

Fig. 11-2

and each of the S obtained is the head of a derivation for the language. This language then satisfies the equation: $\mathfrak{L} = \mathfrak{L}\,a\,\mathfrak{L} \cup b$, which we shall now solve while keeping track of the structural history of the solution. We obtain successively:

$$\mathfrak{L}_0 = \omega$$

$$\mathfrak{L}_1 = \{\omega\,a\,\omega \cup b\} = \{(b)\}$$

$$\mathfrak{L}_2 = \{\{(b)\}\,a\,\{(b)\} \cup b\} = \{((b)\,a\,(b)),\,(b)\}$$

$$\mathfrak{L}_3 = \{\{((b)\,a\,(b)),\,(b)\}\,a\,\{((b)\,a\,(b)),\,(b)\} \cup b\}$$

$$= \{(((b)\,a\,(b))\,a\,((b)\,a\,(b))),\,(((b)\,a\,(b))\,a\,(b)),$$

$$((b)\,a\,((b)\,a\,(b))),\,((b)\,a\,(b)),\,(b)\},\quad \text{etc.}$$

If we eliminate the parentheses, then $\mathfrak{L}_3$ becomes:

$$\mathfrak{L}_3 = \{b\,a\,b\,a\,b\,a\,b,\ b\,a\,b\,a\,b,\ b\,a\,b\,a\,b,\ b\,a\,b,\ b\}.$$

Note that the string b a b a b has been obtained twice. From the viewpoint of set theory, one instance of it is enough. From the viewpoint of structural history, we note that the first instance of it corresponds to the derivation:

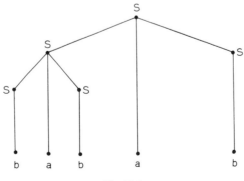

Fig. 11-3

and thus to the description $(((b) a (b)) a (b))$; whereas the second instance
of it has a derivation that is "symmetrical" to the first:

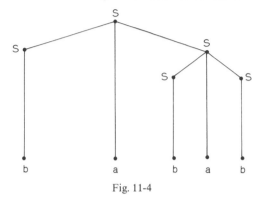

Fig. 11-4

and may be described by $((b) a ((b) a (b)))$.

We have the same parenthesization as with the braces, with the
exception of a few details (which are left to the exercises).

This result can be generalized. In effect, the set $\mathfrak{L}_1$ which was obtained by deleting the non-constant monomials has the derivation:

Fig. 11-5

The set $\mathfrak{L}_2$ makes use of the monomial $\mathfrak{L} a \mathfrak{L}$ again, and this makes
possible the attaching of the terminal derivation of Fig. 11-5 to the non-
terminal derivation:

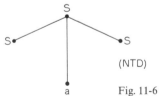

(NTD)

Fig. 11-6

which yields

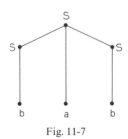

Fig. 11-7

The set $\mathfrak{L}_3$ brings in the non-terminal derivation of Fig. 11-6 once more, and also the possibility of attaching to S the sub-tree of either Figs. 11-5 or 11-7.

The parenthesization by braces represents this process and is therefore equivalent to ordinary parentheses.

Conclusion. Starting from a purely set-theoretic point of view, we have encountered questions of structure and ambiguity. This fact suggests a revision of our concepts and notations, and justifies the introduction of power series that will follow.

We shall first consider languages defined by systems of equations.

11.1.7. System of Equations Associated with a CF-Grammar

Let G be a CF-grammar which generates a CF-language L. We shall now generalize the ideas illustrated thus far by special cases.

To simplify the notation, we shall take the auxiliary vocabulary to contain only three symbols: the axiom S the two non-terminals A and B. It is easily verified that this simplification in no way affects the generality of our argument.

We expressly assume that the grammar contains no rule of the type $A \to E$ (where E is the empty word), no rule of the type $A \to B$, nor any non-terminal symbol that is unproductive at the terminal level. We know that the elimination of such rules or symbols does not affect the generative capacity of a grammar and changes the syntactic descriptions very little or not at all.

Let us order the productions according to their left members, thus obtaining:

$$S \to \Phi_1, \quad S \to \Phi_2, \ldots, S \to \Phi_k;$$
$$A \to \Psi_1, \quad A \to \Psi_2, \ldots, A \to \Psi_1;$$
$$B \to \Theta_1, \quad B \to \Theta_2, \ldots, B \to \Theta_m;$$

where the Φ, Ψ, and Θ are strings from the vocabulary $V = V_A \cup V_T$. With the non-terminal symbols S, A, and B taken in that order, we associate the language variables $\mathfrak{L}$, $\mathfrak{A}$, and $\mathfrak{B}$, respectively. In the strings Φ, Ψ, and Θ we shall replace each occurrence of a non-terminal symbol by the corresponding variable. Then we take the union of the Φ which yields an expression f, the union of the Ψ yielding an expression g, and the union of the Θ yielding an expression h.

Finally, we consider the system of equations:

$$(\sigma) \quad \begin{cases} \mathfrak{L} = f(\mathfrak{L}, \mathfrak{A}, \mathfrak{B}) \\ \mathfrak{A} = g(\mathfrak{L}, \mathfrak{A}, \mathfrak{B}) \\ \mathfrak{B} = h(\mathfrak{L}, \mathfrak{A}, \mathfrak{B}). \end{cases}$$

Example. 1. For the language $S \to a\,S\,a$, $S \to b\,S\,b$, $S \to c$, we obtain the equation $\mathfrak{L} = a\,\mathfrak{L}\,a \cup b\,\mathfrak{L}\,b \cup c$, studied in § 11.1.5.

2. For the grammar:

$$V_A = \{S, A, B\}; \qquad V_T = \{a, b, c, d\};$$

$$\begin{vmatrix} S \to A\,B \\ A \to S\,c \\ B \to d\,B \\ A \to a \\ B \to b \end{vmatrix}$$

we obtain the system:

$$\mathfrak{L} = \mathfrak{A}\,\mathfrak{B}$$
$$\mathfrak{A} = \mathfrak{L}\,c \cup a$$
$$\mathfrak{B} = d\,\mathfrak{B} \cup b.$$

As has been shown for the single equations of the preceding paragraphs, the system (σ) expresses the stability of the language L with respect to the transformation:

$$\mathfrak{L} \to f(\mathfrak{L}, \mathfrak{A}, \mathfrak{B})$$
$$\mathfrak{A} \to g(\mathfrak{L}, \mathfrak{A}, \mathfrak{B})$$
$$\mathfrak{B} \to h(\mathfrak{L}, \mathfrak{A}, \mathfrak{B})$$

which involves the productions only of the grammar G.

We may thus expect to find L in the solution of the system. In this connection, note that $\mathfrak{L}$ is not distinguished in any way: the variables $\mathfrak{A}$ and $\mathfrak{B}$ appear in a similar way to $\mathfrak{L}$. They correspond to the languages obtained by keeping the same rules but taking A and B as axioms, respectively. In fact, the unknown of the system is a triple of languages (L_S, L_A, L_B) having S, A, and B as axioms.

To solve the system, we proceed in the same way as in § 11.1.5. Since every solution necessarily contains the constants on the right, we start from the initial triple: $(\mathfrak{L}_0 = \omega\ \mathfrak{A}_0 = \omega\ \mathfrak{B}_0 = \omega)$ and successively form the triples that the solution must contain:

$$[\mathfrak{L}_1 = f(\mathfrak{L}_0, \mathfrak{A}_0, \mathfrak{B}_0); \qquad \mathfrak{A}_1 = g(\mathfrak{L}_0, \mathfrak{A}_0, \mathfrak{B}_0); \mathfrak{B}_1 = h(\mathfrak{L}_0, \mathfrak{A}_0, \mathfrak{B}_0)]$$
$$\cdots \qquad\qquad \cdots \qquad\qquad \cdots$$
$$[\mathfrak{L}_n = f(\mathfrak{L}_{n-1}, \mathfrak{A}_{n-1}, \mathfrak{B}_{n-1}); \mathfrak{A}_n = \cdots\cdots\cdots ; \mathfrak{B}_n = \cdots\cdots\cdots]$$
$$\cdots \qquad\qquad \cdots \qquad\qquad \cdots$$

We obtain a single triple as the inductive limit, which is the minimal solution of the system. It is necessarily the same as the languages having axioms S, A, and B which are generated by the rules of G.

11.1.8. Example of the Solution of a System

As an example, we shall solve the system mentioned above in Example 2, § 11.1.7.

$$\mathfrak{L} = \mathfrak{A}\,\mathfrak{B}$$

$$\mathfrak{A} = \mathfrak{L}\,c \cup a$$

$$\mathfrak{B} = d\,\mathfrak{B} \cup b.$$

Our computations will record the parenthesization introduced by the process of solution itself. Furthermore, we shall subscript the braces, and the parentheses derived from them, according to the left side of the equation, namely, $\mathfrak{L}$, $\mathfrak{A}$, or $\mathfrak{B}$. However, for simplicity of notation, we shall write 1, 2, and 3 instead of $\mathfrak{L}$, $\mathfrak{A}$, and $\mathfrak{B}$, respectively.

We have, successively:

$$\mathfrak{L}_0 = \omega$$

$$\mathfrak{A}_0 = \omega$$

$$\mathfrak{B}_0 = \omega,$$

$$\mathfrak{L}_1 = \{_1\, \omega\, \omega\} = \omega$$

$$\mathfrak{A}_1 = \{_2\, \omega\, c \cup a\} = \{_2\, a\}$$

$$\mathfrak{B}_1 = \{_3\, d\, \omega \cup b\} = \{_3\, b\},$$

$$\mathfrak{L}_2 = \left\{_1 \{_2 a\}\{_3 b\}\right\} = \left\{_1 \left(_1 (_2 a)(_3 b)\right)\right\}$$

$$\mathfrak{A}_2 = \{_2\, \omega\, c \cup a\} = \{_2\, a\}$$

$$\mathfrak{B}_2 = \{_3\, d\, \omega \cup b\} = \{_3\, b\},$$

$$\mathfrak{L}_3 = \left\{_1 \{_2 a\}\{_3 b\}\right\} = \left\{_1 \left(_1 (_2 a)(_3 b)\right)\right\}$$

$$\mathfrak{A}_3 = \left\{_2 \left\{_1 \left(_1 (_2 a)(_3 b)\right)\right\} c \cup a\right\} = \left\{_2 \left(_2 \left(\left(_1 (_2 a)(_3 b)\right)\right) c\right), a\right\}$$

$$\mathfrak{B}_3 = \left\{_3 d\{_3 b\} \cup b\right\} = \left\{_3 \left(_3 d(_3 b)\right), b\right\},$$

$$\mathfrak{L}_4 = \left\{_1 \left\{_2 \left(_2 \left(\left(_1 (_2 a)(_3 b)\right)\right) c\right), a\right\}\left\{_3 \left(_3 d(_3 b)\right), b\right\}\right\}$$

$$= \left\{_1 \left(_2 \left(_2 \left(\left(_1 (_2 a)(_3 b)\right)\right) c\right)\left(_3 \left(_3 d(_3 b)\right)\right)\right),\right.$$

$$\left.\left(\left(_2 \left(_2 \left(\left(_1 (_2 a)(_3 b)\right)\right) c\right)(_3 b)\right), \left(_1 (_2 a)\left(_3 d(_3 b)\right)\right), \left(_1 (_2 a)(_3 b)\right)\right\}\right.$$

$$\mathfrak{A}_4 = \text{etc.}$$

$$\mathfrak{B}_4 = \text{etc.}$$

We thus obtain a description by parentheses of the languages which are obtained by means of the rules of the CF-grammar considered, starting from the axioms S, A, or B. Let us compare this description with the description given these strings by the CF-grammar itself.

At the first level, we have the derivations:

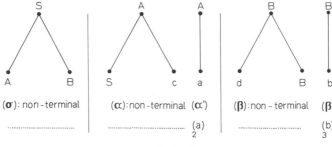

Fig. 11-8

At the second level, we find the derivations (α') and (β') attached to the nodes A and B of the non-terminal tree (σ):

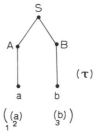

Fig. 11-9

At the third level, in the language with axiom A, we obtain the tree which results from attaching the tree τ (of Fig. 11-9) to the node S of (α):

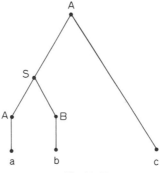

Fig. 11-10

which corresponds to:

$$\left(_2\left(_1\left(_2 a\right)\quad\left(_3 b\right)\right)\quad\quad c\right)$$

Fig. 11-11

In the same way, we obtain a tree by attaching the terminal tree (β') to the node B of the terminal tree (β)

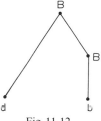

Fig. 11-12

which corresponds to

$$\left(_3 d\quad\quad\left(_3 b\right)\right)$$

Fig. 11-13

At the fourth level, in the language with axiom S, we have all the trees obtained by attaching the terminal trees with vertices A or B thus far encountered to the nodes A and B of the tree (σ) (in Fig. 11-8):

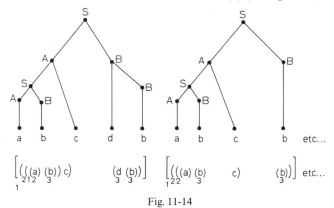

Fig. 11-14

The two systems of parenthesization are thus identical. The reason for this is that, at each iteration of the solution, we reintroduce the fundamental derivation schemata together with the possibility of attaching to the non-terminal nodes the terminal trees formed up to that point. The description is the same, whether the trees are constructed from "bottom to top", as in the solution of the system, or from "top to bottom", as when following the rules of the grammar directly.

11.1.9. Conclusion

To summarize, we can associate with every CF-grammar a system of equations, as many as there are non-terminal symbols. Each equation is of the type $\mathfrak{L} = f(\mathfrak{A}, \mathfrak{B}, \mathfrak{C}, \ldots)$ where f stands for an expression of the first kind. The solution of the system is an ordered set of languages, each of which has as its productions those of the CF-grammar, and as axiom one of the non-terminal symbols.

More briefly, this ordered set of languages is said to satisfy the given grammar. The class of CF-languages and the class of languages defined by the systems of equations in the space described are identical. Furthermore, one way of solving the system brings out a structuring of the strings of the languages, and suggests modifying the purely set-theoretic viewpoint adopted at the outset.

We shall pursue the consequences of this last remark in the next section.

11.2. Languages and Formal Power Series

11.2.0.

The more "algebraic" way of describing the sequence of languages $L_0, L_1, L_2, \ldots, L_n$, and our need to take into consideration degrees of ambiguity suggest introducing polynomials, whose monomials are just the strings belonging to these languages and whose coefficients are positive integers. If the language which is the solution is not finite, the polynomials contain an increasing number of terms of increasingly higher degrees. However, the terms of a given degree do not change after a certain point, and this enables us to continue to the inductive limit in order to obtain power series.

In order to study languages from this new viewpoint, we will now set forth *a priori* the definitions which our preceding empirical work has suggested. We shall also generalize by taking the coefficients to be integers of arbitrary sign; the productiveness of this extension will find an ample justification in what follows.

11.2.1. Power Series

Let $V_T = \{a_i \mid 1 \leq i \leq n\}$ be the terminal vocabulary. The set of finite strings that can be written with such a vocabulary is denumerably infinite. With each sequence $x \in V_T^*$ we associate a related integer by means of a procedure (r). In other words, we take a function, or a mapping (r), whose arguments are on V_T^* and whose values are in Z: $x \xrightarrow{(r)} \langle r, x \rangle \in Z$.

With this mapping we can define the power series r: $r = \sum_x \langle r, x \rangle\, x$

in which each monomial x has as coefficient the integer that was associated with it.

Example. Let $V_T = \{a, b\}$. Writing the terms in order of increasing degree, and in alphabetical order for each degree, we obtain:

$$E, \ a, \ b, \ a\,a, \ a\,b, \ b\,a, \ b\,b, \ a\,a\,a, \ a\,a\,b, \ a\,b\,a, \ldots$$

For each term, we add 1 to its degree and take as its coefficient the remainder mod 3 of the integer so obtained; this yields the power series:

$$r = 1\,E + 2\,a + 2\,b + 0\,a\,a + 0\,a\,b + 0\,b\,a$$
$$+ 0\,b\,b + 1\,a\,a\,a + 1\,a\,a\,b + 1\,a\,b\,a + \cdots.$$

We may also omit the terms with coefficient zero.

A series is said to be *characteristic* if the procedure (r) maps V_T^* onto $\{0, 1\}$, or, in other terms, if the function (r) is characteristic. With every series there can be associated, at least in principle, the characteristic series obtained by keeping the value *zero* for every null coefficient and replacing every non-zero coefficient by *one*.

Given a power series r, the set of strings having a non-zero coefficient is a language L which is called the *support* of the series, and we write: $L = \text{Sup}\,(r)$.

11.2.2. Operations on Power Series

When addition and multiplication are defined for it, the set of power series takes on a ring structure.

Addition. Addition is defined in the usual way. In the series which is the sum of r and r', written $r + r'$, the coefficient of a string is the sum of the coefficients of similar strings: $\langle r + r', x \rangle = \langle r, x \rangle + \langle r', x \rangle$.

Multiplication. Multiplication is also defined in the usual way. However, its non-commutativity must be respected: the factors may only be concatenated, and in order, without permutation. In the product series, written $r\,r'$, the coefficient $\langle r\,r', x \rangle$ is the sum of the partial products $\langle r_i, y \rangle \langle r_j', z \rangle$ such that $y\,z = x$.

We leave to the reader the question of a detailed proof of our assertion concerning the ring structure.

Multiplication by an Integer. The ring of power series has Z as its operator domain; then, clearly, we take the term $n \langle r, x \rangle$ as the general term of the series $n \cdot r$.

11.2.3. Topological Concepts

We shall now specify the transition from polynomials to series and explain a concept of neighborhood.

We shall say that the series r is *equivalent to the series r' modulo the degree n* and write $r \equiv r'$ (mod. deg. n) to mean that (degree of $x \leq n$) $\Rightarrow$ $(r, x) = (r', x)$.

Suppose now that we are given an infinite sequence of series $r_1, r_2, \ldots$ such that for every n, and for every n′ greater than n we have $r_n \equiv r_{n'}$. In this case, the limit of the sequence $r_1, r_2, \ldots$ is well-defined. It is the limit of the sequence of polynomials which are obtained by truncating each r_n of all terms of degree greater than n.

We thus see how the ring of power series can be furnished with a topology.

11.2.4. Series with Positive Coefficients

Aside from the fact that those series whose coefficients are all positive or zero form a semi-ring, we note the following important properties of their supports.

Addition. The coefficient $\langle r + r', x \rangle$, which is the sum of two non-negative integers, is different from zero if one or the other of these integers is not zero.

For positive series, the support of the sum is the union of the supports.

Multiplication. If the support of r contains the string y and the support of r′ the string z, then, since the terms cannot reduce, the support of r r′ contains the string y z. Conversely, if the support of r r′ contains a string x, there exists at least one pair (y, z) of strings such that y z = x. Consequently:

For positive series, the support of the product is the product (in the sense of product of languages) of the supports.

11.2.5. Positive Series and CF-Grammars

The reader has surely noticed that the computations we have carried out in order to set up and solve the system of equations associated with a CF-grammar can be described in a conceptually simple manner by series with non-negative integral coefficients.

We now adopt the convention that the variables $\mathfrak{L}, \mathfrak{A}, \mathfrak{B}, \ldots$ no longer stand for languages in the purely set-theoretic meaning of the term, but for power series. With each series we associate a support, which is a language, and coefficients which describe the relationship of a word to the language and its degree of ambiguity:

0　if the word is not generated at all,

1　if it is generated once,

2　if it is generated in two distinct ways, etc.

The system associated with a CF-grammar is still written:

$$\mathfrak{L} = f(\mathfrak{L}, \mathfrak{A}, \mathfrak{B}, \ldots)$$
$$\mathfrak{A} = g(\mathfrak{L}, \mathfrak{A}, \mathfrak{B}, \ldots)$$
$$\mathfrak{B} = h(\mathfrak{L}, \mathfrak{A}, \mathfrak{B}, \ldots)$$

where f, g, h, etc. are polynomials with coefficients equal to one.

The method given for solving this system remains valid. The successive approximations $(\mathfrak{L}_0, \mathfrak{A}_0, \mathfrak{B}_0, \ldots)$, $(\mathfrak{L}_1, \mathfrak{A}_1, \mathfrak{B}_1, \ldots)$, ... are a special kind of power series, viz., polynomials. Modulo their degree, these polynomials are equivalent to the desired solution, which they approach in the sense of the inductive limit. The reader may take as an exercise the solution of the examples treated in the preceding sections, using the present notation.

We now give an example which is interesting in itself.

Example. We have treated the grammar $S \to S\, a\, S$, $S \to b$, which is ambiguous. On the other hand, the grammar

$$S \to a\, S\, S, \quad S \to b,$$

which corresponds to Polish notation, is not ambiguous. We expect therefore to find a characteristic series. We obtain the equation:

$$\mathfrak{L} = a\, \mathfrak{L}\, \mathfrak{L} + b,$$

which can solved:

$$\mathfrak{L}_0 = \omega$$
$$\mathfrak{L}_1 = b$$
$$\mathfrak{L}_2 = a\,(b)\,(b) + b = a\,b^2 + b$$
$$\mathfrak{L}_3 = a\,[a\,(b)\,(b) + b]\,[a\,(b)\,(b) + b]$$
$$\quad = a\,[a\,(b)\,(b)]\,[a\,(b)\,(b)] + a\,[b]\,[a\,(b)\,(b)]$$
$$\quad + a\,[a\,(b)\,(b)]\,[b] + a\,[b]\,[b] + b;$$

and, without parentheses:
$$L_3 = a^2\,b^2\,a\,b^2 + a\,b\,a\,b^2 + a^2\,b^3 + a\,b^2 + b, \quad \text{etc.}$$

The series is clearly characteristic.

Conclusion. CF-grammars lead to systems whose right sides are polynomials with coefficients equal to 1. CF-languages are the supports of positive series which are obtained by the solution of the system; the coefficients give the degree of ambiguity.

It remains to be seen whether we can give linguistic interpretation to series with terms of arbitrary sign and to systems with coefficients which are not necessarily positive. We shall return to this question in a later chapter devoted to algebraic languages.

11.2.6. Exercises

1. Consider the language defined by the normal grammar:

$$V_A = \{S, A, B\}; \quad V_T = \{a, b, c\}$$

$$\left| \begin{array}{c} S \to a\, A, \ S \to b\, B, \ S \to c \\ A \to S\, a, \ B \to S\, b \end{array} \right|.$$

Form the associated system: solve it by power series. Study the structure obtained, and compare it with the one given.

2. Consider the grammar $S \rightarrow SS$, $S \rightarrow a$, $S \rightarrow b$, where the axiom is S and the terminal symbols a and b.

Solve the equation obtained. Take into consideration its structural history and ambiguities. Give the rule for describing its degrees of ambiguity.

3. Consider the grammar: $S \rightarrow S a S$, $S \rightarrow b$. Show that the general term of the power series which is the solution is

$$\frac{1}{n+1} C_{2n}^{n} (a\, b)^n a.$$

Chapter XII

Context-Sensitive Grammars.
Linear Bounded Automata

12.1. Context-Sensitive Grammars

12.1.1. Linguistic Motivation

Consider a simple sentence having the structure: $NP_1 \, V \, NP_2$ (noun phrase subject, verb, noun phrase object). If NP_1 and NP_2 belong to special classes, such as animate nouns, abstract nouns, etc., the class of verbs V which may appear between NP_1 and NP_2 is *restricted* by these contexts.

This type of situation is frequent in both natural and artificial languages, and this explains the interest of the formalization which follows.

12.1.2. Context-Sensitive Grammars

A context-sensitive grammar is defined by:

1. a finite alphabet V which is the union of two disjunct alphabets V_A (auxiliary) and V_T (terminal);

2. an axiom $S \in V_A$;

3. productions of the form:

$$\varphi_1 A \varphi_2 \rightarrow \varphi_1 \omega \varphi_2, \qquad A \in V_A; \quad \varphi_1, \varphi_2, \omega \in V^*; \quad \omega \text{ non-empty.}$$

A rule is interpreted as follows: in the context which consists of φ_1 on the left and φ_2 on the right, the non-terminal symbol A is rewritten as ω. Note that the CF-grammars belong to this class of grammars if

φ_1 and φ_2 are empty, whence their name "context-free". Just as we abbreviated "context-free" to CF, so we shall abbreviate context-sensitive grammars as *CS-grammars*.

12.1.3. An Immediate Property

The hypothesis that ω is never empty means that every CS-grammar is a special semi-Thue system in which the productions:

$$P \varphi_1 A \varphi_2 Q \to P \varphi_1 \omega \varphi_2 Q,$$

satisfy the additional condition of *non-decreasing degree*. We shall study the reciprocal condition.

12.1.4. Condition of Non-Decreasing Degree

Consider a semi-Thue system on the alphabet $V = V_A \cup V_1$, whose productions $P g_i Q \to P \bar{g}_i Q$ satisfy the condition of non-decreasing degree: $|\bar{g}_i| \geq |g_i|$. Each rule can be replaced by a sequence of context-sensitive rules: $\varphi_1 A \varphi_2 \to \varphi_1 \omega \varphi_2$, which yields

$$g_i = \alpha_1 \ldots \alpha_k$$
$$\bar{g}_i = \beta_1 \ldots \beta_k \ldots \beta_{k+q}$$
$$q \geq 0; \quad \alpha_i, \beta_i \in V.$$

Let us take k new auxiliary symbols

$$\gamma_1, \gamma_2, \ldots, \gamma_{k-1}, \gamma_k$$

and consider the rules:

$$\alpha_1 \alpha_2 \alpha_3 \ldots \alpha_{k-1} \alpha_k \to \gamma_1 \alpha_2 \alpha_3 \ldots \alpha_{k-1} \alpha_k$$
$$\gamma_1 \alpha_2 \alpha_3 \ldots \alpha_{k-1} \alpha_k \to \gamma_1 \gamma_2 \alpha_3 \ldots \alpha_{k-1} \alpha_k$$
$$\cdots \cdots \cdots \cdots \cdots \cdots \cdots \cdots$$
$$\gamma_1 \gamma_2 \gamma_3 \ldots \gamma_{k-1} \alpha_k \to \gamma_1 \gamma_2 \gamma_3 \ldots \gamma_{k-1} \gamma_k$$
$$\gamma_1 \gamma_2 \gamma_3 \ldots \gamma_{k-1} \gamma_k \to \beta_1 \gamma_2 \gamma_3 \ldots \gamma_{k-1} \gamma_k \cdot$$
$$\beta_1 \gamma_2 \gamma_3 \ldots \gamma_{k-1} \gamma_k \to \beta_1 \beta_2 \gamma_3 \ldots \gamma_{k-1} \gamma_k$$
$$\cdots \cdots \cdots \cdots \cdots \cdots \cdots \cdots$$
$$\beta_1 \beta_2 \beta_3 \ldots \beta_{k-1} \gamma_k \to \beta_1 \beta_2 \beta_3 \ldots \beta_{k-1} \beta_k \ldots \beta_{k+q} \cdot$$

If g_i contains any $\alpha_i \in V_T$, we can introduce new auxiliary symbols A_i, where $A_i \to \alpha_i$. With this modification, all the rules are of the type: $\varphi_1 A \varphi_2 \to \varphi_1 \omega \varphi_2$. Further, it is clear that this set of rules implies the rule $g_i \to \bar{g}_i$ and does not increase the generative capacity. Consequently, a semi-Thue grammar satisfying the condition of non-decreasing degree is equivalent to a CS-grammar. To summarize, we have:

Theorem. *The class of CS-grammars is the same as the class of semi-Thue grammars satisfying the condition of non-decreasing degree.*

12.1.5. Recursiveness of the Generated Languages

Proposition. Every grammar G satisfying the condition of non-decreasing degree generates a recursive language.

Proof. With the alphabet X defined, the proposition is evident if all the inequalities in the productions are never equalities. Suppose there are some productions which conserve the degree. The set of words of n letters generated by G has the finite cardinality $N(n)$, where $N(n) \leqq [\text{card}(X)]^n$.

Starting with a word of n letters, let us write all the derivations which do not increase the degree. In each of these derivations, after $N+1$ steps, or even sooner, we shall come upon a word of n letters which has already been derived: there is a *loop*. By excluding such cycling in loops, we shall keep only the "useful" derivations.

For a given integer m, it is clear that the set of useful derivations which, in the grammar G, yield words f such that $|f| \leq m$ is of finite cardinality. The proposition then follows.

12.1.6. Example

$$V_A = \{S, B\} \qquad V_T = \{a, b, c\}$$

$$S \rightarrow a S B c \tag{1}$$

$$S \rightarrow a b c \tag{2}$$

$$c B \rightarrow B c \tag{3}$$

$$b B \rightarrow b b \tag{4}$$

Rules (1) and (2) generate the strings

$$a^n b c (B c)^{n-1}, \qquad n > 0.$$

Rule (3) now applies to these strings and shifts all the c to the right, and all the B to the right of b. Rule (4) then yields a terminal string.

The language generated is $L = \{a^n b^n c^n; n > 0\}$, which has already been shown not to be context-free (§7.2.5).

12.2. Linear Bounded Automata

12.2.1. Definition

A *linear bounded automaton* (abbreviated as l.b. automaton) consists of a computing unit, a read-write head and a tape. It uses an alphabet V to which a special marker is added which serves only to set off the word being examined.

The computing unit has a finite set of states S_j; among them, we distinguish an initial state S_0 and a subset Φ of final states. The read-write head carries out its operations under the control of a finite set of instructions of the type: $(a_i, S_j) \rightarrow (S_k, a_l, M)$. An instruction is interpreted as follows. If the symbol read from tape is a_i, while the computing unit is in the state S_j, then the computing unit switches to the state S_k and the read-write head replaces a_i by a_l and moves one square right if $M = +1$, one square left if $M = -1$, and remains stationary if $M = 0$.

If a_i is the special marker $\#$, then a_l is also this marker.

12.2.2. The Computation

Given a word enclosed between $\#$, the automaton computes as follows:

1. at the start, the computing unit is in the initial state S_0 and the read-write head is scanning the left marker;

2. the automaton applies the instructions;

3. if the read-write head reaches the right marker and the computing unit is in a final state, the word is accepted; otherwise it is rejected.

There are deterministic automata of this type, as well as non-deterministic automata.

12.2.3. The Languages Accepted by l.b. Automata

The following proposition can be stated in connection with the languages accepted by l.b. automata.

Proposition. If $\mathfrak{A}$ is an l.b. automaton, a CS-grammar G can be constructed such that $L(G) = L(\mathfrak{A})$.

Proof. To construct G, we shall take the same terminal vocabulary as that of $\mathfrak{A}$, and for auxiliary vocabulary the set: $V_A^G = \{A_{ij}, S, T, \#\}$, where A_{ij} is associated with the situation (a_i, S_j); S is the axiom of G; T is a new auxiliary symbol; and $\#$ is the marker for enclosing the words.

The rules of G refer to the situations of $\mathfrak{A}$: they carry out the computation of $\mathfrak{A}$, but in reverse order, roughly from right to left. The rules can be divided into three groups.

I. G generates words of the type $\varphi_T A_{if}$ where $\varphi_T \in V_T^*$ and A_{if} corresponds to a terminal situation (a_i, S_f).

$$S \to A\, A_{if} \quad \text{for every terminal situation } (a_i, S_f);$$

$$\left.\begin{array}{l} A \to A\, a_i \\ A \to \quad a_i \end{array}\right\} \quad \text{for every } a_i.$$

II. The rules of this group act upon the strings produced by the rules of group I. They yield a terminal word if and only if there exists a computation of the automaton $\mathfrak{A}$ that accepts this word. The computation ends at the head of the word in the situation (a_i, S_0) or A_{i0}.

1. To the instruction $(a_i, S_j) \to (S_k, a_l, +1)$ there correspond the rules $a_l A_{rk} \to A_{ij} a_r$ for every $a_l \in V_T$.

2. To the instruction $(a_i, S_j) \to (S_k, a_l, -1)$ there correspond the rules $A_{rk} a_l \to a_r A_{ij}$ for every $a_l \in V_T$.

3. To the instruction $(a_i, S_j) \to (S_k, a_l, 0)$ there corresponds the rule $A_{lk} \to A_{ij}$.

III. The rules of this group allow the derivations to end. They are:

$$\# A_{i0} \to \# a_i.$$

It is clear that $L(G) = L(\mathfrak{A})$. The grammar G so constructed is a CS-grammar, but of a particular type: the words appearing in its rules have degree 2 or 1.

12.2.4. CS-Grammars and l.b. Automata

Conversely, it can be shown that with every CS-grammar we can associate an l.b. automaton which accepts this language. To show this, we begin by reducing the grammar to one having rules of only the following types:

$$AB \to CD, \quad A \to C, \quad S \to EF$$

with the additional constraint that if S is the axiom, then for $S \to EF$, $E = S$. In summary, we have the following theorem:

Theorem of Kuroda-Landweber. *The class of languages generated by CS-grammars is equivalent to the class of languages accepted by nondeterministic l.b. automata.*

12.2.5. Properties of Languages Generated by Context-Sensitive Grammars

The main property of the languages studied in this chapter is given by the following proposition:

Proposition. The class of languages accepted by *deterministic* linear bounded automata is a Boolean algebra.

G. H. Matthews has studied a certain number of special cases where all the auxiliary symbols form a single block inside the words (in the course of a derivation) and the beginning and the end of a word are terminal symbols. The languages generated by these grammars are found to be the CF-languages.

Decision Problems. Decision problems are for the most part recursively unsolvable for context-sensitive grammars; among others, the problem of deciding whether the language generated by a context-sensitive grammar is empty, finite, infinite, or context-free. These problems are nevertheless interesting in the case where the derivations can be shown graphically as trees which represent more complex restrictions than those which arise in the CF-languages.

12.3. Classification of the Automata

12.3.1. Linear Bounded Automata

The term linear bounded automaton is due to J. Myhill; its origin becomes evident upon studying the amount of memory such an automaton uses in the course of computation. In the preceding chapters we have studied three large classes of automata, namely: Turing machines, push-down automata, and finite automata. To compute the acceptability of a word, a Turing machine has at its disposal a tape having an unlimited number of squares which can store an unlimited number of symbols. On the other hand, a finite automaton uses only a finite and invariable amount of the memory of the central processing unit (tape is used only for reading). As for the push-down automaton, it uses intermediate results which have been stored on a scratch tape. The length of scratch tape which is necessary cannot be estimated once and for all, for it is a function of the input word f, but we can calculate an upper limit to this function.

Let $n = |f|$ and $k = |x|$, where x is the longest word that can be written with one instruction: it is clear that $k\,n$ is an upper limit for the number of squares which will be needed on the scratch tape. To this variable part a fixed number k' should be added which represents the possibility for the central processing unit to store the list of instructions and a certain number of states.

Since $k\,n + k'$ is a linear function, the push-down automaton belongs to the class of linear bounded automata, but it has special restrictions due to:

  1) the input tape moving in only one direction;

  2) the memory having a push-down structure (strong restriction).

According to the description which we have given of it, a linear bounded automaton can use an arbitrary number of squares in which to write the letters of the word proposed to it. This number is therefore at most equal to n. We also have a fixed number equal to the space used by the central processing unit for storing the program and the states. The upper limit is indeed linear.

It is possible to construct variants of this automaton having an upper limit of the general form $k\,n + k'$.

12.3.2. Hierarchy of Automata

The criterion of the amount of memory needed during computation provides us with an initial hierarchical classification of automata (Fig. 12-1).

To refine this first classification, and in particular, to introduce push-down automata in a natural way, the very concept of computation has to be refined by specifying not only the size but the *structure* of the memory used during the computation. By proceeding in this fashion, subclasses of automata can be defined.

Another direction in which the theory is developing is that of automata operating in real time. We have seen that the operation of a push-down automaton leads to the destruction of the information contained between the top of the stack and the information that is being looked for at any given point in the computation (erasure). Using instructions of the type (e, S_j, A_k), there is the possibility of making use of the memory independently of the input.

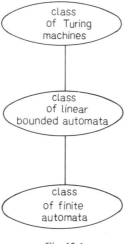

Fig. 12-1

If both the erasure condition and the possibility of disregarding the input are suppressed, then the real-time automaton of Yamada is obtained.

Another important criterion is the deterministic or non-deterministic nature of the automaton; this allows the subclasses to be defined. We recall in this connection that the standard CF-languages are accepted by deterministic automata whereas the most general CF-languages are not. The source for this is to be found in the homomorphism that maps the former into the latter.

12.4. Exercises

12.4.1.

Construct l. b. automata that accept the languages

$$\{a^n b^n a^n | n > 0\}, \quad \{x c x | x \in \{a, b\}^*\};$$

Are these automata deterministic?

12.4.2.

Show that permutations can be effected by means of context-sensitive rules. For example, if we have a language {x c y} given by a grammar G, then we can construct a grammar G' such that $L(G') = \{y\ c\ x\}$.

12.4.3.

Given two l.b. automata $\mathfrak{A}_1$ and $\mathfrak{A}_2$, construct an l.b. automaton which accepts the language $L(\mathfrak{A}_1) \cup L(\mathfrak{A}_2)$. Same question for the language $L(\mathfrak{A}_1) \cap L(\mathfrak{A}_2)$.

The required automaton $\mathfrak{A}$ can be constructed in the following way: begin by writing next to every word f that is proposed another word f' obtained from f by recopying and priming the letters of f. Then one part of $\mathfrak{A}$ (identical to $\mathfrak{A}_1$) will compute the acceptance of f by $\mathfrak{A}_1$, and another part of $\mathfrak{A}$ (identical to $\mathfrak{A}_2$ except for the primes) will compute the acceptance of f' by $\mathfrak{A}_2$.

PART III

The Algebraic Point of View

Chapter XIII

Homomorphisms of Monoids

13.0.

This chapter sets forth some concepts of algebra which will be used frequently in what follows.

13.1. Arbitrary Monoids

13.1.1. The Neutral Element

The concept of a monoid has been defined in §1.1.3, where the reader will notice that a monoid necessarily has a neutral element. More generally, from the technical point of view which interests us here, it is preferable to take every semigroup as having such an element. If a given semigroup **M** does not have a neutral element, it suffices to add a new element to it such that

$$(\forall X \in \mathbf{M})[EX = XE = X];$$

$$EE = E.$$

In this way we form a monoid — its associativity is easily verified — which has the neutral element E and clearly contains the semigroup.

13.1.2. Natural Homomorphism

Let $\mathbf{M} = \{A, B, C, \ldots\}$ be a monoid and $\Re$ an equivalence relation on **M** which is left and right compatible with the operation — in short, a congruence. We have mentioned in Chapter I that $\Re$ divides **M** into disjunct classes which make up the quotient set $\mathbf{M}/\Re$, and that the classes $\bar{A}, \bar{B}, \bar{C}, \ldots$ constitute a new monoid for the induced operation. We gave an example where $\Re$ is a Thue equivalence.

Consider the natural (or canonic) mapping ψ associated with $\Re$ which sets up a correspondence between every $A \in \mathbf{M}$ and its class $\bar{A}$ with respect to $\Re$. Since $\Re$ is a congruence, we have:

$$[A \xrightarrow{\psi} \bar{A} \ \& \ B \xrightarrow{\psi} \bar{B}] \ \Rightarrow \ [AB \xrightarrow{\psi} \bar{A}\bar{B} = \overline{AB}].$$

The image of a compound is given by the composition of the images of each element of the compound. ψ is said to be the *natural homomorphism* associated with $\Re$.

Example. $\mathbf{M}$ is the free monoid on the alphabet $\mathfrak{A} = \{a, b, c\}$, and $\Re$ is the relation which corresponds to equality of degree. The empty word belongs to the class 0, single-letter words to the class 1, etc. $\mathfrak{A}^*/\Re$ is isomorphic to the monoid formed by the set of positive integers, or zero, together with addition. This example now leads us to the following more general considerations.

13.1.3. General Definitions

Let $\mathbf{M}$ and $\mathbf{M}'$ be two monoids, and φ a mapping of the first into (possibly on) the second. φ is said to be a homomorphism of $\mathbf{M}$ into (possibly on) $\mathbf{M}'$ if this mapping is compatible with the operations in the two monoids:

$$[A \xrightarrow{\;\varphi\;} A' \;\&\; B \xrightarrow{\;\varphi\;} B'] \;\Rightarrow\; [AB \xrightarrow{\;\varphi\;} A'B'].$$

We write the set of images as $\mathbf{M}'_1$. Consider the relation $\Re$ on $\mathbf{M}$ defined by: $A_1 \,\Re\, A_2 \Rightarrow (A_1$ and A_2 have the same image under φ).

Clearly, this relation is an equivalence; it divides $\mathbf{M}$ into disjunct classes. Let us write the classes $A, B, C, \ldots$ as $\bar{A}, \bar{B}, \bar{C}, \ldots$ respectively. Firstly, there exists a natural mapping ψ of $\mathbf{M}$ onto $\mathbf{M}/\Re$ which sends every $A \in \mathbf{M}$ onto its class $\bar{A}$. Secondly, there exists a bijection θ of $\mathbf{M}/\Re$ to the set of images $\mathbf{M}'_1$. To the class $\bar{A}$ of all the elements having A' as image there corresponds A' itself — and conversely. What we have just said would still be valid if φ were only a simple mapping; let us now take into account the fact that it is a homomorphism.

Let A_1 and A_2 be two elements in the class of elements $\bar{A}$ which have the image A', and similarly B_1 and B_2 elements in the class $\bar{B}$ corresponding to B'. Since φ is a homomorphism, we have:

$$\varphi(A_1 B_1) = \varphi(A_1)\,\varphi(B_1) = A'B'$$
$$= \varphi(A_2)\,\varphi(B_2) = \varphi(A_2 B_2).$$

The compounds $A_1 B_1$ and $A_2 B_2$ have the same image and therefore, for $\Re$, belong to the same class. The class to which a two-element compound belongs depends only on the classes of each component:

Theorem. *With every homomorphism φ of a monoid $\mathbf{M}$ on or in another there can be associated a congruence $\Re$ defined by their common images.*

With the congruence $\Re$, we have the same situation described in § 13.1.2. There exists a natural homomorphism of $\mathbf{M}$ on $\mathbf{M}/\Re = \bar{\mathbf{M}}$, which is a monoid. The bijection θ of $\bar{\mathbf{M}}$ to $\mathbf{M}'_1$, the set of images, is compatible with the operations:

$$[A' \xleftrightarrow[\theta^{-1}]{\theta} \bar{A} \;\&\; B' \xleftrightarrow[\theta^{-1}]{\theta} \bar{B}] \;\Rightarrow\; [A'B' \xleftrightarrow[\theta^{-1}]{\theta} \bar{A}\bar{B}].$$

θ is an isomorphism.

Finally, we obtain the following diagram:

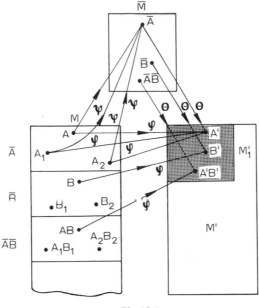

Fig. 13-1

13.1.4. Classification of Homomorphisms

We shall keep the notation of the preceding paragraph. The nature of φ, *qua* mapping, can be made more explicit with the help of an additional hypothesis. This leads us to the following definitions:

1. *φ is not surjective.* If there exist elements of $\mathbf{M}'$ which are not obtained as the image of some element of $\mathbf{M}$, we have the proper inclusion $\mathbf{M}_1' \subset \mathbf{M}'$. This can be specified by speaking of a homomorphism of $\mathbf{M}$ strictly in $\mathbf{M}'$:

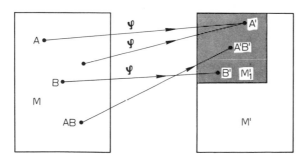

Fig. 13-2

2. *φ is surjective.* When each element of **M**′ is obtained at least once as the image of some element of **M**, we have the equality **M**′ = **M**′₁, and φ is said to be a *homomorphism of* **M** *on* **M**′ or, in brief, an *epimorphism:*

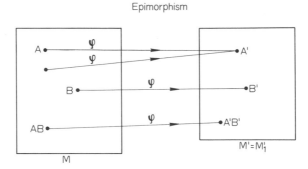

Fig. 13-3

3. *φ is injective.* When the image A′ of an element A is the image of this element only, φ is said to be a *monomorphism* of **M** in **M**′:

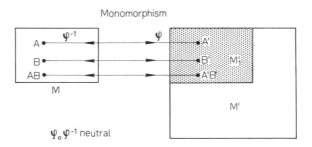

Fig. 13-4

4. *φ is bijective.* When every element of **M**′ is obtained as the image of one, and only one, element of **M**, φ is said to be an isomorphism of **M** on **M**′:

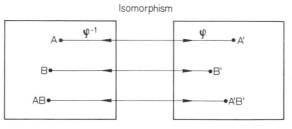

Fig. 13-5

Examples. 1. **M** is the free monoid on an alphabet $\mathfrak{A}$ and **M′** is the finite monoid (in this case, the group) {p, i} defined by the table:

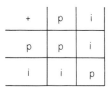

+	p	i
p	p	i
i	i	p

Fig. 13-6

We obtain an epimorphism by mapping the words of even degree onto p and those of odd degree onto i.

2. **M** is the monoid of positive integers or zero together with the rule of addition; **M′** is the free monoid on {a, b}. We obtain a monomorphism by mapping 0 onto the empty word, 1 onto a, 2 onto a a, ... n onto a^n.

*The case where **M** coincides with **M′**.*

When the homomorphism φ maps the monoid **M** in (possibly onto) itself, we say *endomorphism* instead of homomorphism and *automorphism* instead of isomorphism. However, we still use the word monomorphism for a bijection, compatible with the operation, of **M** onto one of its proper subsets.

We remark at once that this last concept is not empty.

Example. **M** is the free monoid on {a, b}. We set up a correspondence between each word and the word obtained by repeating each occurrence in the given word: a yields a a; a b b yields a a b b b b, etc. The correspondence is bijective and compatible with concatenation. This is just how one goes about spelling a word by repeating each letter.

13.1.5. Kernel of a Homomorphism

We suppose that the monoids **M** and **M′** each have a neutral element (if necessary, by adjunction), E and E′ respectively. Let φ be a homomorphism of **M** into (possibly onto) **M′**; set $\varphi(E) = E_1$.

Since φ is a homomorphism, we have:

$$\varphi(EA) = \varphi(E)\,\varphi(A) = E_1\,\varphi(A),$$

$$\varphi(AE) = \varphi(A)\,\varphi(E) = \varphi(A)\,E_1.$$

But $EA = AE = A$ since E is the neutral element; hence

$$E_1\,\varphi(A) = \varphi(A)\,E_1 = \varphi(A).$$

Consequently, E_1 is neutral for the monoid $\mathbf{M}_1$, the set of images, but we cannot conclude from this, without any additional hypothesis, that E_1 is identical to E (see exercise 1.4.4).

We can assert that $E_1 = E'$ when we know that $E' \in \mathbf{M}'_1$ (in particular, in the case where the homomorphism is an epimorphism). In effect, we have, in $\mathbf{M}'_1$:

$E'E_1 = E_1$ from the neutrality of E',

$E'E_1 = E'$ from the neutrality of E_1, whence $E_1 = E'$.

In what follows, we shall make the hypothesis that $E_1 = E'$ unless the contrary is explicitly stated.

In group theory, the kernel of a homomorphism φ which maps a group $\mathbf{G}$ into (possibly onto) a group $\mathbf{G}'$ is the set of elements $\mathbf{H}$ which have their image on the neutral element of $\mathbf{G}'$. A classic result of the theory is that the kernel is a distinguished subset and determines the homomorphism completely.

In the case of monoids, the situation is more complicated: it is (generally) impossible to reconstruct a homomorphism starting only from the class of the canonically associated congruence. There is no objection to calling the class to which the neutral element of the source monoid belongs the *kernel of a homomorphism*. Although less used than in group theory, the concept of a kernel is nonetheless important and we shall have more than one occasion to make use of it. The rôle which the kernel plays in a given case depends on the rôle of the neutral element in the image monoid, and, in the last analysis, it is the image which counts.

13.2. Congruence and Equivalences Associated with a Language

13.2.1. Congruence by Good Contexts

Let $\mathfrak{A}$ be an alphabet, $\mathfrak{A}^*$ the free monoid on $\mathfrak{A}$, $\Lambda \subset \mathfrak{A}^*$ a language, and lastly $M \in \mathfrak{A}^*$ an arbitrary word. It may happen that there exist two words $A \in \mathfrak{A}^*$ and $B \in \mathfrak{A}^*$ such that the word AMB belongs to Λ. In this case we shall say that the ordered couple (A, B) is a *good context for M with respect to Λ*.

Examples. Let $\mathfrak{A} = \{a, b, c\}$. The language Λ is the mirror language $\Lambda = \{X c \tilde{X} \mid X \in \{a, b\}^*\}$. For the word $a c$, $(b, a b)$ is a good context with respect to Λ. The set of good contexts comprises all the contexts of the form $(X, a \tilde{X})$ and only these.

For the word $a c a$, the good contexts form the set $(X, \tilde{X})$, which comprises in particular (E, E) where E is the empty word. For the word $a c c b$, no context is good with respect to Λ; we say that the set of good contexts is empty.

Notice that if a set of good contexts contains the empty context, it is not empty!

We shall define a relation $\equiv_\Lambda$ on the free monoid $\mathfrak{A}$. We set $M \equiv_\Lambda P$ to mean that the set of good contexts for M with respect to Λ is equal to the set of good contexts for P with respect to Λ. In other words, the relation $\equiv_\Lambda$ means

1. either there exists no good context for M or for P;

2. or that there exist good contexts for M and for P, and that every context that is good for the one is good for the other, and conversely.

This can be written in the more condensed form:

$$[M \equiv_\Lambda P] \Leftrightarrow (\forall X \in \mathfrak{A}^*), (\forall Y \in \mathfrak{A}^*)[XMY \in \Lambda \Leftrightarrow XPY \in \Lambda].$$

Example. $\mathfrak{A} = \{a, b\}$ and Λ is the finite language $\Lambda = \{a\,a\,a, a\,b\,a\}$. We have $a \equiv_\Lambda b$, the set of good contexts being $\{(a, a)\}$. Further, we have $a\,a\,a \equiv_\Lambda a\,b\,a$, the set of good contexts being $\{(E, E)\}$. Finally, we have $b\,a\,b \equiv_\Lambda b\,b\,b$, the set of good contexts being $\varnothing$.

It is clear that the relation $\equiv_\Lambda$ is an equivalence. Let us examine its behaviour with regard to concatenation. Suppose we have $P \equiv_\Lambda M$. If A and B are two arbitrary words, let us compare A M B and A P B. With every context (X, Y), whether it is good for A M B and A P B or not, we can associate the context $(X A, B Y)$ for M and P. We therefore have (the parentheses are used only to indicate groupings):

$$X(A\,M\,B)\,Y \in \Lambda \Leftrightarrow (X\,A)\,M\,(B\,Y) \in \Lambda$$

$$\Leftrightarrow (X\,A)\,P\,(B\,Y) \in \Lambda$$

$$\Leftrightarrow X\,(A\,P\,B)\,Y \in \Lambda.$$

Every context that is good for A M B is also good for A P B and conversely. If there is no good context for the one, then there is none for the other. Hence:

$$P \equiv_\Lambda M \Rightarrow A\,P\,B \equiv_\Lambda A\,M\,B.$$

The relation $\equiv_\Lambda$ is therefore a congruence. We shall call it the congruence via good contexts with respect to Λ.

Example.
$$\mathfrak{A} = \{a, b\}; \quad \Lambda = \{a^m\,b^n\,a^p \mid 1 \leq m, 1 \leq n, 0 \leq p\}.$$

The words which do not belong to Λ have an initial segment either of the form b^r, $1 \leq r$, or of the form $a^m\,b^n\,a^p\,b^r$, $1 \leq m, 1 \leq n, 1 \leq p, 1 \leq r$. They belong to a single class corresponding to the empty set (of good contexts).

The words of Λ can be divided into two classes: the class of $a^m\,b^n$, with the contexts $(a^x, b^y\,a^z)$, and the class of $a^m\,b^n\,a^p$, $1 \leq p$, with the contexts (a^x, a^z). We see that Λ is the union of these classes.

The relation $\equiv_\Lambda$ divides $\mathfrak{A}^*$ into disjunct classes and defines a quotient set $\mathfrak{A}^*/\equiv_\Lambda$ which is a monoid for the operation induced by concatenation. If we have $M \in \Lambda$ and $M \equiv_\Lambda P$, we deduce from this that the

11*

context (E, E), which is good for M, is also good for P, whence $P \in \Lambda$. Together with the word M which it contains, Λ contains the whole class of M.

Theorem. *With respect to the congruence via good contexts that it defines, a language Λ is a union of classes.*

Example. Cf. the preceding example.

13.2.2. A Property of this Congruence

We shall prove the following theorem:

Theorem. *Every congruence defined on $\mathfrak{A}^*$ and such that Λ is a union of classes with respect to it is finer than $\equiv_\Lambda$ (or coincides with $\equiv_\Lambda$).*

Let $\mathfrak{R}$ be such a congruence; we shall prove that $A \mathfrak{R} B$ implies $A \equiv_\Lambda B$. We have, in effect:

$$[A \mathfrak{R} B \,\&\, XAY \in \Lambda] \;\Rightarrow\; [XAY \mathfrak{R} XBY \,\&\, XAY \in \Lambda]$$

because Λ, being a union of classes, contains XBY if it contains XAY.

If there exist any, every good context of A is a good context of B such that $A \mathfrak{R} B$. If there is no good context for the one, there cannot be a good context for the other: Q.E.D.

13.2.3. Equivalence via Good Finals

Starting with the congruence $\equiv_\Lambda$ and taking the empty word on the left (right) in the pair making up the context, we obtain an equivalence via good finals (initials). Since these concepts are important, we shall present them in detail without using the congruence $\equiv_\Lambda$.

Let Λ be a language, a subset of the free monoid $\mathfrak{A}^*$. Consider a word $M \in \mathfrak{A}^*$. It may happen that by concatenating some word $X \in \mathfrak{A}^*$ to the right of M we obtain a word $MX \in \Lambda$. In this case we shall say that X is *a good final for M with respect to Λ*.

Example. Let $\mathfrak{A} = \{a, b, c\}$ and Λ be the mirror language $Ac\tilde{A}$, where A stands for a word written in the alphabet $\{a, b\}$.

For the word a a b c, there exists one good final, and only one: b a a.

For the word a a b, every word of the form $Bc\tilde{B}$ b a a is a good final.

For the word a a b c b a a, only the empty word is a good final.

For the word a a b c b b, no word is a good final: the set of good finals for this word is empty

The reader will observe that if the empty word E is a good final for A, the set of good finals of A is not empty.

Let us now define the following relation between the words of $\mathfrak{A}^*$:

$A \mathfrak{J}_\Lambda B \Rightarrow$ A and B have the same set of good finals with respect to Λ.

This relation, which is obviously an equivalence, is true in just two cases, and only these two:

1. neither A nor B have good finals;

2. every good final of A is a good final of B, and conversely.

Suppose A and B satisfy $A \mathfrak{J}_A B$; let $C \in \mathfrak{A}^*$ be an arbitrary word. Consider the words AC and BC. If the set of good finals of A and that of B are empty, then those of AC and BC are necessarily empty. If X is a good final for AC, we have $ACX \in \Lambda$, hence CX is a good final for A. Since it is a good final for A, it is also a good final for B and we have $BCX \in \Lambda$, hence X is a good final for BC.

This case-by-case test establishes that the relation $\mathfrak{J}_A$ is compatible on the right with concatenation. By considering the initials of words we would obtain an analogous relation $\mathfrak{T}_A$ which is compatible on the left with concatenation.

It is easy to see that Λ is a union of classes with respect to $\mathfrak{J}_A$. In effect, $M \in \Lambda$ implies that the set of good finals of M contains the empty word E. Every word equivalent to M for $\mathfrak{J}_A$ contains the empty word E. Every word equivalent to M for $\mathfrak{J}_A$ has E as a good final, hence belongs to Λ. If Λ contains a word, it contains the entire class of this word. To summarize, we have obtained the following proposition.

Proposition. Giving a language $\Lambda \subset \mathfrak{A}^*$ defines in $\mathfrak{A}^*$ an equivalence relation $\mathfrak{J}_A$ via good finals ($\mathfrak{T}_A$ via good initials) which is compatible on the right (left) with concatenation. The language Λ itself is a union of classes for $\mathfrak{J}_A$ ($\mathfrak{T}_A$).

13.2.4. A Property of the Relation $\mathfrak{J}_A$

The relation $\mathfrak{J}_A$ has then the following two properties:

1. It is compatible on the right with concatenation.

2. Λ is a union of classes for this relation.

It is easily seen that every relation $\mathfrak{R}$ having these two properties is finer than $\mathfrak{J}_A$ (or coincides with it).

Let $\mathfrak{R}$ be such a relation; we shall prove that $A \mathfrak{R} B$ implies $A \mathfrak{J}_A B$. In effect, we have:

$$[A \mathfrak{R} B \,\&\, AC \in \Lambda] \Rightarrow [AC \mathfrak{R} BC \,\&\, AC \in \Lambda]$$

by the compatibility on the right of $\mathfrak{R}$; then,

$$[AC \mathfrak{R} BC \,\&\, AC \in \Lambda] \Rightarrow [AC \in \Lambda \,\&\, BC \in \Lambda].$$

For, Λ being a union of classes, if Λ contains AC it also contains BC.

If there exist any, every good final of A is a good final for every B such that $A \mathfrak{R} B$, and conversely. And finally, if there is no good final for the one, there cannot be any for the other. Q.E.D.

Theorem. *The equivalence relation via good finals with respect to a language Λ is the least fine of the equivalence relations which are compatible on the right with concatenation and such that Λ is a union of classes.*

13.3. Introduction to Codes

13.3.1. Definition

Let X and Y be two finite alphabets containing at least two letters each. Every monomorphism of Y* into X* is called a *coding*. Like every homomorphism, a monomorphism is given by the images of the generators of Y*, i.e., the letters of Y. The set of images of the letters of Y is the *code* used for the coding.

Example. Let $Y = \{x, y, z, t\}$ and $X = \{0, 1\}$. For the images of x, y, z and t we shall take 00, 01, 10, 11, respectively (i.e., the first four binary numbers). Clearly, we are defining a monomorphism of Y* into X*. If a word of X* is the image of a word of Y*, then it is the image of only that word. For example, 11 01 01 01 00 can be *decoded* as t y y y x.

If the images of the letters of Y are taken at random, we obtain a homomorphism which is not necessarily a monomorphism.

Example. With the same alphabets as in the preceding example, let us take 0, 1, 10, 11 (i.e., the first four integers in binary notation) as the images of x, y, z, and t, respectively. Then 10 is the image of z and also of y x: there is no longer a *unique decoding*.

Hence $\{00, 01, 10, 11\}$ is a code, but $\{0, 1, 10, 11\}$ is not.

13.3.2. A Necessary and Sufficient Condition for Coding

A necessary and sufficient condition for $A \subset X^*$ to be a code is the condition:

$$(L)(\forall f \in X^*)[(A^* f \cap A^* \neq \varnothing \ \& \ f A^* \cap A^* \neq \varnothing) \Rightarrow (f \in A^*)].$$

Proof. In order to establish the proposition (L) $\Leftrightarrow$ (A is a code), we shall prove the equivalent proposition: (A is not a code) $\Leftrightarrow \neg$(L).

1. (A is not a code) $\Rightarrow \neg$(L).

If A is not a code, then there exists a set of words in A* having at least two readings, and in this set, a subset of words of minimum degree. Let

$$m = a_{i_1} \ldots a_{i_n} = a_{j_1} \ldots a_{j_p} \tag{1}$$

be such a word. The minimality of m implies that $a_{i_1} \neq a_{j_1}$. Then, with no loss of generality, we can suppose that $|a_{i_1}| < |a_{j_1}|$, whence:

$$a_{j_1} = a_{i_1} h, \quad h \in X^*, \quad |h| \neq 0. \tag{2}$$

From (1) and (2) we conclude:

$$a_{i_2} \ldots a_{i_n} = h \, a_{j_2} \ldots a_{j_p}. \tag{3}$$

However, (2) implies $A^* h \cap A^* \neq \varnothing$, (3) implies $h A^* \cap A^* \neq \varnothing$, whereas (3) together with the minimality of m implies that $h \notin A^*$. This means that (L) cannot be satisfied.

2. $\neg(L) \Rightarrow$ (A is not a code).

By hypothesis, there exist: $f \in X^*$, $g \in A^*$, $h \in A^*$, $g' \in A^*$, $h' \notin A^*$ with $g f = h$, $f g' = h'$, $f \notin A^*$. $f \notin A^*$ implies that f is not empty, hence h is also not empty. By simplifying on the left if necessary we can arrange for g and h not to have the same initial in A^*. Then the relations $g f g' = h g' = g h'$, $g \neq h$ imply that A is not a code.

13.3.3. Exercises on Codes

1. Show that condition (L) can be written in the form:

$$(\forall f \in X^*) [A^* f \cap f A^* \cap A^* \neq \varnothing \Rightarrow f \in A^*].$$

2. The algorithm of Sardinas and Patterson.

If A is a subset of X^*, construct the sequence of sets $A_0, A_1, ..., A_n, ...$ defined in the following way:

(a) $A_0 = A$;

(b) $f \in A_{i+1}$, if and only if there exists some $f \in X^*$, some $g \in A_i$ and some $a \in A$ with $g f = a$ or $a f = g$.

Show that a necessary and sufficient condition for A to be a code is $(\forall i \geq 1) [A_i \cap A = \varnothing]$. From this, derive an automatic procedure for deciding whether a set A is a code. Show that there is only a finite number of different A_i.

Chapter XIV

More about Kleene Languages

14.1. The Standard K-Languages

14.1.1. Definition

Let V_T be a terminal alphabet. We define a language K_S by the following conditions:

1. the words of K_S begin with a letter chosen from a fixed set I (the set of initials);

2. the words of K_S end with a letter chosen from another fixed set J (the set of finals);

3. the words of K_S contain none of the two-letter words which appear in a given set $\Delta \subset V_T \times V_T$.

Example. The alphabet is $V_T = \{a, b, c, d, f\}$; the initials are to be chosen from the letters of $I = \{a, b, c\}$ and the finals from $J = \{c, f\}$. In order to represent the set of excluded two-letter words conveniently, we shall draw up a table of the cartesian product $V_T \times V_T$. We write 0 for the entries corresponding to the forbidden transitions, and 1 for those corresponding to the permitted transitions. We shall also write V_T in the order: $\{a, b, c, f, d\}$ so as to group together the elements of I on the one hand, and J on the other. Under these conditions, we can represent Δ and its complement by a table such as the following:

1st letter \ 2nd letter	a	b	c	f	d
a	0	0	1	0	1
b	0	1	1	1	0
c	0	0	0	0	1
f	0	0	1	1	1
d	1	1	1	1	0

Initials: a, b, c. Finals: c, f.

Fig. 14-1

We shall prove that the languages obtained under these conditions are special K-languages which are called *standard* K-languages.

More technically, the set of words of V_T which begin with a letter of I and end with a letter of J is a *quasi-ideal*; it is given by the formula: $I V_T^* \cap V_T^* J$.

The set of forbidden two-letter words is a *two-sided ideal* given by the formula: $V_T^* \Delta V_T^*$.

The language K_S is then identical to the intersection of the quasi-ideal with the complement of the two-sided ideal:

$$K_S = [I V_T^* \cap V_T^* J] \cap [V_T^* \setminus V_T^* \Delta V_T^*].$$

14.1.2. System of Equations Generating K_S

Given the language K_S defined by the quadruple: (V_T, I, J, Δ), with

$$V_T = \{a_\lambda \mid 1 \leq \lambda \leq n\};$$

$$I = \{a_{\alpha_1}, \ldots, a_{\alpha_i}\};$$

$$J = \{a_{\beta_1}, \ldots, a_{\beta_j}\}.$$

For the case where some letters appear as both initials and finals, we set

$$I \cap J = \{a_{\gamma_1}, \ldots, a_{\gamma_K}\}.$$

In order to characterize Δ, the set of forbidden transitions, we make use of the delta function $\delta(\lambda, \mu)$ such that:

$$\delta_{(\lambda, \mu)} = 0 \qquad \text{if } a_\lambda\, a_\mu \text{ is forbidden},$$

$$\delta_{(\lambda, \mu)} = 1 \qquad \text{if } a_\lambda\, a_\mu \text{ is allowed}.$$

This function was used in the example of the preceding paragraph; it gives the elements of the transition matrix.

We now propose to construct a power series S having K_S as support. It will be useful to introduce the power series $A_1, \ldots, A_n$, as many series as there are terminal letters $a_1, \ldots, a_n$. To be precise, we associate with the letter $a_\lambda \in V_T$ the non-commutative power series A_λ such that:

1. all the words of the support of A_λ can be concatenated to the right of a_λ: if a word of A_λ begins with a_μ, the the transition $a_\lambda\, a_\mu$ is allowed and we have $\delta_{(\lambda, \mu)} = 1$.

2. the words of the support of A_λ contain only the allowed two-letter words.

3. the words of the support of A_λ end with a letter of J.

We now set up a system of $n+1$ equations whose left-hand sides are $S, A_1, \ldots, A_n$. The first of these equations is:

$$S = a_{\alpha_1} A_{\alpha_1} + \cdots + a_{\alpha_i} A_{\alpha_i} + a_{\gamma_1} + \cdots + a_{\gamma_\kappa}.$$

It guarantees that the words of K_S do indeed begin with the fixed initials and that K_S contains (possibly) the single-letter words of $I \cap J$.

The n other equations are built on the same model:

$$(\forall \lambda)\, 1 \leq \lambda \leq n,$$

$$A_\lambda = \sum_\mu \delta_{(\lambda, \beta_\mu)}\, a_{\beta_\mu} + \sum_\mu \delta_{(\lambda, \mu)}\, a_\mu A_\mu.$$

We see that:

1. the first sum contains those of the finals which can be concatenated with a_λ.

2. the second sum contains all the pairs such that a_μ can be concatenated on the right of $a_\lambda (a_\lambda\, a_\mu\, \Delta)$, which corresponds with what we expect of A_λ.

The reader can verify that the system of equations formulated in this way generates K_S (and the auxiliary languages) unambiguously. It is immediately clear that this system corresponds to a K-grammar (right-linear), which justifies the assertion that K_S is a K-language.

Example. Consider again the language K_S given as an example in the first paragraph. The alphabet contained five letters a, b, c, d, f, so that there are six non-terminal letters, namely, the axiom S and the five auxiliaries A, B, C, D, F.

Then the system contains six equations which we will write on six lines. Five columns are allowed for the monomials of the type a A, b B, etc., and two columns for the terminal letters c and f. We then obtain the system:

		Initials		Finals
	S=	aA+bB+cC		+c
The double-barred portion	A=	cC	+dD	+c
	B=	bB+cC+fF		+c+f
corresponds to the	C=		dD	
	F=	cC+fF	+dD	+c+f
transition matrix	D=	aA+bB +cC+fF		+c+f

Fig. 14-2

Upon inspection, the system is seen to contain the initials, the finals, and the transition matrix (the squares containing the monomials a A, etc.).

14.1.3. Exercises

1. Give a complete treatment of the standard K-language given by:

$$V_T = \{a, b, c\}; \quad I = \{a, b\}; \quad J = \{c\},$$

$$\Delta = \{b\,c, c\,a, c\,b, c\,c\}.$$

Write the system, solve it, and give a simple characterization of the language.

2. Give sufficient conditions for a quadruple $\{V_T, I, J, \Delta\}$ to yield an empty language, for example:

a) "poorly chosen" initials (give an example);

b) "poorly chosen" finals (give an example).

14.2. Characterization and Properties of Standard K-Languages

14.2.1.

The result obtained so far for the standard K-languages can be summarized as follows.

Every standard K-language is generated by a system of right-linear equations defined on a terminal alphabet $V_T = \{a_\mu | 1 \leq \mu \leq n\}$, and an auxiliary alphabet $V_A = \{A_\lambda | 0 \leq \lambda \leq n\}$, and satisfies the conditions (KS):

1. the non-terminal A_0, which is the axiom of the language, appears in just one equation, and only as the left-hand side;

2. all the monomials which appear on the right-hand sides are either of the form $a_\mu A_\mu$, or are single-letter words.

Consider now a system of this type. If we write it out methodically by rows and columns, as we did in the example of § 14.1.2, a set of initials, a set of finals and a transition matrix stand out clearly: the system thus defines a standard K-language.

Theorem. *A characteristic property of the standard K-languages is that they can be defined by a system having the particular type of structure specified by the conditions* (KS).

14.2.2. Associated Automaton

It can be easily shown (and the proof is left to the reader) that the finite automaton associated with a standard K-language via a system of the type (KS) is a deterministic automaton.

Furthermore, since the forbidden transitions are provided by a list of two-letter words, it suffices to store just *one* letter in the memory in order to test by iteration whether a word belongs to the language or not. It follows from this that the automaton is 1-definite (cf. § 10.3.3); we can also say that *a standard K-language is 1-definite.*

14.2.3. Applications to Arbitrary K-Languages

The interest of the standard K-languages derives not only from their own simplicity but more especially from the fact that they enable us to describe the structure of an arbitrary K-language simply. In effect, we have the following important proposition:

Theorem. *Given an arbitrary* K-*language* Λ, *we can always find a standard* K-*language* L *and a homomorphism* φ *such that* $\varphi(L) = \Lambda$.

We shall now prove this proposition.

First point. We know that every K-language corresponds to a finite automaton, possibly non-deterministic, and that with every finite non-deterministic automaton we can associate a finite deterministic reading automaton which accepts (generates) the same language (cf. § 10.3.1.). We can therefore suppose that Λ is generated (accepted) by such an automaton.

We can also arrange for this automaton to have no rule $(a_i, A_j) \rightarrow A_0$ for $i \neq 0$, or in other words, for the return to the initial state to be made on the necessary condition that a_0 be read.

Second point. The standard K-languages are 1-definite. We shall therefore construct a 1-definite automaton, starting from the automaton which generates Λ. To this end, we take as our new alphabet the couples (a_i, A_j) which appear in the rules (a_i, A_j, A_k) of the second automaton and for the internal states we take once more the couples $[a_i, A_j]$. Thus, to each letter there corresponds a "homonymous" state and vice-versa.

If the first automaton has the rule:

$$(a_i \quad , \quad A_j , \quad A_k)$$

then:

$$((a_i, A_k), [a_l, A_j], [a_i, A_k]),$$

is a rule of the second automaton, for every *l*.

This automaton is clearly 1-definite since it switches to the state which is homonymous with the letter just read. If we take $[a_0, A_0]$ as the initial state we obtain an automaton which generates a standard K-language L. The homomorphism φ which maps (a_i, A_j) onto a_i maps L onto Λ.

Remark. We have sketched a proof which uses automata as auxiliaries. This method seems more intuitive to us for a first presentation. In fact, we can proceed directly from the normalized system generating Λ to the system (KS) generating L by algebraic substitutions. We associate the monomial $(a_i, A_j) [a_i, A_j]$ with the monomial $a_i A_j$, the symbol $[A_0]$ with the symbol A_0, and the symbols (a_k, A_0) with the symbols a_k.

These operations transform the system of $n + 1$ equations and $n + 1$ unknowns into a system of $n + 1$ equations and $m\,n + 1$ unknowns. Then, with each equation having left-hand side A_p $(p \neq 0)$ we associate m equations having the same right-hand sides but with left-hand sides:

$$[a_1, A_p], \; [a_2, A_p], \ldots, [a_m, A_p].$$

Aside from some minor variations, we find substantially what has already been done above using automata.

14.3. Algebraic Characterization of the K-Languages

14.3.0.

Let us first recall some results concerning the K-languages which we established or mentioned in Chapter 9.

Giving a K-grammar defines a K-language; if this grammar generates the language recursively from left to right, then there exists another K-grammar, a dual of the first one, which generates the same language recursively from right to left — and vice-versa. With every K-grammar we can associate canonically a finite automaton which generates (accepts) the same language — and vice-versa. With every finite non-deterministic automaton we can associate a deterministic automaton which generates (accepts) the same language.

The same K-language can be generated by several different grammars or several different automata. The properties of a K-language which is determined by some grammar or automaton may therefore not be entirely specific to that language. To avoid this drawback, we shall seek a purely algebraic characterization of the K-languages considered as subsets of a free monoid.

To this end, we shall begin with a finite automaton which is introduced for heuristic reasons but which will disappear in the course of the argument.

14.3.1. Partitions Linked to a Finite Automaton

The Transition Function. Let us consider a finite automaton given by:

1. an alphabet $\mathfrak{A} = \{a_i \mid 1 \leq i \leq n\}$;
2. a set of states $\Sigma = \{S_j \mid 0 \leq j \leq p\}$;
3. a set of initial states $\Sigma_\alpha \subset \Sigma$ and a set of final states $\Sigma_\omega \subset \Sigma$;
4. a transition function f defined by a set of rules of the type $(a_i, S_j) \to S_k$.

The transition function is defined on a subset of $\mathfrak{A} \times \Sigma$; the situations relating to the complement subset do not appear in the rules and, insofar as reading is concerned, lead to a halt. By convention, we shall adjoin to the states of Σ the blocking state \$: the transition function then takes its arguments on $\mathfrak{A} \times \Sigma$ and its values in (possibly on) $\Sigma \cup \{\$\}$.

Let us now extend this transition function f onto the domain $\mathfrak{A}^* \times \Sigma$, where $\mathfrak{A}^*$ designates the free monoid on $\mathfrak{A}$. Let M be a word of $\mathfrak{A}^*$ and S_j a state; then the extended function f_g has the value $f_g(M, S_j)$, the state in which the automaton terminates when, having begun in the state S_j, it has read, or tried to read, the word M from left to right.

More precisely, let $M = b_1 \ldots b_q$, $b_i \in \mathfrak{A}$; we shall compute $u_1 = f(b_1, S_j)$. If $u_1 = \$$, we have $f_g(M, S_j) = \$$; if $u_1 = S_k$, then we set $f(b_2, S_k) = u_2$, and continue in this way until the automaton blocks or the last letter b_q is read.

A function f_d which corresponds to reading from right to left can be defined in an analogous way.

Example. Given the automaton defined by

$$\mathfrak{A} = \{a, b\}; \quad \Sigma = \{S_0, S_1, S_2, S_3\}; \quad \Sigma_\alpha = \{S_0\}; \quad \Sigma_\omega = \{S_2, S_3\}$$

and the function f given by the table of Fig. 14-3. This automaton can be represented by the graph Fig. 14-4; it corresponds to the language

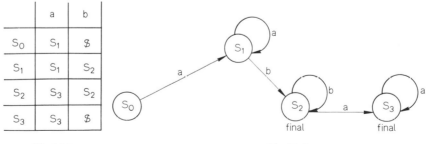

	a	b
S_0	S_1	\$
S_1	S_1	S_2
S_2	S_3	S_2
S_3	S_3	\$

Fig. 14-3   Fig. 14-4

$\{a^m b^n a^q \mid 1 \leq m, 1 \leq n, 0 \leq q\}$. We have:

$$f_g(a\,b\,b\,a, S_0) = S_3; \quad f_g(a\,b\,a\,b, S_0) = \$;$$
$$f_g(a\,b\,b\,a, S_1) = S_3; \quad f_g(a\,b\,b\,b, S_1) = S_2 \quad \text{etc.}$$

14.3.2. Partition Defined by a Finite Automaton

Let us take a finite automaton with an alphabet $\mathfrak{A}$ and the function f_g associated with the left-to-right reading of the words of $\mathfrak{A}^*$. With S_i standing for a state, let us consider the relation $\mathfrak{G}$ which is defined on $\mathfrak{A}^*$ by the condition:

$$(\forall S_i)\, A \,\mathfrak{G}\, B \;\Leftrightarrow\; f_g(A, S_i) = f_g(B, S_i).$$

Clearly, $\mathfrak{G}$ is an equivalence relation. Suppose the words A and B satisfy the relation $\mathfrak{G}$ and C is an arbitrary word. Then, if we have

$$f_g(A, S_i) = f_g(B, S_i) = S_k$$

we also have:

$$f_g(A\,C, S_i) = f_g(C, S_k) = f_g(B\,C, S_i).$$

The choice of the initial and final states specifies the automaton and associates a language with it by marking off distinguished classes. It follows from this that the relation $\mathfrak{G}$ is compatible with concatenation on the right.

The number of classes for $\mathfrak{G}$ in $\mathfrak{A}^*$ is equal to n^n at most (n is the number of states), hence the quotient set $\mathfrak{A}^*/\mathfrak{G}$ is finite. We also say that *the index of the relation $\mathfrak{G}$ is finite.*

By its very definition, the automaton specified accepts a word if it begins reading in one of the states of the set of initial states and finishes reading in one of the states of the set of final states. Consequently, the classes of $\mathfrak{G}$ which correspond to the states of Σ_ω belong to the language generated (accepted) by the automaton. Consider then — and it is possible to reduce to this case by a slight modification — the case where the set Σ_α comprises the single state S_0. Then the language generated (accepted) by the automaton is the union of the classes which correspond to the states of Σ_ω.

Starting with the function f_d, we would have an equivalence $\mathfrak{D}$, analogous to $\mathfrak{G}$, which is compatible with concatenation on the left. To summarize, we have the following proposition:

Proposition. Defining a finite automaton with alphabet $\mathfrak{A}$ canonically specifies, in the free monoid $\mathfrak{A}^*$, a relation $\mathfrak{G}$ ($\mathfrak{D}$) of finite index which is compatible on the right (left) with concatenation. The K-language generated (accepted) by the automaton is the union of a certain number of these classes.

Example. Consider the automaton defined in the preceding paragraph. The language which it generates (accepts) is the union of the language:

$$\{a^m \, b^n \, | \, m \geq 1, \, n \geq 1\} \quad \text{corresponding to the state } S_2,$$

and the language:

$$\{a^p \, b^q \, c^r \, | \, p \geq 1, \, q \geq 1, \, r \geq 1\} \quad \text{corresponding to } S_3.$$

We have just established that it is possible to find, in connection with a free monoid, a pair made up of a language Λ and an equivalence $\mathfrak{R}$ such that:

1. The relation $\mathfrak{R}$ is compatible on the right (left) with concatenation.
2. The language Λ is a union of classes for $\mathfrak{R}$.
3. The index of $\mathfrak{R}$ is finite.

Now we have already seen a very general relation having the properties 1. and 2., namely, the congruence via good contexts with respect to Λ. We have also seen that this congruence $\equiv_\Lambda$ is the least fine of all those having properties 1. and 2.

Suppose that Λ is a K-language; we define a relation $\mathfrak{G}$ as described above by means of a finite automaton which generates Λ. The result can itself be applied to $\mathfrak{G}$: it is finer than $\mathfrak{J}_\Lambda$. But then, since $\mathfrak{G}$ has a finite index, the index of $\mathfrak{J}_\Lambda$, which is less than that of $\mathfrak{G}$, is also finite.

Corollary. The equivalence relation via good finals with respect to a K-language Λ has a finite index. It is less fine than any equivalence relation $\mathfrak{G}$ which is associated with the left-to-right reading of an automaton accepting Λ.

14.3.3. Automaton with a Minimal Number of States

Reconsideration of the Hypothesis of Finiteness. Having characterized $\mathfrak{J}_\Lambda$ as the least fine of the relations which have properties 1. and 2. of § 14.3.2, we now re-introduce the hypothesis of finiteness:

3. The index of $\mathfrak{J}_\Lambda$ is finite.

We shall show that Λ is then necessarily a K-language. $\mathfrak{A}^*/\mathfrak{J}_\Lambda$ is finite; let us consider an automaton such that there is a bijection between the states of the automaton and the classes of $\mathfrak{A}^*/\mathfrak{J}_\Lambda$. If $A \in \mathfrak{A}^*$, we write the class of A as $\bar{A}$, and the state "homonymous" with $\bar{A}$ as $[A]$. To the empty word E there corresponds the class $\bar{E}$ and the initial state $[\bar{E}]$. The final states correspond to the words $M \in \Lambda$.

The transition function f is defined by the rule $f[a_i, [\overline{M}]] = [\overline{M \, a_i}]$. This rule is justified by the compatibility of $\mathfrak{J}_\Lambda$ with concatenation on the right. We can extend this transition function into a function f_g and we see that $f_g[M, [\bar{E}]] \in \Sigma_\omega$ if and only if $M \in \Lambda$.

The automaton so constructed accepts Λ which therefore is a K-language. Furthermore, since the number of states is equal to the index of $\mathfrak{J}_\Lambda$, this number is minimal.

Theorem. *If the index of the equivalence relation via good finals is finite, the language is a K-language. There exists a canonical procedure which enables us to construct an automaton having a minimal number of states which is capable of generating (accepting) this language.*

14.3.4. Use of a Congruence

We shall now make use of congruences instead of simple equivalence relations.

14.3.5. Congruence Defined by a Finite Automaton

Given a finite automaton with alphabet $\mathfrak{A}$ and a left-to-right transition function f_g. We define on $\mathfrak{A}^*$ the relation:

$$A \, \mathfrak{U} \, B \; \Leftrightarrow \; (\forall S \in \Sigma) \; [f_g(A, S) = f_g(B, S)].$$

Clearly, this relation is an equivalence that is compatible with concatenation on the right. It is also compatible with concatenation on the left, for, if the automaton reads C in CA and in CB, it ends in the same state either because C can be read or because it blocks the automaton.

A and B are said to be congruent for the automaton $(\mathfrak{U})$. If $(\mathfrak{U})$ generates (accepts) Λ, the relation $\mathfrak{U}$ is finer than $\equiv_\Lambda$.

The number of classes for $\mathfrak{U}$ is finite. In effect, when S runs through Σ, $f_g(A, S)$ takes its values in Σ. Therefore, a class is a word written in the alphabet Σ and containing card (Σ) occurrences. Hence the index of $\equiv_\Lambda$ is finite.

Theorem. *For a K-language, the congruence defined by good contexts has a finite index.*

14.3.6. The Converse Theorem

In order for the automaton $(\mathfrak{U})$ to accept a word A, it is necessary and sufficient that there exist $S \in \Sigma_\alpha$ and $S' \in \Sigma_\omega$ such that $f_g(A, S) = S'$. But then $(\mathfrak{U})$ accepts all the words which are congruent to A: hence Λ is a union of classes for $\mathfrak{U}$.

Then the following question arises: let Λ be a language such that the relation $\equiv_\Lambda$ has a finite index and Λ is the union of certain classes of $\equiv_\Lambda$. Is it possible to construct a finite automaton $\mathfrak{U}$ which accepts Λ? In other words, is Λ a K-language? This problem can be reduced to one that has already been solved, for the congruence via good contexts is finer than the equivalence via good finals.

Let us first justify this assertion. In effect, we have:

$$A \equiv_\Lambda B \Leftrightarrow (\forall X)(\forall Y)[X A Y \in \Lambda \Leftrightarrow X B Y \in \Lambda]$$

hence, by substituting the empty word for X:

$$A \equiv_\Lambda B \Rightarrow (\forall Y)[(A Y) \in \Lambda \Leftrightarrow B Y \in \Lambda],$$

and so finally $A \equiv_\Lambda B \Rightarrow A \mathfrak{J}_\Lambda B$.

Since the index of $\equiv_\Lambda$ is finite, the index of $\mathfrak{J}_\Lambda$ is necessarily finite and the theorem of §14.3.3 applies. We thus obtain the following theorem:

Theorem. *For the language Λ to be a K-language it is necessary and sufficient that the congruence via good contexts with respect to Λ have a finite index.*

Now we have already observed that $\equiv_\Lambda$ is the least fine of the congruences with respect to which Λ is a union of classes. For the index of $\equiv_\Lambda$ to be finite, it suffices that the index of such a congruence be finite. We then have the following corollary.

Corollary. For the language Λ to be a K-language, it is necessary and sufficient that there exist a congruence with respect to which Λ is a union of classes and which has a finite index.

14.3.7. Formulation by Homomorphism

The existence of a congruence $\mathfrak{R}$ on a monoid **M** specifies a quotient set **M/$\mathfrak{R}$** and a natural mapping of each $A \in \mathbf{M}$ onto its class $\bar{A} \in \mathbf{M}/\mathfrak{R}$. Let us suppose that A_1 and A_2, on the one hand, and B_1 and B_2 on the other, belong to the classes $\bar{A}$ and $\bar{B}$ respectively.

$$\bar{A}_1 = \bar{A}_2 \Rightarrow \overline{A_1 B_2} = \overline{A_2 B_2} \quad \text{(compatibility on the right)};$$

$$\bar{B}_1 = \bar{B}_2 \Rightarrow \overline{A_1 B_1} = \overline{A_1 B_2} \quad \text{(compatibility on the left)}.$$

Hence

$$[\bar{A}_1 = \bar{A}_2 \,\&\, \bar{B}_1 = \bar{B}_2] \Rightarrow \overline{A_1 B_1} = \overline{A_2 B_2}.$$

At the level of classes, it is possible to define an operation induced by the one which operates in **M**: $\overline{AB}$ is the class of the $A_i B_i$, $A_i \in \bar{A}$, $B_i \in \bar{B}$. The induced operation is associative and provides **M/$\mathfrak{R}$** with a monoid structure. The natural mapping of **M** onto **M/$\mathfrak{R}$**, say φ, is compatible with the two operations:

$$\varphi(A B) = \varphi(A) \, \varphi(B)$$

and so is a *homomorphism.*

More generally, let θ be a homomorphism that maps a monoid **M** onto a monoid **M'**. Then by definition:

$$[A \xrightarrow{\ \theta\ } A' \ \& \ B \xrightarrow{\ \theta\ } B'] \Rightarrow A\,B \xrightarrow{\ \theta\ } A'\,B'.$$

Let us set $A_1 \ \Re \ A_2$ if and only if A_1 and A_2 have the same image under θ. The relation $\Re$ is obviously an equivalence; furthermore, since θ is a homomorphism, $\Re$ is compatible on the left and on the right with the operation of **M**. Hence $\Re$ is a congruence.

We observe that we can go from **M**/$\Re$ to **M'** via an isomorphism: A' corresponds to the class of elements which have A' for image.

Inverse Image for a Homomorphism. If **P'** is a subset of **M'**, we shall write as $\theta^{-1}(\mathbf{P'})$ the set of elements of **M** whose image belongs to **P'**. In particular, $\theta^{-1}(A')$, for $A' \in \mathbf{M'}$, is the class of those elements which have their image on A'. If we denote this class by A we have $\theta^{-1}(\theta(A)) = A$.

If **P** is a subset of **M**, let us look for a necessary and sufficient condition that $\theta^{-1}(\theta(\mathbf{P})) = \mathbf{P}$. As before, let $\Re$ be the congruence naturally associated with the homomorphism θ. A sufficient condition is that **P** be a union of classes for $\Re$. This is also a necessary condition since the set $\theta^{-1}(\theta(\mathbf{P}))$ contains, together with each $A' \in \theta(\mathbf{P})$, the class whose image is A'.

Theorem. *If θ denotes a homomorphism of monoids, a necessary and sufficient condition for $\theta^{-1}(\theta(\mathbf{P})) = \mathbf{P}$ to obtain is that **P** be a union of classes with respect to the congruence $\Re$ associated with θ.*

Application to the K-Languages. In order for the language Λ to be a K-language, it is necessary and sufficient that the following proposition be true:

(1) There exists a congruence $\Re$ on the free monoid $\mathfrak{A}^*$ with respect to which Λ is a union of classes and which has a finite index.

If (1) is true, the monoid $\mathfrak{A}^*/\Re$, which is the homomorphic image of $\mathfrak{A}^*$ under the natural homomorphism associated with $\Re$, is finite and we have $\varphi^{-1}(\varphi(\Lambda)) = \Lambda$. More generally, let us suppose that there exists a homomorphism θ of the free monoid $\mathfrak{A}^*$ onto a finite monoid **M**. Then the congruence $\Re$ naturally associated with θ defines a quotient monoid $\mathfrak{A}^*/\Re$ which is isomorphic to **M** (cf. Fig. 14-5).

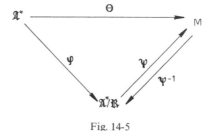

Fig. 14-5

If we have $\theta^{-1}(\theta(\Lambda))=\Lambda$ then we also have $\varphi^{-1}(\varphi(\Lambda))=\Lambda$, and vice-versa — since ψ is an isomorphism. Then the proposition (1) is equivalent to:

(2) There exists a finite monoid **M** and a homomorphic mapping θ of $\mathfrak{A}^*$ onto **M** such that $\theta^{-1}(\theta(\Lambda))=\Lambda$.

Finally, this whole section can be summarized in the following theorem.

Theorem. *In order for the language $\Lambda \subset \mathfrak{A}^*$ to be a K-language, it is necessary and sufficient that there exist a homomorphism θ of $\mathfrak{A}^*$ onto a finite monoid **M** with the condition: $\theta^{-1}(\theta(\Lambda))=\Lambda$.*

14.3.8. K-Languages and Graphs

Let X be an alphabet and A, B $\subset$ X, V $\subset$ X^2. The set: $AX^* \cap X^*B \setminus X^*VX^*$ is a standard K-language. Recall that it is made up of those words of X*

1. which contain just one letter and are in $A \cap B$;

2. or which begin in A and end in B, but contain no two-letter words which appear in V.

We call a *graph* a couple of the type $\langle G, R \rangle$ where

1. G is a set whose elements are called *vertices;*

2. R is a subset of $G \times G$ whose elements are called *edges.*

Given two subsets H and K of G, we use the term *path leading from H to K* for every sequence of vertices which either can be reduced to some unique element of $H \cap K$ or else contains several vertices $x_1, \ldots, x_i, \ldots, x_n$ with $x_1 \in H$, $x_n \in K$ and $(\forall i \in \{1, \ldots, n-1\})$ $[(x_i, x_{i+1}) \in R]$.

Identifying G with X, it is easily seen that the set of paths leading from H to K is nothing else than the standard K-language defined on X by specifying H, K $\subset$ X and $V = X^2 \setminus \{x\,y \,|\, (x, y) \in R\}$.

14.4. Transduction

14.4.1. One-Sided Transduction

We will now consider the concept of one-sided transduction, which we have already discussed, from another point of view for later generalizations.

Let $X = \{x_i \,|\, 1 \leq i \leq m\}$ be an input alphabet, $Y = \{y_j \,|\, 1 \leq j \leq n\}$ an output alphabet and $\Sigma = \{s_k \,|\, 1 \leq k \leq p\}$ a set of states. We are also given a transition mapping:

$$\text{(tr):} \quad \Sigma \times X \to \Sigma,$$

which associates a state, written s x, with the pair (s, x). Finally, we have a mapping:

$$\eta: \quad \Sigma \times X \to Y,$$

which associates $\eta(s, x) \in Y$ with the pair (s, x).

By a one-sided left transduction from the state s_{k_1} is meant a mapping of X* into Y* which is obtained in the following way. Given a word $f \in X^*$: $f = x_{i_1} \dots x_{i_\lambda}$. To the first letter x_{i_1} there corresponds the letter $\eta(s_{k_1}, x_{i_1})$, and a state: $s_{k_2} = s_{k_1} x_{i_1}$. To the second letter x_{i_2} there corresponds the letter: $\eta(s_{k_2}, x_{i_2})$, and a state: $s_{k_3} = s_{k_2} x_{i_2}$, and so on, by induction.

Clearly, to each $f \in X^*$ there corresponds a word of Y*. To simplify the notation, we write the initial state as s (without subscript). We shall use the notation $\eta(s, f)$ for the image of f: it is the *transduced image* of f by the transduction $[X, Y, \Sigma, (tr), \eta]$ starting from the state s.

Let $\Gamma \subset X^*$ be a formal language. We shall write $\eta(s, \Gamma)$ for the set: $\{\eta(s, f) | f \in \Gamma\}$ which we shall call the transduction of Γ. Finally, let $\Delta \subset Y^*$ be a language on the output alphabet; there *may* be words of X* whose image belongs to Δ. We shall set:

$$\eta^{-1}(s, \Delta) = \{f \in X^* | \eta(s, f) \in \Delta\}.$$

This notation should not lead the reader astray: in order for its use to be legitimate, it is not required that every word of Δ be obtained as an image.

14.4.2. Transduction of the Language X*

Let us start by studying the language $\eta(s, X^*)$ which is the transduction of X*. To each $f \in X^*$ there corresponds a transduction $\eta(s, f)$ and a state s_f in which the transduction of f ends.

Let $g \in Y^*$. If $g \in \eta(s, X^*)$, this word is the transduction of the words $f_1, \dots, f_i, \dots$. Let us adjoin to g the set σ_g which is the union of the states $s_{f_1}, \dots, s_{f_i}, \dots$ in which it is possible to terminate after writing the last letter of g. The set σ_g is an element of the set of subsets of Σ. If $g \notin \eta(s, X^*)$, we set $\sigma_g = \varnothing$.

We write $g \sim g'$ to mean that $\sigma_g = \sigma_{g'}$.

1. This relation is an equivalence relation.

2. $\eta(s, X^*)$ is the union of classes such that $\sigma_g \neq \varnothing$.

3. Since the index of this relation is less than or equal to the cardinality of $\mathfrak{P}(\Sigma)$, it is finite.

4. This relation is compatible with concatenation on the right.

In effect, let us suppose that $g \sim g'$, and then compare g h with g' h. If g can be obtained by starting from some f and ending in the state s_α and h can be obtained by starting from some u and beginning in the state s_α, then there exists an f' and we can obtain g' h by using f' u. The transductions end in the same state.

By virtue of these four conditions (cf. Chapter X) $\eta(s, X^*)$ is a K-language. Furthermore, the equivalence relation via good finals for $\eta(s, X^*)$ is less fine than (or at best coincides with) the relation $\sim$.

We see that $\eta(s, X^*)$ is already structured; hence, we understand that it is possible for a language not to be the exact transduction of some $\Gamma \subset X^*$, even if this language is a subset of $\eta(s, X^*)$, if it does not follow the natural structure.

14.4.3. Transduction of a K-Language

The language X^*, which is a K-language, has a K-language as its transduction. Let us now study the transduction of a K-language $\Gamma \subset X^*$.

We know that the equivalence relation via good finals with respect to Γ partitions X^* into a finite number of classes and that Γ itself is a union of classes. Let $f \in \Gamma$. The word f belongs to a certain class γ_f and causes the transduction to end in the state s_f. Let $g \in Y^*$. If $g \in \eta(s, X^*)$, this word comes from a set of f_i to which there corresponds a set of couples (γ_{f_i}, s_{f_i}). If $g \notin \eta(s, X^*)$, we adjoin the empty set to it.

Let us set $g \sim_\Gamma g'$ to mean that the set adjoined to g is identical with the set adjoined to g'.

1. This relation is an equivalence relation.

2. $\eta(s, \Gamma)$ is the union of classes for which the class of γ_f belongs to Γ.

3. The index is finite.

4. This relation is compatible with concatenation on the right.

It suffices to repeat what has been said in § 14.4.2 and to add that the class of f u is identical with that of f' u in the equivalence via good finals.

It follows from all this that $\eta(s, \Gamma)$ is a K-language. We see how the equivalence classes defined by this language are related to the natural classes of $\eta(s, X^*)$. Thus, if a K-language $\Delta \subset Y^*$ defines classes which 'cut across' the natural classes, it is not the transduction of any K-language $\Gamma \subset X^*$, for every Γ yields 'either too much or not enough'.

14.4.4. Study of $\eta^{-1}(s, \Delta)$, where Δ is a K-Language

When $\Delta \subset Y^*$ is a K-language, the set of words whose image is in Δ is also a K-language. This can be shown by examining the equivalence $f \sim_\Delta f'$ which is obtained by taking the class of $\eta(s, f)$ for good finals with respect to Δ to be identical with that of f'.

14.4.5. A Result for $\eta(s, X^*)$

We have seen that $\eta(s, X^*)$ is a K-language. One might ask the following question: given an alphabet Y and a K-language $\Delta \subset Y^*$, is it possible to construct a transduction such that $\eta(s, X^*)$ is this K-language Δ?

The answer is negative. For example, if $Y = \{a, b\}$, it is easily seen that no transduction maps X^* onto $a^* b$. In order to accomplish this, we would have to abandon the deterministic nature of the transducer.

14.4.6. Product of One-Sided Transductions

A one-sided right transduction can be defined in the same way as a one-sided left transduction: it suffices to read in the opposite direction. It is convenient to write the transition mapping as follows: $(tr'): X \times \Sigma' \to \Sigma'$ which maps (x, s') onto a state written as $x\,s'$. It is then possible to take the composition of left or right one-sided transductions: the first maps X^* into Y^*, the second Y^* into Z^*, etc.

The following is one result: If $\Lambda \subset Z^*$ is a K-language, a left transduction and a right transduction can be found whose product maps X^* onto Λ.

This can first be proven for a standard K-language $I\,Z^* \cap {}^*Z\,J \backslash Z^* V Z^*$ (recall that I is the set of initials, J the set of finals, and V the set of forbidden two-letter words). Then we treat the general case with the help of a homomorphism, and this is compatible with the transduction.

14.4.7. Two-Sided Transduction

A two-sided transduction of X^* into Y^* requires two transition mappings for two sets of states:

$$(tr): \quad \Sigma \times X \to \Sigma,$$
$$(s, x) \to s\,x;$$
$$(tr'): \quad X \times \Sigma' \to \Sigma',$$
$$(x, s') \to s'\,x;$$

and a rewriting mapping:

$$(\Sigma, X, \Sigma') \to Y,$$
$$(s, x, s') \to \eta(s, x, s').$$

Given a word $x_{i_1} \dots x_{i_{k-1}} x_{i_k} x_{i_{k+1}} \dots x_{i_r}$, in order to find the image of x_{i_k}, we must find the left state (in Σ) corresponding to the left-to-right reading of the initial segment and the right state (in Σ') corresponding to the right-to-left reading of the terminal segment. The left initial state and the right initial state should be specified.

14.4.8. Two-Sided Transduction and K-Languages

The results obtained for a one-sided transduction apply here: if Γ is a K-language, $\eta(s, \Gamma, s')$ is a K-language, and if $\Delta \subset Y^*$ is a K-language, $\eta^{-1}(s, \Delta, s')$ is also a K-language.

To prove these propositions, the representation of a transduction by a directed graph is useful. The vertices correspond to the triples (s, x, s'). Then there exists a directed edge going from (s_i, x_j, s'_k) to $(s_\alpha, x_\beta, s'_\gamma)$ if and only if $s_\alpha = s_i\,x_j$ and $s'_k = x_\beta\,s'_j$.

14.4.9. Exercises

1. *Transducer yielding a standard K-language for* X*. We let X and Y coincide, and begin by constructing a transducer which maps X* into $(X \cup \{\omega\})^*$, where ω is a special symbol.

There are two states s_1 and s_2, and as many states $[x_i]$ as there are letters x.

The rules are as follows. For the transitions:

$$s_1 x = [x] \quad \text{for} \quad x \in I$$
$$s_1 x = s_2 \quad \text{for} \quad x \notin I$$
$$[x_1] x_2 = x_2 \quad \text{for} \quad x_1 x_2 \notin V$$
$$[x_1] x_2 = s_2 \quad \text{for} \quad x_1 x_2 \in V$$

for writing:

$$\eta(s_1, x) = e \quad \text{for} \quad x \notin I$$
$$\eta(s_1, x) = x \quad \text{for} \quad x \in I$$
$$\eta(s_2, x) = e$$
$$\eta([x_i], x_j) = \omega \quad \text{for} \quad x_i x_j \in V$$
$$\eta([x_i], x_j) = x_j \quad \text{for} \quad x_i x_j \notin V.$$

Finish the transducer by testing it on ω and on J.

2. Let η be a one-sided left transduction of X* into Y* and μ a one-sided right transduction of Y* into Z*.

Does there exist a right μ' and a left η' such that $\eta \mu = \mu' \eta'$? (The authors do not know of any canonical construction of μ' and η').

3. A transduction $|X, Y, \Sigma, \Sigma', \text{tr}, \text{tr}', \eta|$ is faithful if and only if we have: $(\forall y \in Y^*)(\forall s)(\forall s') [\text{card } \eta^{-1}(s, y, s') < \infty]$.

Is it possible to associate a faithful transduction with every two-sided transduction?

Chapter XV

More about Context-Free Languages

15.1. Dyck Languages

15.1.1. The Free Group

Let $\mathfrak{A} = \{a, b, \ldots\}$ and $\mathfrak{A}' = \{a', b', \ldots\}$ be two finite, disjunct alphabets of the same cardinality whose letters are coupled two-by-two: a with a', etc. We set $\mathfrak{B} = \mathfrak{A} \cup \mathfrak{A}'$.

With E the empty word, we take the system $\mathfrak{R}$ of Thue relations:
$\mathfrak{R}$: $a\,a' \sim a'\,a \sim E$, $b\,b' \sim b'\,b \sim E, \ldots$ These relations allow classes to
be defined, and we know that $\mathfrak{B}*/\mathfrak{R}$ is a monoid.

Furthermore, this monoid is a group. In effect, given an arbitrary
word A it is always possible to find a word $\bar{A}$ such that $A\,\bar{A} \sim \bar{A}\,A \sim E$.
For this, it suffices to take the word $\tilde{A}$, the mirror image of A, and to
replace every primed letter by a letter without primes, and vice-versa.

Example. For $A = a\,b\,a'\,b'\,a\,b\,b$, $\tilde{A} = b\,b\,a\,b'\,a'\,b\,a$, and $\bar{A} =$
$b'\,b'\,a'\,b\,a\,b\,a'$.

Hence the class of A has the class of $\bar{A}$ as its inverse.

We shall now prove that this group $\mathfrak{B}*/\mathfrak{R}$ is isomorphic to the free
group generated by $\mathfrak{A}$ and specify the canonical homomorphism that
maps $\mathfrak{B}*$ onto the free group.

15.1.2. Representation of a Class of $\mathfrak{B}*/\mathfrak{R}$

A word is said to be *irreducible* if it contains no occurrence of a letter
which is contiguous to an occurrence of the coupled letter.

Example. $a\,b\,a'\,b'\,a\,b$ is irreducible, but $a\,b\,b'\,a\,b$ is not.

Then the empty word is irreducible. We shall now establish the
following result:

Proposition. *Every equivalence class contains one irreducible word and
only one.*

Only uniqueness has to be proven. We first establish a lemma.

Lemma 1. *The only irreducible word that is equivalent to the empty
word is the empty word itself.*

Two words will be called contiguous if we can obtain one from the
other by just one application of a rule. If we say that a word A is equivalent
to the empty word E, this is the same as saying that there exists a string
of contiguous words starting from A and ending on E. Reversing this
procedure, we are sure to obtain A by constructing this string in the
opposite direction, starting from E, and systematically forming the
words contiguous to E, then those contiguous to these, etc.

The words contiguous to E are $a\,a'$, $a'\,a$, etc. To obtain the words
contiguous to these, we can reduce them — but then we have E once more
— or insert, wherever possible, one of the words $a\,a'$, $a'\,a$, ... Generally
speaking, it suffices to proceed stepwise by *incrementation* and not by
simplification, since any simplification leads to a word obtained in the
preceding step.

Example. Starting with a a′ b b′, we can insert a a′ between a a′ and b b′ to obtain a a′ a a′ b b′. If we simplify this result, which we now write as a *a′ a* a′ b b′, by reducing the italicized elements, we have a a′ b b′ again.

It follows from this that we shall never find an irreducible word in the class of E.

We shall now establish a second lemma.

Lemma 2. *If there existed words which were at the same time irreducible, equivalent, and different, then there would exist words which are non-empty, irreducible and equivalent to the empty word.*

Let A and B be two words which are equivalent, irreducible and different. We may suppose that they do not begin with the same letter; if they did, we would simplify until the initial letters were different. Then we have: $A = x\,A_1$, $B = y\,B_1$, $x \neq y$.

Under these conditions, it is certain that the word $\bar{A}\,B$ is irreducible. Now the hypothesis $A \sim B$ implies $\bar{A} \sim \bar{B}$: it suffices to carry out the bar operation on the string of equivalences.

Hence $\bar{A}\,B \sim \bar{A}\,A \sim E$. Q.E.D. The proposition we wish to prove follows at once from Lemmas 1 and 2.

15.1.3. Canonical Homomorphism

We assume that it is known how to form a free group having $\mathfrak{A}$ as a system of generators (cf. exercise no. 3 in § 15.1.10 on this).

The canonical homomorphism γ which maps $\mathfrak{B}^*$ onto the free group is such that $E \to 1$, $a \to a$, $a′ \to a^{-1}$. $\gamma(f) = \gamma(f′) \Rightarrow f$ and f′ can be reduced to the same irreducible word.

Under these conditions, the set $\gamma^{-1}(1)$, the kernel of this homomorphism, is the set of words which reduce to E upon cancelling pairs of contiguous and coupled letters. It is called the *Dyck language* defined on $\mathfrak{B} = \mathfrak{A} \cup \mathfrak{A}′$, and we shall write it as D*.

15.1.4. Restricted Dyck Language

We obtain a *restricted* Dyck language by cancelling only the pairs a a′, b b′, etc., but not the pairs a′ a, b′ b, ... As we have already observed (cf. § 1.3.2), a restricted Dyck language is a familiar object in mathematical use. It suffices to take the unprimed letters as different types of left parentheses and the primed letters as the right parentheses associated with them.

15.1.5. Nature of the Dyck Languages

This interpretation by means of parentheses, and its 'generalization' for the unrestricted Dyck languages makes it clear that the Dyck languages are CF-languages. As an example of a restricted Dyck language, we have for instance the grammar:

$$S \rightarrow SS; \quad S \rightarrow a S a', b S b', \text{ etc.}; \quad S \rightarrow a a', b b', \text{ etc.}$$

For the word a b b a a' b' c c' b b' b' a' we have the tree in Fig. 15-1:

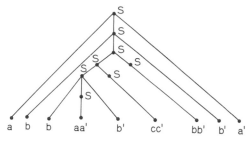

Fig. 15-1

but also the tree of Fig. 15-2:

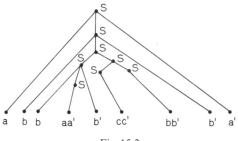

Fig. 15-2

Such a grammar is therefore ambiguous. This is why we shall under-take a more thorough study of the Dyck languages in order to provide them with an unambiguous and better structured grammar.

15.1.6. Factorization Into Dyck-Prime Words

A word $d \in D^*$ is said to be *Dyck-prime* if it has no proper left factor in D^*. We would obtain an equivalent definition if we replace left factor by right factor.

Example. a' b a a' b b' b' a is Dyck-prime, whereas a b b' a' b b' is not.

Theorem. *Every word of a Dyck language can be factorized uniquely into a product of Dyck-prime words.*

The theorem is evident for a Dyck-prime word. Suppose now that we are given a word d which is not Dyck-prime and has two distinct factorizations: $d = f_1 f_2 \ldots f_\lambda = g_1 g_2 \ldots g_\mu$.

If $|f_1|=|g_1|$, then $f_1 = g_1$ and we can simplify.

If $|f_1|<|g_1|$, then g_1 is not Dyck-prime.

15.1.7. Structure of Dyck-Prime Words

Let $g = x f y$ be a Dyck-prime word whose first and last letters are x and y, respectively. In the course of cancellation, x cancels with y and cannot cancel with any other letter — otherwise the word would have a proper left factor, contrary to the hypothesis. Hence y is coupled with x, which we indicate by writing $y = \bar{x}$.

Furthermore, f belongs to the Dyck language and so can be factorized into a product of Dyck-prime words: $f = f_1 f_2 \ldots f_m$. f_1 itself is of the form $x_1 f_1' \bar{x}_1$, with $x_1 \neq \bar{x}$, or else g would not be Dyck-prime. In the same way we have $f_2 = x_2 f_2' \bar{x}_2$, with $x_2 \neq \bar{x}$, etc.

We write D_y for the set of Dyck-prime words that begin with the letter y (and so end with y). Then every Dyck-prime word can be written uniquely in the form:

$$g = x f_1 \ldots f_m \bar{x},$$

$$f_i \in D_{x_i}; \quad x_i \neq \bar{x}; \quad i = 1, \ldots, m.$$

Example. $a\ b'c\,c'b\ a\,a'\ c'a'a\,c\ a'$

We shall call the set of all the Dyck-prime words D. The language D^*, by virtue of the theorem of unique factorization, is the free monoid on D. This fact justifies the notation we have adopted.

15.1.8. Unambiguous Grammar of a Dyck Language

We shall now give an unambiguous CF-grammar of a Dyck language, in the form of a system of equations. For simplicity of notation, we restrict ourselves to the alphabet $\{a, a', b, b'\}$; this will not affect the generality of the line of argument.

We introduce the non-terminal symbols $D_{a'}, D_a, D_b, D_{b'}$, which have the meaning defined in § 15.1.7.

D_a comprises, as well as the word $a\,a'$, all the words of the form: $a f_1 \ldots f_m a'$, with $f_i \in D_{x_i}$, $x_i \neq a'$. We take this into account by writing the equation:

$$D_a = a A a' + a a' \qquad (1\,a)$$

where A is another non-terminal symbol corresponding to a language. This last language comprises $D_{a'}, D_b, D_{b'}$ and, more generally, every product whose factors belong to $D_{a'}, D_b$, and $D_{b'}$. This yields the equation:

$$A = (D_a + D_b + D_{b'})(A + E) \qquad (2\,a)$$

where E stands for the empty word.

As for the Dyck language, D*, it corresponds to the equation:

$$D^* = (D_a + D_{a'} + D_b + D_{b'}) D^* + E. \tag{3}$$

The equations of type (1) and (2), and equation (3) provide the Dyck language with an unambiguous grammar, since this grammar generates words from left to right which are factorized into a product of Dyck-prime words.

Example. Let us consider once more the word a b b a a' b' c c' b b' b' a' which was treated in § 15.1.5. The derivation tree (Fig. 15-3) is unique.

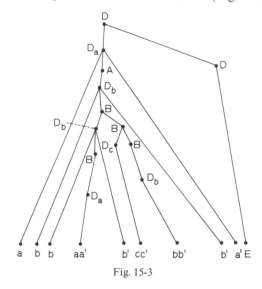

Fig. 15-3

15.1.9. Unambiguous Grammar for a Restricted Dyck Language

It suffices to consider the sets D_a, D_b, etc. (and to exclude $D_{a'}$ etc.). We no longer need to make a distinction between A, B, ... since in any case we no longer take into consideration any set beginning with a primed letter. We then obtain:

$$D_a = a \, U \, a' + a \, a'$$
$$D_b = b \, U \, b' + b \, b'$$
$$U \ = (D_a + D_b)(U + E)$$
$$D_r = (D_a + D_b) \, D_r + E,$$

with the axiom D_r (restricted Dyck).

Example. The example in § 15.1.8, in which we intentionally used only D_r, can serve once more. It suffices to replace A and B in this example by U.

15.1.10. Exercises

1. We write as $\bar{f}$ the word derived from f by taking its mirror image and then reversing the primes on the letters; the alphabet is X.

Let us set $U = \{f\bar{f}|f \neq E\}$ and $V = \{v \in U|v \notin UXX^*\}$. In other words, the words $v \in V$ are irreducible in U and have no proper left factor in U.

Prove that every $f\bar{f} \in U$ can be factorized uniquely into a product of irreducible elements.

2. A code A on X is said to be complete if and only if there exists no subset A', $A \subset A' \subset X^*$, which is itself a code.

Let Δ be the set of Dyck-prime words on an alphabet $X = \{\mathfrak{A} \cup \mathfrak{A}'\}$. Show that Δ, *qua* code, is complete.

3. *A definition of the free group.* Let $\mathfrak{A} = \{a, a', b, b' ...\}$ be an alphabet consisting of $2n$ letters coupled two by two, as we have already seen in connection with Dyck languages (cf. § 1.3.2.). We take the Thue relations $a\,a' = a'\,a = E$, etc.

For a word to be irreducible, it is necessary and sufficient that no occurrence of a letter be contiguous with an occurrence of the coupled letter. We consider the set of irreducible words, including the empty word E, and provide this set with an operation (which is written as a period).

Given the irreducible words X and Y, we define their product $X \cdot Y$ by means of the following algorithm:

a) Concatenate X and Y to form XY;

b) Examine the occurrences at their juncture:

If they involve non-coupled letters, write $X \cdot Y = XY$, exit; otherwise take the new X and the new Y obtained by cancelling the last and the first occurrences respectively, and return to b).

Examples.

$$X = a\ b\ a'\ c\ b,\ Y = c',\ X \cdot Y = a\ b\ a'\ c\ b'\ c'$$
$$X = a\ b\ a',\ Y = a\ b',\ X \cdot Y = a$$
$$X = b\ a\ c',\ Y = c\ a'\ b',\ X \cdot Y = E.$$

Prove that the set of irreducible words, together with this operation, has the structure of a group. Since only associativity is not immediately clear, one may proceed as follows:

Let X, Y, and Z be three irreducible words. The following equality must be proven: $(X \cdot Y) \cdot Z = X \cdot (Y \cdot Z)$. The result is trivially true if one of the words is empty. Now prove the equality if the middle word consists of just one letter. Then iterate on the degree of the middle word.

Take the theorem to be proven for $|Y| = m - 1$. Then set $Y = Y_1\,y$ with $|Y_1| = m - 1$ and $y \in \mathfrak{A}$. Then:

$$X \cdot (Y \cdot Z) = X \cdot [(Y_1 \cdot y) \cdot Z] = X \cdot [Y_1 \cdot (y \cdot Z)], \quad \text{etc.}$$

15.2. Standard CF-Languages

15.2.1. Definition

The language obtained by taking the intersection of a Dyck language and a standard K-language Q is called a *standard CF-language*. We shall write D* for the Dyck language and set: $C_S = D^* \cap Q$.

We have already proven in § 10.6.3. that the intersection of a CF-language with a K-language is indeed a CF-language; this justifies the definition above. We also gave a procedure there which allowed a CF-grammar to be constructed for this intersection. It will be noted that this grammar is unambiguous if the grammars of the K- and CF-languages in question are unambiguous.

Example. The alphabet is {a, b, a', b'}; Q is defined by the initials {a, b}; the forbidden transitions are those which make a shift from a primed to an unprimed letter. Then the intersection is given by:

$$C_S = \{f\bar{f} \mid f \in \{a, b\}^*\},$$

where f has the meaning specified in § 15.1.7.

15.2.2. Restrictions Imposed on the Standard CF-Languages

The restrictions to which C_S is subjected are of two quite different kinds. Those which come from Q are purely local; an automaton whose memory is limited to the last letter read is sufficient to check whether these restrictions are satisfied.

Those which come from D* can have arbitrarily far-reaching effects; to check them, an automaton is required whose memory is not strictly bounded. On the other hand, these are not restrictions between non-contiguous elements: they express the parenthetically intricate structure D*.

Consequently, we see that the standard CF-languages have a rather simple structure which can be grasped intuitively. Such simplicity makes them interesting, but their importance comes from the following theorem.

15.2.3. Fundamental Theorem for the CF-Languages

Theorem. *With every CF-language L we can associate a Dyck language D* (possibly a restricted Dyck language D_r), a standard K-language Q and a homomorphism φ such that: $L = \varphi(D^* \cap Q)$.*

In other words, every CF-language can be obtained by a homomorphism starting from a suitably chosen standard CF-language.

Example. The mirror language $f\tilde{f}$ on {a, b} can be obtained from the standard CF-language $f\bar{f}$ (cf. the example in § 15.2.1) by the homomorphism:

$$\varphi: \quad \begin{array}{l} a \to a; \ a' \to a, \\ b \to b; \ b' \to b. \end{array}$$

The proof of this theorem will require a prior definition and a proposition.

Definition. We shall call a grammar *simple* if all of its rules are of the form:

$$\xi_i = \sum_l d_{i,l} + \sum_{j,k} a_{i,j,k} \ b_{i,j,k} \ \xi_j \ \bar{b}_{i,j,k} \ c_{i,j,k} \ \xi_k \ \bar{c}_{i,j,k} \ \bar{a}_{i,j,k}$$

where the lower-case latin letters stand for terminal letters which are all different (N. B.) and the Greek letters for non-terminal symbols.

Proposition 1. Whatever the grammar G that generates a language L, there exists a simple grammar G′ generating a language L′, and a homomorphism φ such that $L = \varphi(L')$.

Sketch of the proof. If G contains a rule of the form: $\xi_i \to u \ \xi' \ v \ \xi'' \ w \ \xi'''$, where u, v, and w are terminal words, we introduce a non-terminal ζ and the rules: $\xi_i \to \zeta \ w \ \xi'''$, $\zeta \to u \ \xi' \ v \ \xi''$. If G contains the rule: $\xi_i \to u \ \xi' \ v$ we introduce a non-terminal η and the rules: $\xi_i \to u \ \xi' \eta$, $\eta \to v$.

In this way we make all the non-terminal productions quadratic: $\xi_i \to u \ \xi \ v \ \xi' \ w$. We then introduce, for each different triple (u, v, w) the relations: $u = a \ b$, $v = \bar{b} \ c$, $w = \bar{c} \ \bar{a}$, and the homomorphism φ such that:

$$\begin{array}{lll} \varphi(a) = u, & \varphi(b) = e, & \varphi(\bar{b}) = v, \\ \varphi(c) = e, & \varphi(\bar{c}) = w, & \varphi(\bar{a}) = e. \end{array}$$

Then, if the grammar G′ contains the rules $\xi_i \to a \ b \ \xi \ \bar{b} \ c \ \xi' \ \bar{c} \ \bar{a}$, φ yields the rules of G again, and we have $L = \varphi(L')$.

We can now take up the proof of the main theorem. Given a CF-grammar that generates the CF-language L, we first construct a simple grammar G′. With the grammar G′ we canonically associate a K-language R and a Dyck language D*:

1. The allowed two-letter words of R consist of the following forms:

$$\begin{array}{lll} a_{i,j,k} \ b_{i,j,k}; & b_{i,j,k} \ d_{j,l}; & b_{i,j,k} \ a_{j,l,m}; \\ c_{i,j,k} \ d_{k,l}; & c_{i,j,k} \ a_{k,l,m}; & \\ \bar{a}_{i,j,k} \ \bar{b}_{l,i,k}; & \bar{a}_{i,j,k} \ \bar{c}_{l,m,i}; & \\ \bar{b}_{i,j,k} \ c_{i,j,k}; & \bar{c}_{i,j,k} \ \bar{a}_{i,j,k}; & \\ d_{i,l'} \ \bar{b}_{l,j,m}; & d_{i,l'} \ \bar{c}_{l,m,i}. & \end{array}$$

2. The Dyck language D* is the set $\gamma^{-1}e$ for the homomorphism

$$\gamma: X^* \to \Gamma$$
$$\gamma \ d_{i,l} = \gamma \ u \ \bar{u} = e$$

with u running through $\{a_{i,j,k}, b_{i,j,k}, c_{i,j,k}\}$.

The $d_{i,l}$ can be taken as the couples d $\bar{d}$.

Then the main theorem is an immediate consequence of proposition 2:

Proposition 2. We are given the simple grammar defined by a set of rules:

$$\xi_i = \sum_l d_{i,l} + \sum_{j,k} a_{i,j,k}\, b_{i,j,k}\, \xi_j\, \bar{b}_{i,j,k}\, c_{i,j,k}\, \xi_k\, \bar{c}_{i,j,k}\, \bar{a}_{i,j,k};$$

we are also given D* and R, the Dyck language and the K-language canonically associated with G. Then the language L'_1 associated with the non-terminal ξ_i satisfies the equation:

$$L'_i = D^* \cap R \cap \left\{ \bigcup_{j,k} a_{i,j,k}\, X^* \bigcup_l d_{i,l} \right\}.$$

The proof of this proposition can be carried out in two stages. We give an outline of the proof.

First Stage. Consider first the grammar: $\xi = d + a\, b\, \xi\, \bar{b}\, c\, \xi\, \bar{c}\, \bar{a}$ which is obtained by disregarding the subscripts and retaining just one non-terminal symbol; we shall prove the proposition for this special case first. A diagram of R is shown in Fig. 15-4.

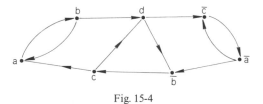

Fig. 15-4

L′ is made up of d(d $\bar{d}$) and of a *certain* set of Dyck-prime words that begin with a and satisfy the restrictions on R. Let

$$L'' = D^* \cap R \cap \{a\, X^* \cup d\};$$

L″ is made up of d and of *all* the Dyck-prime words of the kinds in question. We must show that L′=L″. This is done by induction: starting from d, we assume the result to be true for the factors of the word examined. We make use of the fact that a Dyck-prime word can be written uniquely as a $f_1 \ldots f_m\, \bar{a}$, with $f_i \in D_{x_i}$ (cf. § 15.1.7).

Second stage. We check that the preceding proof is valid when subscripts are introduced, i.e., that the constraints on the subscripts are compatible and consistent with the preceding constraints.

Conclusion. The language: $Q_i = R \cap \left\{ \bigcup_{j,k} a_{i,j,k}\, X^* \bigcup_l d_{i,l} \right\}$, is a standard K-language. Since we already have $L_i = \varphi(L'_i)$, we now have $L_i = \varphi(D^* \cap Q_i)$.

15.2.4. Consequences of the Fundamental Theorem

We have already shown that the class of CF-languages is not closed under the operations of complementation and intersection and we have seen that in general the CF-languages are not deterministic. The algebraic characterization which the fundamental theorem confers upon the CF-languages sheds light on the origin of this situation.

Consider the subclass of standard languages $D_r \cap Q$, where D_r and Q run through, respectively, the class of restricted Dyck languages and the class of standard K-languages with respect to a free monoid: the irregularities relating to closure or acceptance by an automaton disappear. In the case of the linear standard CF-languages, it is clear that the intersection can be constructed, for this problem can be reduced to the construction of the intersection of two regular languages; it is also clear that the result is a linear standard language. We also observe that these languages are deterministic.

The irregularities of the general class of CF-languages originate in the homomorphism φ. The following is what can be said about the undecidable properties due to the homomorphism.

We have seen that if $\mathfrak{A}^*$, $\mathfrak{B}^*$ are two free monoids, and φ and ψ two arbitrary homomorphisms of $\mathfrak{A}^*$ into $\mathfrak{B}^*$, there is no *general* procedure for determining whether or not there exists a word $f \in \mathfrak{A}^*$ such that $\varphi(f) = \psi(f)$. This is the algebraic statement of Post's result (the correspondence problem). Moreover, this result can be strengthened and extended to monomorphisms, i.e., to the case where we can go back from $\varphi(f)$ and from $\psi(f)$ to a single f. This explains the recursive unsolvability of the intersection problem.

15.3. Equivalence of the CF-Languages and the Languages accepted by Pushdown Automata

15.3.0.

We have already shown in Chapter 9 (cf. § 9.3) that every CF-language is accepted by a pushdown automaton. We shall now study the converse.

15.3.1. Theorem

Every language accepted by a pushdown automaton is a CF-language.

Here too we shall give only a general outline of the proof. Consider a pushdown automaton $\mathfrak{A}$ such as has been described in Chapter 9. It is defined by a set of instructions $\mathfrak{A}: \{(b, S_i, a_k) \rightarrow (S_j, x)\}$. Starting from $\mathfrak{A}$, we will construct a finite one-sided transducer $\mathfrak{T}$ (cf. § 10.6) in the following way:

1. For each rule of $\mathfrak{A}: (b, S_i, a_k) \rightarrow (S_j, x)$, $x \neq \sigma$, $\mathfrak{T}$ has the same rule.

2. For each rule of $\mathfrak{A}: (b, S_i, \sigma) \rightarrow (S_0, \sigma)$, $\mathfrak{T}$ has the rule:

$$(b, S_i, \sigma) \rightarrow (S_0, \sigma').$$

3. For each rule of $\mathfrak{A}$: $(b, S_i, a_k \neq \sigma) \to (S_j, \sigma)$, $\mathfrak{T}$ has the rules:

$$(b, S_i, a_k) \to (S_j, a_k \, a'_r \, a_r)$$

for every element a_r of the alphabet.

It can be checked, case by case, that $\mathfrak{A}$ accepts a word f if and only if $\mathfrak{T}(f)$ belongs to the restricted Dyck language on the a_h and the a'_h. Let L be the language that $\mathfrak{A}$ accepts; then we have:

$$\mathfrak{T}(L) = \{D_r \cap \mathfrak{T}(\mathfrak{A}^*)\},$$
$$L = \mathfrak{T}^{-1}(D_r \cap \mathfrak{T}(\mathfrak{A}^*)).$$

Now:

1. $\mathfrak{A}^*$ is regular; the transduction of a K-language is another K-language (cf. § 10.6.1); hence $\mathfrak{T}(\mathfrak{A}^*)$ is regular.

2. The intersection of a K-language and a CF-language is a CF-language (§ 10.6.3); hence $\mathfrak{T}(\mathfrak{A}^*) \cap D_r$ is a CF-language.

3. The transduction of a CF-language is a CF-language, hence $\mathfrak{T}^{-1}(D_r \cap \mathfrak{T}(\mathfrak{A}^*))$ is a CF-language, and the theorem is proven.

We have thus proven the theorem which was only stated in § 9.3.3. In view of its importance, we shall state it here again.

Theorem. *The class of languages accepted (generated) by pushdown storage automata is identical with the class of CF-languages.*

15.3.2. Remark about Ambiguity

Consider the homomorphism φ which maps a standard CF-language onto an arbitrary CF-language. The standard CF-language, which is structured by its 'natural' grammar, is not ambiguous; the arbitrary CF-language may possibly be ambiguous if its description is given by a grammar obtained from a construction (D^*, Q, φ).

The degree of ambiguity of a word f is equal to the cardinality of the set of words that φ maps onto it:

$$\text{degree of ambiguity of } f = \text{card } [\varphi^{-1}(f)].$$

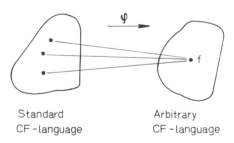

Standard   Arbitrary
CF-language   CF-language

Fig. 15-5

15.4. Exercises

15.4.1.

Given a Dyck language on the alphabet {a, b, ...; a', b', ...} and a standard K-language defined by equations as in § 14.1.2, how many equations are necessary to define the corresponding CF-language if the procedure for the construction of the intersection given in § 10.6.3 is used?

15.4.2.

Restricted standard CF-languages. The *restricted* standard CF-languages are obtained by imposing the following additional conditions.

1. Every transition from an unprimed letter to an unprimed letter implies the existence of the "reverse" transition between the corresponding primed letters; for example, a b implies b' a'.

2. The only allowed transitions of the type x y' are the type x x'.

First question. Construct a transition table, arranging the rows in the order a, b, c, ..., a', b', c', ... and the columns in the order a', b', c' ... a, b, c, ... Then the table divides itself naturally into four sections $\mathfrak{A}, \mathfrak{A}'$; $\mathfrak{A}', \mathfrak{A}'$; $\mathfrak{A}, \mathfrak{A}$; $\mathfrak{A}', \mathfrak{A}$. How are conditions 1. and 2. expressed in the table so constructed?

Second question. The transitions of the type x' y are not subject to any special restrictions. We shall examine their influence on the nature of C_S.

a) Suppose there is no restriction of the type x' y; show that the language is linear.

b) Suppose there are transitions of the type x' y, but no sequence can be found that makes a closed "loop": x' y, y' z, ..., v' w, w' x. Show that the language is metalinear.

c) If there exist one or more sequences that loop, the language is of the most general type.

Third question. Given the set of initials and the transition table, construct C_S directly.

15.4.3.

Are the standard CF-languages deterministic?

15.4.4.

CF-languages can be classified according to two criteria: ambiguous or unambiguous, deterministic or nondeterministic. Are all four classes non-empty? Give examples.

15.4.5.

Consider the language L on $\{a, b\}^*$: $L = \{x c y | |x| = |y| \ \& \ x \neq \tilde{y}\}$. Show that its complement with respect to $\{a, b\}^*$ is a CF-language. Show that $L_1 = \{x c y | x \neq y\}$ is a CF-language.

15.4.6.

Carry out the general computations of § 15.2.3 (grammar and fundamental theorem of the CF-languages) in the special case of the double-mirror-image language (cf. § 7.4.3).

Chapter XVI

Algebraic Languages

16.1. More about Formal Power Series

16.1.0.

In Chapter 11 the concept of a formal power series whose terms are associative but not commutative monomials was introduced from a heuristic point of view. We then indicated (somewhat intuitively) some of the applications that could be made of power series to the CF-languages.

In this section, we shall take up these same power series again, more rigorously, for new applications. We shall develop the theory in a rather general way, taking the domain Ω of the coefficients to be a ring. The reader will make the appropriate modifications if Ω is only a semi-ring. For the moment, the most important applications involve the cases $\Omega = \mathbf{Z}$ and $\Omega = \mathbf{N}$.

Although this chapter has been written as simply as possible, the reader is supposed to have a smattering of "modern" mathematics; in particular, it would be very useful for the reader to be acquainted with the formal presentation of polynomials in one or more commutative variables. If this is not the case, we caution the reader against the error of confusing polynomial with *polynomial function*.

In a polynomial such as $3x^2 + 2x + 1$, the letter x does not necessarily stand for a variable which must take on its values in some particular domain. It stands for a variable, or, if one likes, the special polynomial reduces to the monomial x. A polynomial can be used to make a polynomial function, and many other entities as well.

16.1.1. Associative Polynomials

Given the alphabet $X = \{x_i \mid 1 \leq i \leq n\}$, we first form the free monoid X^* generated by the letters x_i. Recall that each word $x_{i_1} \ldots x_{i_r}$ has a degree in x_1, a degree in x_2, etc., and a total degree, or multi-degree, which is the sum of the preceding degrees (the empty word, written e, has zero degree).

Given also $\Omega = \{\alpha, \beta, \ldots\}$, a commutative (associative) ring having a unit element, we can construct the *free associative algebra* $\Omega[X^*]$. For $\alpha \in \Omega$ and $f \in X^*$, αf is an *associative monomial* of coefficients α. The *product* of two monomials αf and βg (taken in that order) is $(\alpha \beta)(f g)$, $(\alpha \beta)$ being defined in Ω and $(f g)$ in X^* by concatenation.

The elements of $\Omega[X^*]$ are *associative polynomials* in the x_i, with coefficients in Ω. A polynomial has the form:

$$P = \alpha_1 f_1 + \cdots + \alpha_r f_r, \quad \alpha_i \in \Omega, \quad f_i \in X^*$$

and comprises a *finite* number of terms with non-zero coefficients. Moreover, it is possible to introduce terms of the form $0 f$, where 0 stands for the null element of Ω.

The sum of two polynomials is obtained by the usual rule: if P and Q contain the similar monomials αf and βf respectively, $P + Q$ contains the monomial $(\alpha + \beta) f$, and the sum $(\alpha + \beta)$ is carried out in Ω. $P + Q$ contains no other terms than those formed by this rule; the possibility of introducing terms of the form $0 f$ makes the rule applicable in all cases.

It will be observed that every polynomial is then the sum of its monomials considered as special polynomials. In this way, the use of the sign $+$ in writing a polynomial is justified *a posteriori*.

Multiplication, which is associative but not commutative, is defined by the rule:

$$\left(\sum_{i=1}^{r} \alpha_i f_i \right) \left(\sum_{j=1}^{s} (\beta_j g_j) \right) = \sum_{i=1, j=1}^{r, s} (\alpha_i \beta_j)(f_i g_j).$$

It is clear that $\Omega[X^*]$ is a ring and that its null element is the null polynomial (all of whose coefficients are zero). The element $1 e$, where 1 is the unit element of Ω, is the neutral polynomial for multiplication.

16.1.2. Composition of Polynomials

Let Y be an alphabet; it may be that $Y = X$. Let $f \in \Omega[X^*]$, and $g_i \in \Omega[Y^*]$ with $i = 1, \ldots, n$; $n = \text{card}(X)$. Since we have addition and multiplication at our disposition, we can define the compound polynomial: $f(g_1, \ldots, g_n)$.

Example. Let $f(x_1, x_2) = x_1 x_2$; then $f(g_1, g_2) = g_1 g_2$ which proves that the ordinary product can be considered as given by a special case of composition.

The mapping φ such that $\varphi: x_i \to g_i(y_1, \ldots, y_n)$ is a homomorphism of $\Omega[X^*]$ into $\Omega[Y^*]$. We have the following situation: the letters $A_1, \ldots, A_n$ which make up the alphabet $\mathfrak{A}$ stand for variables taking their values on $\Omega[T^*]$, where $T = \{t_1, \ldots, t_m\}$.

We also have a mapping of $\Omega[\mathfrak{A}^*]$ into $\Omega[\{\mathfrak{A} \cup T\}^*]$ defined by:

$$\sigma: \quad A_j \to g_j(t_1, \ldots, t_m, A_1, \ldots, A_n).$$

This mapping induces a mapping into $\Omega^n[T^*]$, for, if we have an n-tuple of polynomials $[(s_1), \ldots, (s_n)]$ as initial value, we can deduce from it another n-tuple by means of σ.

Example.
$$\mathfrak{A} = \{A, B\}, \qquad T = \{a, b\}$$
$$A \to a + A\,b\,B + B\,b\,A$$
$$B \to \qquad A\,b\,A + B\,b\,B.$$

To the pair $(0, 0)$ there corresponds the pair $(a, 0)$, to the pair (b, a) the pair $(a + b^2\,a + a\,b^2, b^3 + a\,b\,a)$, etc.

16.1.3. Power Series

We shall now construct the *large algebra* $\Omega[[X^*]]$ which extends $\Omega[X^*]$. Its elements are the power series:

$$\alpha_1 f_1 + \cdots + \alpha_n f_n + \cdots$$

in which there may be an infinite number of different monomials with non-zero coefficients.

Addition is defined as it was for the polynomials.

To define multiplication we order the series by increasing degree. A word $h = x_{i_1} x_{i_2} \ldots x_{i_k}$ can be factored either into $e\,h$, or $(x_{i_1})(x_{i_2} \ldots x_{i_k})$, etc. A monomial in h appears in the product with a coefficient of the form $\Sigma \, \alpha_i \, \beta_j$ which corresponds to all the factorizations of h into a word of the first series followed by a word of the second. To determine the coefficient of h in the product series, a *finite* number of terms must be added together: hence the product of two series is definable.

It is easily seen that $\Omega[[X^*]]$ is a ring. This large algebra contains a subset that is isomorphic to $\Omega[X^*]$; we shall identify this isomorphic subset with $\Omega[X^*]$, which amounts to considering a polynomial as a special series.

16.1.4. Valuation of the Space of Power Series

In every power series other than the null series (possibly after reduction of similar terms), there exists one class of homogeneous monomials, and just one, with non-zero coefficients and whose multidegree is *minimal*. We shall call this minimal multidegree the *order* of the series.

Example. Let $X = \{x, y\}$; the series are written in order of increasing degree. The series $e + x\,y + x^2\,y^2 + \cdots + x^n\,y^n + \cdots$ contains the empty word, hence its order is 0 (zero). The series

$$x\,x + y\,y + x\,y\,x + y\,x\,y + \cdots + x\,y^k\,x + y\,x^k\,y + \cdots$$

is of order 2, which is the multidegree of x x and y y.

We complete this definition by taking the order of the null series to be $+\infty$.

Addition. When two series are added together, if the order of one is less than (and not equal to) the order of the other, then the smaller of the two orders is the order of the sum.

If the series have the same order, two cases are possible: either the smallest degree terms do not all cancel out, and so the order of the sum is the same as the order of either of the series, or else they all cancel out and the order of the sum is greater than the order of either of the series.

The case where one (at least) of the two series is the null series presents no difficulty and we have the following result:

Lemma 1. *The order of the sum of two series* (s) *and* (s') *satisfies the inequality:* order $[(s) + (s')] \geq$ min [order [(s)], order [(s')]].

Multiplication. When two series are multiplied, two terms of minimal degrees give a term of minimal degree (the sum of the preceding) if Ω contains no divisors of zero. Otherwise, the multidegree of the minimal term in the product may be greater than the sum.

Lemma 2.   order $[(s)(s')] \geq$ order [(s)] + order [(s')].

There is always equality if the ring Ω is an integral ring.

Valuation of $\Omega[\![X^*]\!]$. Let us choose a real number greater than 1, for example 2. Starting with the order of a series (s), let us define the function val [(s)] by the rule val $[(s)] = 2^{-\text{order }[(s)]}$.

Example. For the series which were studied in the preceding example, we obtain, respectively: $2^0 = 1$ and $2^{-2} = \frac{1}{4}$.

By virtue of this definition we obtain for the null series, (s_0):

$$\text{val } [(s_0)] = 2^{-\infty} = 0.$$

Let us add two series (s) and (s'). We have:

$$\text{val } [(s) + (s')] = 2^{-\text{order }[(s) + (s')]},$$

but

$$\text{order } [(s) + (s')] \geq \text{min } [\text{order } [(s)], \text{order } [(s')]]$$

which yields:

Lemma 3.   val $[(s) + (s')] \leq$ Max [val [(s)], val [(s')]].

Examples. (s) begins with x and (s') with x y. Then (s)+(s') begins with x. We have:

$$\text{val } [(s)] = 2^{-1}, \text{ val } [(s')] = 2^{-2}$$
$$\text{val } [(s)+(s')] = 2^{-1}.$$

The relation holds with equality.

If (s) begins with $x + x\,y + \cdots$ and (s') with $-x + x\,y + \cdots$, we have:

$$\text{val } [(s)] = 2^{-1}, \quad \text{val } [(s')] = 2^{-1}$$
$$\text{val } [(s)+(s')] = 2^{-2}.$$

The relation holds with inequality.

There follows immediately from Lemma 2:

Lemma 4. In $\Omega[[X^*]]$ we have: val $[(s)(s')] \leq$ val $[(s)] \cdot$ val $[(s')]$. It is left as an exercise for the reader (exercise 16.4.1) to show that val $[(s)]$ is a *norm* for the ring $\Omega[[X^*]]$.

16.1.5. Distance of Two Series

Given two series (s) and (s'), we shall call distance of these two series, written $d[(s), (s')]$, the number:

$$d[(s), (s')] = \text{val } [(s)-(s')].$$

This distance has the following properties:

I. $d[(s), (s)] = 0$. In effect, $d[(s), (s)] = \text{val}[(s_0)] = 0$.

II. $d[(s), (s')] = d[(s'), (s)]$.

III. $d[(s), (s'')] \leq \text{Max } [d[(s), (s')], d[(s'), (s'')]]$.

In effect, we have $(s)-(s'') = [(s)-(s')] + [(s')-(s'')]$, and it suffices to apply Lemma 3.

It will be noted that III is stronger than the triangle inequality:

IIIa. $d[(s), (s'')] \leq d[(s), (s')] + d[(s'), (s'')]$.

However, I, II and IIIa are characteristic of a distance function (which justifies the name distance given d at the outset).

A space for which a distance is defined is a *metric* space; if the stronger inequality III obtains, the space is called *ultrametric*. Furthermore, the greatest value that the distance between two series can have is 1, hence the space is *bounded*, of diameter 1.

Proposition. If the space of power series is provided with the distance derived from the order, it is ultrametric.

16.1.6. Limit of a Sequence of Series

Given a distance, we can define the concept of limit precisely. Let $(s_1), \ldots, (s_p), \ldots$ be a sequence of power series, and let (s) be a *fixed* series. The series (s_p) is said to tend towards (s) as p approaches infinity if and only if $d[(s_p)-(s)]$ tends towards zero.

In particular, let P_0, P_1, ..., P_r, ... stand for a sequence of homogenous polynomials, the degree being equal to the subscript. The sequence:

$$P_0$$
$$P_0 + P_1$$
$$\cdots\cdots\cdots$$
$$P_0 + P_1 + \cdots + P_r$$
$$\cdots\cdots\cdots\cdots$$

is a sequence of polynomials, hence a sequence of series, which tends (in the sense defined above) towards the series which can be written

$$P_0 + P_1 + \cdots + P_r + \cdots.$$

Then let (s_1), (s_2), ... be arbitrary series of order 1, 2, ... etc. The sequence

$$(t_0) = P_0 + (s_1)$$
$$(t_1) = P_0 + P_1 + (s_2)$$
$$\cdots\cdots\cdots\cdots\cdots$$
$$(t_r) = P_0 + P_1 + \cdots + P_r + (s_{r+1})$$

tends towards the same series.

Two series are said to *equivalent for order r* if their difference is of order $r + 1$, at least. We can say:

Proposition. The limit of a convergent sequence (t_0), ..., (t_r) is not changed if each series (t_r) is replaced by a series which is equivalent to it for order r.

16.1.7. Completeness of the Space $\Omega[[X^*]]$

Recall the statement of Cauchy's criterion for an infinite sequence of elements (s_1), (s_2), ..., (s_n), ... in a metric space. This criterion is:

$$(\forall \varepsilon > 0)(\exists N)[p > N \ \& \ q > N \ \Rightarrow \ d[(s_p), (s_q)] < \varepsilon].$$

Every convergent sequence satisfies Cauchy's criterion. A space in which every Cauchy sequence converges is said to be complete. Let us prove that $\Omega[[X^*]]$ is complete.

Let (s_n) be a Cauchy sequence. By using the ε of the criterion, a subscript n_1 can be found such that all series with $n > n_1$ are equivalent for order 1, then a subscript n_2 such that all series with $n > n_2$ are equivalent for order 2, etc. This defines a sequence of polynomials which converges towards a series (s); the sequence of (s_n) converges towards (s).

16.1.8. Quasi-Regularity. Star Operation

A series for which the coefficient of the empty word is zero is called *quasi-regular*. By virtue of this definition, the null series is quasi-regular.

Let (s) be a quasi-regular series; its terms of smallest multi-degree have degree 1, at least. For $(s)^2$, the terms of smallest degree have degree 2, at least, etc. The order of $(s)^p$ tends to infinity with p.

Let (s_0) be the null series. What has just been said proves that $d[(s)^p, (s_0)]$ tends to zero, hence $(s)^p$ tends towards the null series. Now consider the sequence:

$$(t_1) = (s)$$
$$(t_2) = (s) + (s)^2$$
$$(t_3) = (s) + (s)^2 + (s)^3.$$
$$\dots\dots\dots\dots\dots$$

It satisfies Cauchy's criterion and tends to a limit which we write as $(s)^*$. For this series, the following relations are obvious:

$$(s) + (s)^2 + \cdots + (s)^p + \cdots = (s)^*$$
$$(s) + (s)^*(s) = (s) + (s)(s)^* = (s)^*.$$

If we set:

$$(s') = e - (s)^*, \quad (s'') = e + (s)^*$$

then we have:

$$(s')(s'') = e - (s) - (s)(s)^* + (s)^* = e.$$

Conversely, let (s') be a series in which the coefficient of the empty word is the unit element of Ω. Writing successively $(s) = e - (s')$, then $(s)^*$, and finally $(s'') = e + (s)^*$, we obtain the *inverse* of (s'). The possibility of taking the inverse of a series can be extended, if Ω is a field, to every series in which the empty word has a non-zero coefficient. In this case, every polynomial of $\Omega[X^*]$, of the type Q(X) with $Q(0) \neq 0$, has an inverse in $\Omega[[X^*]]$. It follows from this that this latter ring contains all the quotients $P(X) \cdot \dfrac{1}{Q(X)}$ and $\dfrac{1}{Q(X)} \cdot P(X)$, $Q(0) \neq 0$, i.e., a subset of the so-called *rational series*. $(s)^*$ is called the *quasi-inverse* of (s).

16.1.9. Substitution of Power Series

Given two alphabets X and Y. Is it possible to substitute for every y_j in a series $(t) \in \Omega[[X^*]]$ some $(s_j) \in \Omega[[X^*]]$? If (t) is a polynomial, this is possible without any restriction. If (t) is a series, this is possible only if the (s_j) are quasi-regular (the proof is left as an exercise).

Example. The computation of $(s)^*$ is nothing else than the substitution of (s) into the series: $1 \cdot Y + 1 \cdot Y^2 + \cdots + 1 \cdot Y^n + \cdots$.

16.1.10. N-Tuples of Power Series

Let n be a fixed positive integer. The ordered n-tuples of power series belonging to $\Omega[[X^*]]$ make up a space in which the distance can be taken as the sum of the distances of the components.

Since polynomials are special cases of power series, what we have established with regard to series can throw some light on the composition of polynomials. Let us return to the situation considered in § 16.1.2. To simplify the notation, we shall study couples of series or polynomials, but this will not affect the generality of the argument.

A and B stand for variables which take their values on $\Omega[X^*]$ and we have the mapping:

$$A \to \sigma(x_1, \ldots, x_m, A, B),$$
$$B \to \tau(x_1, \ldots, x_m, A, B).$$

This mapping induces a mapping of $\Omega^2[X^*]$ onto itself: starting from a point $M(P, Q)$, we obtain the point:

$$M(P', Q') = (\sigma(x_1, \ldots, x_m, P, Q), \quad \tau(x_1, \ldots, x_m, P, Q)).$$

Let us see what happens for the distances. We start with the points (P_1, Q_1), (P_2, Q_2) whose distance is $d(P_1, P_2) + d(Q_1, Q_2)$. For their transforms we have the distance $d(P'_1, P'_2) + d(Q'_1, Q'_2)$.

Now:

$$d(P_1, P_2) = \mathrm{val}(P_2 \quad P_1)$$
$$d(P'_1, P'_2) = \mathrm{val}(P'_2 - P'_1)$$

and

$$P'_2 - P'_1 = \sigma(x_1, \ldots, x_m, P_2, Q_2) - \sigma(x_1, \ldots, x_m, P_1, Q_1).$$

The monomials which result from those which contain neither A nor B cancel out. *Suppose that neither A alone nor B alone contains a monomial in e* (hypothesis of elevation). Under these conditions, the minimal multidegree increases by an integer whose value is determined by the polynomial σ, hence the distance is multiplied by a reduction factor λ_1 which is less than (but not equal to) 1.

We come to a similar conclusion for the distance $d(P_1, P_2) + d(Q_1, Q_2)$ by taking $\lambda = \max(\lambda_1, \lambda_2)$. In summary,

$$d(M'_1, M'_2) = \lambda \, d(M_1, M_2), \quad 0 < \lambda < 1.$$

This mapping is therefore a contraction mapping. We shall make use of this result in § 16.2.

16.1.11. Power Series in Commutative Variables

It is clear that we could have developed an analogous theory by allowing the generators to be commutative; instead of X^* we would have considered the Abelian monoid generated by X.

With every computation carried out in $\Omega[[X^*]]$ there corresponds a computation obtained by assuming commutativity. More exactly, there exists a ring homomorphism which maps every $f \in X^*$ onto its Abelian class.

Example. Let Ω be the ring of rational integers. Consider the polynomial $f(x, y, a) = a + x y^2$ and the computation which consists of forming the following sequence of iterates:

$$Y_0 = 0 \, e, \ldots, Y_n = f(x, Y_{n-1}, a).$$

With non-commutative variables we have:

$$Y_0 = 0 \, e$$
$$Y_1 = a$$
$$Y_2 = a + x \, a^2$$
$$Y_3 = a + x (a + x \, a^2)^2 = a + x \, a^2 + x \, a \, x \, a^2 + x^2 \, a^3 + x^2 \, a^2 \, x \, a^2.$$

With commutative variables we have:

$$\overline{Y}_0 = 0 \, e$$
$$\overline{Y}_1 = a$$
$$\overline{Y}_2 = a + a^2 \, x$$
$$\overline{Y}_3 = a + a^2 \, x + 2 \, a^3 \, x^2 + a^4 \, x^3.$$

16.2. Algebraic Series

16.2.0. About the Use of the Word Algebraic

Given a commutative field K and the ring K [x] of commutative polynomials on K, consider an equation: $a_0 \, x^n + \cdots + a_n = 0$, which has no solution in K.

If we let θ stand for a new element that satisfies this equation, then $K(\theta)$ is an *algebraic extension* of K.

Example. K is the field of rational numbers and the equation is $x^2 - 2 = 0$. If we now introduce a symbol θ such that $\theta^2 - 2 = 0$, it then follows that $x^2 - 2 = x^2 - \theta^2 = (x + \theta)(x - \theta)$. We also know how to find the other root, $-\theta$.

When dealing with a field of numbers which are known to have values either in R or in C, we can identify θ with some particular real or complex number.

Example. In the preceding example, we can identify θ with $\sqrt{2} = 1.41421\ldots$.

The numbers that are roots of a polynomial equation with rational coefficients are called *algebraic*. It can be shown that π is not an algebraic number. π satisfies only *series* equations like:

$$x - \frac{x^3}{3!} + \frac{x^5}{5!} - \frac{x^7}{7!} + \cdots + (-1)^p \frac{x^{2p+1}}{(2p+1)!} + \cdots = 0.$$

The word algebraic is used in the same way with regard to fields of functions.

Example. $Q(x)$ is the field of the rational fractions with rational coefficients. We can extend this field by means of a function y such that $y = x \, y^2 + 1$. This function is algebraic.

A power series should not be confused with a function related to a series. A series can be used to represent a function if we know how to associate a sum with that series. In classical analysis, the "ordinary" sum, which is defined when the series is convergent, is used. The radius of convergence is defined, etc.

We retain the formal point of view; it is natural to say that the power series which satisfies a *finite* algebraic equation is algebraic. In non-commutative structures we shall continue to use the word algebraic with the same meaning.

16.2.1. Special Systems

Let $X = \{x_i \mid 1 \leq i \leq m\}$ be the base alphabet and $\mathfrak{A} = \{A_j \mid 1 \leq j \leq n\}$ be an alphabet used for writing polynomials or power series on $\Omega[[X^*]]$. Also, let σ_j be polynomials on $\Omega[\{\mathfrak{A} \cup X\}^*]$. We shall consider systems of the form $A_j = \sigma_j$, $j = 1, \ldots, n$; we seek solutions in $\Omega^n[[X^*]]$.

The systems studied in Chapter 11 are special cases of these systems (a stronger justification is given in what follows). We assume in addition that the hypothesis of elevation is satisfied (§ 16.1.10).

These systems can be solved by the method of successive approximations. This method is based on the following theorem.

Theorem. *Let* E *be a complete metric space and* f *a contraction mapping of* E *into itself. The equation* $x = f(x)$ *has a solution* a, *and just one solution. For every* $x_0 \in E$, *the sequence of successive transforms of* x_0 *converges to* a.

Proof. The proof of the general theorem is left as an exercise. In the case of a *bounded* space, such as the one we are studying, it is enough to remark that the sequence $f^n(E)$ is a decreasing series and that the diameter of $f^n(E)$ is $\leq \lambda^n$ (the diameter of E).

Remark. In the examples given in chapter 11, we started with a value ω, which was an "annihilator" element that corresponds to $0\,e$, for example. This was done for intuitive reasons; in fact, we can start from any value at all, but then information-less items are carried along.

Example. Consider once more the case of the "polish" grammar $S = a\,S\,S + b$ studied in § 11.2.5, but starting from another value, for example a:

$$S_0 = a$$
$$S_1 = a^3 + b$$
$$S_2 = a(a^3 + b)(a^3 + b) + b$$
$$= a^7 + a^4\,b + a\,b\,a^3 + a\,b\,b + b.$$

It is seen that we have a "heavy" sequence of S_r, where S_r, for order r, is equivalent to the "good value".

Theorem. *Given an algebraic system* $A_j = \sigma_j$, $j = 1, \ldots, n$ *where the polynomials* σ_j *contain no monomials in* e *nor any monomials of multidegree* 1 *in the* A_i, *there exists just one n-tuple of series of* $\Omega[[X^*]]$ *that satisfies this system (and which can be obtained by successive approximations).*

Every series contained in the solution of an algebraic system is called an *algebraic* series.

16.3. Applications to Languages

16.3.0.

We shall take for Ω the ring Z of rational integers. Some applications have already been given in chapter 11. We shall now interpret some new results.

16.3.1. Subtraction of Two Languages

Consider the non-commutative equation

$$S = a - S\,b\,S \qquad \text{(F)}$$

and the following approximations:

$$S^{(0)} = a$$
$$S^{(1)} = a - S^{(0)}\,b\,S^{(0)} = a - a\,b\,a$$
$$S^{(2)} = a - S^{(1)}\,b\,S^{(1)} = a - (a - a\,b\,a)\,b\,(a - a\,b\,a)$$
$$= a - a\,b\,a + 2\,a\,b\,a\,b\,a - a\,b\,a\,b\,a\,b\,a.$$
$$\cdots\cdots\cdots\cdots\cdots$$

The power series which is the solution of (F) has positive and negative coefficients.

Let us set $S = S^+ - S^-$ and substitute in (F); there results

$$S^+ - S^- = a - (S^+ - S^-)\,b\,(S^+ - S^-)$$
$$S^+ - S^- = a - (S^+\,b\,S^+ - S^+\,b\,S^- - S^-\,b\,S^+ + S^-\,b\,S^-)$$
$$S^+ - S^- = a + S^+\,b\,S^- + S^-\,b\,S^+ - (S^+\,b\,S^+ + S^-\,b\,S^-).$$

Now consider the system:

$$\left|\begin{array}{l} S^+ = a + S^+\,b\,S^- + S^-\,b\,S^+ \\ S^- = S^+\,b\,S^+ + S^-\,b\,S^- \end{array}\right| \qquad \text{(F')}$$

(F') has positive coefficients, and will have as solution a pair of power series all of whose coefficients are positive, say (σ^+, σ^-); if σ is the power series which is the solution of (F), we have: $\sigma = \sigma^+ - \sigma^-$. We can associate two grammars with (F'): G^+ with axiom S^+, and G^- with axiom S^-. With this example in view, we can interpret the notion of subtraction for languages.

Consider the two CF-grammars G^+ and G^- each of which generates words having a certain degree of ambiguity, say $\langle \alpha, f \rangle$ where $f \in L(G^+)$ and α is the degree of ambiguity of f with respect to G^+, and $\langle \beta, g \rangle$ where $g \in L(G^-)$ and β is the degree of ambiguity of g with respect to G^-. We shall say that $G^+ - G^-$ generates words with degrees of ambiguity that can be positive or negative. When $f = g$, the degree of ambiguity corresponding to the word generated is $\alpha - \beta$.

The decomposition given above as an example is in fact quite general: with every system having both positive and negative coefficients we can associate two systems which have positive coefficients and their difference.

Example. Consider another example. Given $L_m = \{a^n c a^n | n \geq 0\}$ generated by $S = a\,S\,a + c$, and L'_m generated by $(G): S = a\,S\,a + c - a^k c a^k$.

L'_m can be obtained as the difference of the languages generated by the equations:

$$(G^+): S^+ = a\,S^+\,a + c$$
$$(G^-): S^- = a\,S^-\,a + a^k c a^k$$
$$L(G^+) = \{a^n c a^n | n \geq 0\}$$
$$L(G^-) = \{a^n c a^n | n \geq k\}$$
$$L'_m = L(G^+) - L(G^-) = \{a^n c a^n | 0 \leq n < k\}.$$

The language L'_m is finite; applying the method of successive approximations to (G) we see that all the words built around $a^k c a^k$ are subtracted and so disappear since the series solutions of (G^+) and (G^-) are characteristic.

16.3.2. Rational Languages

We have already seen (§ 16.1.8) that $Z[\![X^*]\!]$ contains the quotients of the form $\dfrac{P(x_1, \ldots, x_m)}{Q(x_1, \ldots, x_m)}$ for which Q contains the empty word with coefficient 1 (or -1). The supports of such series are *rational languages;* they correspond to the case where the system can be solved by linear methods.

The right-hand sides of the equations are linear in the unknowns and the coefficients are all on the same side of the unknowns.

Example. Computation of non-commutative rational functions.

Consider the system of rational equations:

$$A = b\,B - c\,C + c \tag{1}$$
$$B = a\,b\,B + c\,A \tag{2}$$
$$C = b\,A - c\,C. \tag{3}$$

We shall write the unit element as 1. Eq. (2) yields:

$$(1 - a\,b)\,B = c\,A; \quad B = \frac{c\,A}{1 - a\,b} = (1 + (a\,b)^*)\,c\,A$$

and similarly, Eq. (3) gives:

$$(1+c)\,C = b\,A, \quad C = \frac{b\,A}{1+c} = (1+(-c)^*)\,b\,A.$$

Substituting into (1), we have:

$$A = b(1+(a\,b)^*)\,c\,A - c(1+(-c)^*)\,b\,A + c$$
$$A = b(1+(a\,b)^*)\,c\,A - c(1+(-c)^*)\,b\,A + c$$
$$[1 - b(1+(a\,b)^*)\,c + c(1+(-c)^*)\,b]\,A = c$$

whence

$$A = \frac{c}{[1 - \{b(1+(a\,b)^*)\,c - c(1+(-c)^*)\,b\}]}$$
$$= [1 + \{b(1+(a\,b)^*)\,c - c(1+(-c)^*)\,b\}^*]\,c$$

and similar expressions for B and C.

This computation was possible only because of the particular form of the monomials: they are linear in the variables, and they have all their coefficients on the same side of the variable. The effect of this latter property is that there is no ambiguity as to the place of the multipliers and divisors. If in a system of equations there were two-sided monomials, or monomials of the kind a A and A a at the same time, then expressions like $A = \dfrac{b}{1-a}$ could have two interpretations: $b(1+a^*)$ or $(1+a^*)\,b$.

16.3.3. Algebraic Languages

The support of an algebraic series is an *algebraic language*. The criteria: "algebraic or rational" and "positive or negative coefficients of the systems" enable us to distinguish four classes of languages.

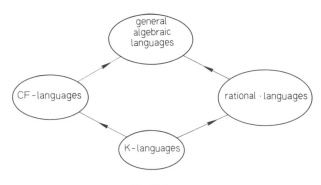

Fig. 16-1

These are proper inclusions: there are rational languages which are not K-languages but which are CF-languages.

16.3.4. Hadamard Product of Two Series

There is one operation on languages for which we do not yet have an interpretation in terms of series, namely, the operation of intersection of two languages. Let us recall the definition of the Hadamard product of two power series (in commutative variables).

Given two functions defined by a Taylor series expansion

$$f = a_0 + a_1 x + a_2 x^2 + \cdots + a_n x^n + \cdots$$
$$g = b_0 + b_1 x + b_2 x^2 + \cdots + b_n x^n + \cdots. \tag{T}$$

The Hadamard product of f by g is:

$$f \odot g = a_0 b_0 + a_1 b_1 x + a_2 b_2 x^2 + \cdots + a_n b_n x^n + \cdots$$

and the theorem of Jungen concerning the functions of a variable of classical analysis can be stated as follows. If

a) f is rational and g is rational, $f \odot g$ is rational;

b) f is rational and g is algebraic, $f \odot g$ is algebraic;

c) f is algebraic and g is algebraic, $f \odot g$ may or may not be algebraic.

Consider the following generalization of the value of the Hadamard product. Let σ_1 and σ_2 be two non-commutative power series, let f be a word of the support of σ_1 and of the support of σ_2, and α and β the degrees of ambiguity of f in σ_1 and σ_2, respectively. We have:

$$\sigma_1 \odot \sigma_2 = \sum_f \alpha \beta f.$$

From the definition, it is obvious that the Hadamard product of two series corresponds to the intersection of the supports of these two series:

$$\text{Sup}(\sigma_1 \odot \sigma_2) = \text{Sup}(\sigma_1) \cap \text{Sup}(\sigma_2).$$

The theorem of Jungen, generalized to the case of non-commutative functions, becomes:

Theorem of Jungen-Schützenberger. *If:*

a) σ_1 *is rational and* σ_2 *is rational,* $\sigma_1 \odot \sigma_2$ *is rational;*

b) σ_1 *is rational and* σ_2 *is algebraic,* $\sigma_1 \odot \sigma_2$ *is algebraic;*

c) σ_1 *is algebraic and* σ_2 *is algebraic,* $\sigma_1 \odot \sigma_2$ *may or may not be algebraic.*

This theorem also generalizes the results concerning the intersections of CF-languages and K-languages. We have the following important property:

Consider a homomorphism of the words of a language onto monomials in commutative variables; the results that we have given for non-commutative power series are preserved by such a homomorphism. Clearly, such a homomorphism transforms a system of non-commutative equations into a classical system of the type (T).

16.4. Exercises

16.4.1.

A function defined on a ring $U = \{a, b, c \ldots\}$ and having real values is a *norm* if it satisfies the following conditions:

1) $\qquad\qquad\qquad (\forall\, a \in U)\, [\varphi(a) \geq 0]$
2) $\qquad\qquad\qquad \varphi(a) = 0 \Leftrightarrow a = 0$
3) $\qquad\qquad\qquad \varphi(a + b) \leq \varphi(a) + \varphi(b)$
4) $\qquad\qquad\qquad \varphi(1) \quad = 1$
5) $\qquad\qquad\qquad \varphi(a\, b) \quad \leq \varphi(a)\, \varphi(b).$

Show that val $[(s)]$ is a norm for $\Omega\,[\![X^*]\!]$.

16.4.2.

Prove that the choice of the number greater than (but not equal to) 1 which was used to define the function val $[(s)]$ has no fundamental importance.

16.4.3.

Justify the assertion of § 16.1.9, namely, that the substitution of the series (s_j) into another series is possible if the former are quasi-regular.

16.4.4.

Generate the language $\{x^p\, y^q \,|\, p, q > 0,\, p \neq q\}$

    a) by an algebraic procedure;
    b) by a CF-grammar.

16.5. Applications of Equations to Combinatorial Geometry

16.5.0.

The theory of formal grammars finds some interesting applications in the domains of combinatorial geometry and combinatorial analysis. We shall limit our discussion to one example which shows how such an application enables us to study a classical problem from a new point of view.

16.5.1. A Decomposition Problem

Given a Jordan polygon (i.e., a simply connected topological polygon with an inside and an outside) whose n vertices have been labelled, in how many ways can it be decomposed into triangles by non-intersecting diagonals (except for intersections at the vertices)?

Example. The case of a pentagon can be handled straightforwardly and leads to the following five decompositions:

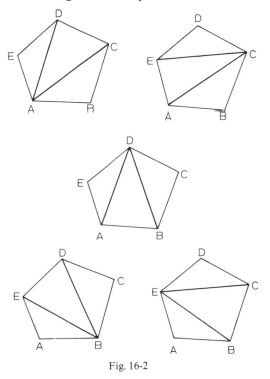

Fig. 16-2

Let us first sketch a "classical" solution to this problem. Let f(m) be the number of decompositions for an m-sided polygon. Consider a polygon P having n sides; using the function f, we shall calculate the number of decompositions that have a fixed (acceptable) triangle in common. If we exclude this common triangle, there remain inside P, in the general case, two polygons having p and q sides, with $p+q=n+1$; then the number we are seeking is $f(p)\,f(q)$. One of the polygons may be empty; in this case, the number is $f(n-1)$. Taking $f(2)=1$, we obtain just one rule: $f(p)\,f(q)$; $p+q=n+1$.

Let us hold constant one of the sides of the polygon $A_1 A_2 \ldots A_n$, for example $A_1 A_2$, while allowing A_i to run through the set of all the other vertices.

14*

All the triangles $A_1 A_2 A_i$ are different, and a triangulation containing $A_1 A_2 A_i$ differs from a triangulation containing $A_1 A_2 A_j$, $i \neq j$. Summing with respect to the subscript i, we obtain the recursion relation:

$$f(n) = f(2) f(n-1) + \cdots + f(i) f(n-i+1) + \cdots + f(n-1) f(2).$$

The case of a triangle gives $f(3) = 1$ immediately, which enables us to make an iterative calculation of $f(n)$.

Example. $f(4) = f(2) f(3) + f(3) f(2) = 2$
$\quad\quad\quad\quad f(5) = f(2) f(4) + f(3) f(3) + f(4) f(2) = 5.$

One next thinks of determining the generating function:

$$y = f(2) x^2 + f(3) x^3 + \cdots + f(n) x^n + \cdots$$

for which the coefficient of x^n would yield $f(n)$... but the reasoning used above gives hardly any clue as to how to go about this. The rest of the classical solution comes under the heading of "wizardry".

We shall see how the "grammatical" method, on the other hand, leads to a very *natural* solution.

16.5.2. Solution Using a Grammar

The basic idea consists in generating the triangulated polygons in the same way that the words of a language are generated. If the grammar is unambiguous, it will provide us with a count of the triangles as a by-product. The method that follows is a result of the application of simple ideas, in order to make the triangles "sprout".

Let us consider the "polish" grammar $S \to aSS$, $S \to b$, which is known to be unambiguous, and attribute to the symbols and the productions the following semantic values.

1. S is taken to be a directed topological segment which we shall call virtual, and represent as:

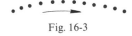

Fig. 16-3

2. aSS is taken to be a directed topological triangle having a side a, which is called real, and two virtual sides S and S. The correspondence is indicated in the figure:

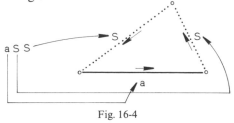

Fig. 16-4

3. A production that consists of replacing some S by a SS means: construct a triangle a SS whose real side a coincides, *direction included*, with the S in question, and which is located outside the polygon thus far constructed.

It is easy to show by recursion that this last condition can always be satisfied: the application of the rule is not subject to any restrictions of context.

Example. We give, side by side, the derivation tree and the translation of the word.

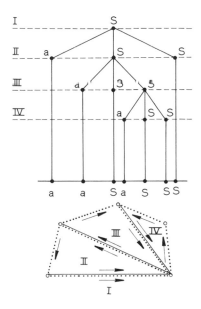

Fig. 16-5

4. A production that consists in replacing S by b means: replace the "virtual" side S by a "real" side b. This terminal production closes the polygon on the side where it was applied.

It is clear that every terminal word corresponds to a correctly triangulated polygon. All the a, except the first, represent diagonals and all the b represent sides. It can be easily shown by recursion that

$$\text{(number of S or of b)} = \text{(number of a)} + 1.$$

Furthermore, there are as many triangles as there are a. We thus have the classical result once more, namely, that the number of triangles is equal to two less than the number of sides or to the number of diagonals plus one.

Example. The word

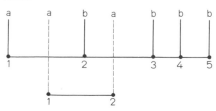

Fig. 16-6

represents a pentagon decomposed into three triangles by two diagonals.

Note that naming and orienting one side of a polygon suffices for labelling the entire polygon. Consequently, every terminal word of degree n in a corresponds to *one* triangulation of a labelled polygon with n + 2 sides. Conversely, two different words of degree n in a correspond to different triangulations. And every triangulation can be found by the procedure described above.

Example. Consider once more the pentagon ABCDE in which we mark the side AB; we obtain the following correspondences:

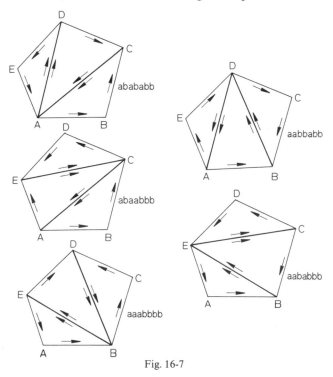

Fig. 16-7

In order to generate the sequence of all the triangulated polygons without repetition, it suffices to find the sequence of words generated by the grammar: $S \to b$, $S \to a b b$, i.e., to solve the non-commutative equation $S = b + a S S$. The computation has already been carried out (Chapter 11). We obtain the non-commutative power series:

(s): $b + a b b + a b a b b + a a b b b + a a b b a b b + \cdots$.

If we do no more than count the decompositions of polygons, then since the number of sides of a polygon is equal to the degree in a of the word plus two, we see that the number of triangulations of a polygon with $n + 2$ sides is equal to the coefficient of x^n in the commutative series deduced from (s).

It suffices to consider the homomorphism: $a \to x$, $s \to y$, $b \to 1$, $x y = y x$. The function y satisfies the equation $y = 1 + x y^2$; we obtain:

$$y = 1 + x + 2 x^2 + 5 x^3 + \cdots.$$

Example. For a pentagon, $n + 2 = 5$. Then we must take the coefficient of x^3, which yields 5.

16.5.3. Exercises

1. Given a triangle A B C. By taking an interior point and connecting it to the three vertices A, B, and C, the triangle can be decomposed into three other triangles, each of which can be decomposed in turn, etc.

Study this *ternary triangulation*. The grammar

$$\begin{vmatrix} T \to (T T T) \\ T \to (t) \end{vmatrix}$$

can be used.

2. Study the decomposition of a polygon with $2n$ sides into quadrilaterals by means of non-intersecting diagonals.

Transformational Grammars

1. About Formal Grammars and Natural Languages

Many of the concepts which have been described in this book have their origin in the study of the natural languages.

Certain operations carried out on sentences of every-day language have been formalized in logic: "It is false that ... : ⌐"; "... or ... : ∨"; "... and ...: ∧"; "if ... then ...: ⊃"; "... is equivalent to ...: ≡"; etc., where the periods stand for sentences.

The concept of a Markov chain (related to that of a K-language) was elucidated following statistical studies of the patterns of vowels and consonants in literary texts.

The formal grammars developed by Chomsky (1959; CF-grammars and context-sensitive grammars) represent a culmination of efforts devoted to obtaining rigorous and completely explicit descriptions of certain grammatical regularities (Harris, 1946 – 1951).

The goal contemplated by modern linguistics is the construction of grammars for natural languages which are completely specified by an automaton, a formal grammar, or an algebraic construction. The requirement that the descriptions have such forms is entirely justified from the theoretical point of view: the linguist seeks to describe the mechanisms that enable man to produce and to understand speech. These mechanisms make up the grammatical intuition of a linguistic community and are only imperfectly described in traditional grammars.

The formalization should make apparent the regularities of a language, contain very general rules (liable to only a minimum of exceptions), and, by comparing the grammars of very diversified types of natural languages, should define universal mechanisms amenable to mathematical analysis. From a practical point of view, the various applications to information processing which might be envisaged with the help of linguistic analyses carried out on computers presuppose the availability of very complete formalized grammars.

During the last 15 years, a significant amount of work which has been carried on with the idea of achieving formalized descriptions having solid empirical bases has shown that the various combinatorial systems which we have described here present numerous drawbacks when one attempts to describe syntactic phenomena in a significant way. These drawbacks, due principally to the fact that these systems are not sufficiently specialized, disappear in large part when the descriptive technique known as transformational analysis is used (Chomsky, 1957, 1962, 1965; Harris, 1952, 1957, 1964).

The fundamental idea of this analysis is that every sentence of a natural language can be described in terms of elementary sentences (often called "kernel" sentences in the literature) and certain operations of combination on these elementary sentences; these operations are the transformations. The kernel sentences in turn can be decomposed into simpler elements which are words, or better, roots and affixes. In fact, the atomic elements of these descriptions are more abstract elements defined in such a way as to have compact and regular descriptions which require only a minimal number of atoms.

It will be noted that this approach is simply the traditional scientific method for describing any physical phenomenon. A similar method had been universally adopted by the rationalist grammarians of the 17th and 18th centuries, but it was then neglected for two hundred years during which period it was severely criticized by means of exceedingly dubious arguments.

An example of a transformation as it was very clearly described in the grammar of Port-Royal is the following. The sentence

(1) Dieu invisible a créé le monde visible
can be analyzed as follows:

(2) Dieu qui est invisible a créé le monde qui est visible.

(3) (i)   Dieu a créé le monde.
    (ii) Dieu est invisible.
    (iii) Le monde est visible.

(3) is a set of three kernel sentences; (2) is made up of the matrix sentence (3 i), or principal proposition, into which the two subordinate propositions (3 ii) and (3 iii) have been inserted. This operation of insertion constitutes a transformation. (1) is obtained from (2) by applying a deletion transformation.

The superiority of this type of description becomes evident when it is compared with a description in terms of a CF-grammar, for example, which latter is in widespread use in present-day linguistics.

2. CF-Grammars and Transformations

Consider the following rules, written in the form of equations; the meaning of the auxiliary symbols is clear:

$$\text{(A)} \left|\begin{array}{l} S = NP\,VP \\ NP = Art\,N_c + N_{pr} \\ VP - V\,NP + est\,Adj \\ Art = le \\ \quad V = a\ cré\acute{e} \\ \quad N_c = monde \\ N_{pr} = Dieu \\ Adj = visible + invisible \end{array}\right| \left.\begin{array}{l} N_c \equiv common\ noun; \\ N_{pr} \equiv proper\ noun \\[2em] \\ \end{array}\right\} lexical\ rules.$$

The CF-grammar (A) generates 8 sentences that can be written in the following condensed form:

(Dieu + le monde)(a créé (Dieu + le monde) + est (visible + invisible)).

The parentheses are not supposed to delimit structures; they are used only to indicate a non-commutative product.

To obtain sentences (1) and (2), rules must be added to (A) which introduce noun modifiers:

$$\text{(B)} \left|\begin{array}{ll} \text{(B1)}\ NP = Art\,N_c\,Adj + N_{pr}\,Adj; & \text{adjectival modifiers} \\ \text{(B2)}\ NP = Art\,N_c\,qui\,VP + N_{pr}\,qui\,VP; & \text{relative modifiers}. \end{array}\right.$$

The grammar (A, B) contains recursive symbols and generates infinitely many sentences containing relative clauses embedded in each other. The relative clauses of the type "qui V NP" allow such embeddings. This description is based on a linguistic concept of noun modifiers that is quite different from the transformational concept. Here, the rules of (B) introduce these modifiers directly and each of the two types (B1) and (B2) is introduced independently. The transformational treatment, however, shows that the adjectives in (1) and (2) have the same status, with the exception of a deletion rule.

We shall now consider a transformational grammar which generates L(A, B) and is made up of:

1. the CF-grammar (A) which generates the kernel sentences;

2. transformations (C) defined on structures which are either kernels, or else structures obtained by prior transformations.

a) binary transformations (operating on a pair of sentences); the insertion of relatives is an example of a binary transformation. It can be formulated in the following way:

(C1): $X\,N_1\,Y$, $Art\,N_2\,VP \rightarrow X\,N\,qui\,VP\,Y$, where $N_1 = N_2 = N$; X and Y are the contexts of N_1 in the main clause;

b) unary transformations (operating on a single sentence). Deletion of "qui est" is an example of a unary transformation which can be written:

(C 2) X N qui est Adj Y → X N Adj Y.

An objection to this type of analysis may at once be made, namely, that the rules we have introduced have a very complicated form, are very difficult to study, and accomplish no more than did the rules (B); furthermore, whereas the grammar (A, B) is homogeneous, (A, C) is heterogeneous.

3. Extension of the Grammars

The objection just mentioned is only apparent. In effect, if we wish to extend our description to other data than those of L(A, B), to data which take into account the existence of restrictions between certain parts of speech: restrictions of agreement in gender, number and person, or class restrictions between subject and verb, then the grammars (A, B) and (A, C) must be modified. These modifications are extremely cumbersome in the case of CF-grammars, but can be effected quite elegantly in the case of transformational grammars.

Thus, in order to treat just gender and number, (A) must be modified so as to describe the agreements article-noun, subject-verb, noun-attributive adjective, noun-predicative adjective. (A) then becomes (A'), where the meaning of the subscripts used in the augmented auxiliary alphabet is evident:

$$S = NP_{sing} VP_{sing} + NP_{pl} VP_{pl}. \tag{A'1}$$

This rule is valid only for sentences without the verb "être". For sentences with the verb "être", the gender agreement restriction yields the rules:

$$
\begin{aligned}
S = NP_{masc\ sing}\ est\ Adj_{masc\ sing} + NP_{fem\ sing}\ est\ Adj_{fem\ sing} \\
+ NP_{masc\ pl}\ sont\ Adj_{masc\ pl} + NP_{fem\ pl}\ sont\ Adj_{fem\ pl}.
\end{aligned} \tag{A'2}
$$

The noun phrases which appear in (A'1) and (A'2) are of the same kind, and this cannot be made explicit unless the NP of (A'1) are written twice, once for each gender. Such a duplication of the NP in (A'1) would be very inelegant linguistically, since the gender has nothing to do with subject-verb agreement. Moreover, gender and number are generally unrelated parameters, so that the following rules are preferable:

$$
\begin{aligned}
NP_{sing} &= NP_{masc\ sing} + NP_{fem\ sing} \\
NP_{pl} &= NP_{masc\ pl} + NP_{fem\ pl}.
\end{aligned} \tag{A'3}
$$

A solution using verb phrases differentiated by gender is even more cumbersome than the solution just outlined.

We also have the following rules:

$$NP_{\text{masc sing}} = \text{le } N_{\text{c masc sing}} + N_{\text{pr masc sing}}$$

$$NP_{\text{masc pl}} = \text{les } N_{\text{c masc pl}} + N_{\text{pr masc pl}}$$

$$NP_{\text{fem sing}} = \text{la } N_{\text{c fem sing}} + N_{\text{pr fem sing}}$$

$$NP_{\text{fem pl}} = \text{les } N_{\text{c fem pl}} + N_{\text{pr fem pl}}$$

$$VP_{\text{sing}} = V_{\text{sing}}(NP_{\text{sing}} + NP_{\text{pl}})$$

$$VP_{\text{pl}} = V_{\text{pl}}(NP_{\text{sing}} + NP_{\text{pl}})$$

and the lexical rules:

$$V_{\text{sing}} = \text{a créé}; \qquad\qquad V_{\text{pl}} = \text{ont créé}$$

$$N_{\text{c masc sing}} = \text{monde} + \cdots; \quad N_{\text{c masc pl}} = \text{mondes} + \cdots$$

$$N_{\text{pr masc sing}} = \text{Dieu} + \cdots; \quad N_{\text{pr masc pl}} = \text{Dieux} + \cdots$$

$$N_{\text{pr fem sing}} = \text{nature} + \cdots; \quad N_{\text{c fem pl}} = \text{natures} + \cdots$$

$$Adj_{\text{masc sing}} = \text{visible} + \text{invisible} + \text{beau} + \text{loyal} \ldots$$

$$Adj_{\text{fem sing}} = \text{visible} + \text{invisible} + \text{belle} + \text{loyale} \ldots$$

$$Adj_{\text{masc pl}} = \text{visibles} + \text{invisibles} + \text{beaux} + \text{loyaux} \ldots$$

$$Adj_{\text{fem pl}} = Adj_{\text{fem sing}}\, \text{s}.$$

By no means do these rules account for numerous "irregular" morphological phenomena.

The rules (B) become

$$NP_{\text{masc sing}} = \text{le } N_{\text{c masc sing}}\, Adj_{\text{masc sing}} + N_{\text{pr masc sing}}\, Adj_{\text{masc sing}}$$
$$NP_{\text{masc sing}} = (\text{le } N_{\text{c masc sing}} + N_{\text{pr masc sing}})\, \text{qui } (VP_{\text{sing}} + \text{est } Adj_{\text{masc sing}}),$$

(B′)

plus six other equations corresponding to the other possible combinations of gender and number.

It is easily seen that the introduction of the contrasting subclasses animate-inanimate, concrete-abstract will cause the number of rules of (A′, B′) to increase rapidly. In the form (C) we gave of the transformational rules, a rapid increase in the number of rules is also possible but, in view of the absence of any *a priori* formal restrictions on these rules, they can be modified in a very natural way so as to describe L(A′, B′) without any increase in their number.

We shall modify (A) to (A′) in the following way. We consider the subscripts attached to the auxiliary symbols as markers to which the rules can refer: with every N, for example, we shall associate three binary subscripts corresponding to the three contrasting categories: common-proper, masc-fem, sing-pl. A rule may make mention of N alone: N x x x, or it may mention the second subscript of N: N x masc x, or else the first and third subscripts of N: N c x pl, etc. A noun may not be selected from the dictionary unless all its subscripts have been specified.

Then we have the rules:

$S = NP\ VP.$

$NP = Art\ x\ x\ N\ x\ x\ x$; the two subscripts of Art and the last two of N are *gender* and *number*. The first subscript of N is the *type*.

$VP = V\ x\ x\ NP + V\ x\ x\ \hat{e}tr\ Adj\ x\ x$; the two subscripts of V are *person* and *number*, être is a subscript that classifies verbs, and Adj has the subscripts *gender* and *number*.

These subscripts are specified by the rules:

$$type\ \ \ \ = c + pr$$
$$gender = masc + fem$$
$$number = sing + pl$$
$$person = 1 + 2 + 3.$$

Next we have the context-sensitive rules

$Art\ x\ x\ Npr\ x\ sing = E\ Npr\ x\ sing$; in certain cases, no article before a singular proper noun. The rule is in fact much more complicated.

$Art\ x\ x\ N\ x\ gender\ number = Art\ gender\ number\ N\ x\ gender\ number$. This rule recopies onto the article the gender and number attached to N. It is independent of the type, and allows articles to be placed in front of Npr. In order to obtain all the correct forms, a detailed classification of Npr is required.

(A″) $N\ x\ x\ number\ V\ x\ x = N\ x\ x\ number\ V\ 3\ number$; subject-verb agreement.

   $N\ x\ gender\ number\ V\ x\ x\ \hat{e}tr\ Adj\ x\ x = N\ x\ gender\ number\ V\ x\ x\ \hat{e}tr$ $Adj\ gender\ number$; when the verb has the subscript être, the adjective agrees with the subject.

We also have the lexical rules:

$$V\ 3\ sing\ \hat{e}tr\ \ \ = est\ \ + devient\ \ \ \ + \cdots;$$
$$V\ 3\ pl\ \hat{e}tr\ \ \ \ \ = sont + deviennent + \cdots;$$
$$Art\ masc\ sing = le;$$
$$Art\ fem\ sing\ \ = la;$$
$$Art\ x\ pl\ \ \ \ \ \ \ \ = les;$$
$$Npr\ masc\ sing = Dieu$$

as well as the other lexical rules mentioned in the description of (A′).

The context-sensitive rules just given are of a special type and do not satisfy the definitions given in Chapter 12. In effect, these rules do not rewrite a symbol but merely assign values to symbols by using the available information which is carried by the N. With these conventions, the rule (C1) requires no modification, if it is understood that the appearance of the symbol N in (C1) means that no reference is made to the three subscripts. Modifying (C2) in the following way

$$X \text{ N qui V x x êtr Adj Y} \rightarrow X \text{ N Adj Y} \qquad (C'2)$$

also covers all the cases.

This system of subscripts simplifies our transformational grammar for two reasons:

we use context-sensitive rules which refer to these subscripts, and this exceeds the capabilities of CF-grammars;

the transformations operate independently of certain subscripts, which enables us to obtain a very general applicability of the rules and to account for the fact that type, gender, number and person are parameters that are independent of each other, which does not appear in the CF-rules.

Whereas more refined classifications are the cause of a considerable proliferation in the number of CF rules and require the CF grammars to be completely rewritten every time a new parameter is introduced in the descriptions, these same refinements modify only the context-sensitive rules of the component (A'') in the transformational grammar without any modification of the transformational rules.

The only advantage in using CF-grammars for linguistic descriptions is the simplicity in writing programs of syntactic analysis, based upon such grammars, for the computer. However, the restricted form of the rules deprives the linguistic analyses in terms of CF-trees of any theoretical interest, and their practical interest would become apparent only if it were possible to really implement such descriptions for a natural language, which is far from the actual case. In fact, even if these descriptions were worked out there is every reason to believe that the linguistic analyses would have such a form as to be unusable, for much interesting information is in many cases very difficult to represent in a CF-tree.

An example of such a difficulty of representation is given by the sentence

(a) *Jean obtient de Pierre l'autorisation de partir* (John obtains from Peter permission to leave).

A CF-tree can give the following information in a natural way:

Jean is the subject of *obtient*.

Pierre is the prepositional object of *obtient*.

L'autorisation de partir is the direct object of *obtient*.

Partir is a noun complement of *autorisation*.

However, from the way that this sentence is understood it is clear that there are other relations which are not so simply expressed:

Jean is the subject of *partir*. This can be shown by the fact that the two sentences

J'obtiens de Pierre l'autorisation de m'absenter (I obtain from Peter permission to absent myself)

Il obtient de Pierre l'autorisation de s'absenter (He obtains from Peter permission to absent himself)

are correct, but

* *Il obtient de Pierre l'autorisation de m'absenter* (He obtains from Peter permission to absent myself)

is not.

Another relation contained in (a) is that *Pierre* gives *l'autorisation de partir*. This can be established from the fact that

* *Jean obtient de Pierre votre autorisation de partir* (John obtains from Peter your permission to leave)

is not acceptable.

These last two relations cannot be given naturally by a CF-grammar. The natural way of expressing them would be to say that (a) "contains" the sentence

(b) *Pierre autorise Jean à partir* (Peter permits John to leave) and that a certain process of nominalization and restructuring of (b) enables us to derive (a) from (b).

Operations of this kind can be described by the transformational rules, although sentence (a) does present certain problems which have not yet been satisfactorily resolved.

4. Problems Related to Transformations

The main idea of transformational analysis is that two levels of linguistic "atoms" are used in the description of sentences. A first level is made up of morphemes (word stems, flexional endings) upon which the CF-rules or context-sensitive rules operate to form larger units. At this level, elementary sentences (or structures) are formed. These elementary sentences constitute the atoms for the second level, where they are modified and combined with each other by means of the transformational rules to form complex sentences. Whereas the elementary sentences are of finite length, on this second level complex sentences may also be modified and combined with each other. Since the transformations are defined recursively, the length of the sentences which they generate is not bounded.

We took the liberty of effecting some rather profound modifications of the grammar (A, C) which resulted in a certain economy in the number of rules. On the other hand, the modifications made on (A, B) were imposed by the condition that only CF-rules could be used. This liberty of manipulation of the transformations is in fact the central problem of the grammar.

Certain syntactic mechanisms emerge from the empirical studies carried out on various natural languages, and experience shows that the more transformational data one has, the less latitude there is for the formulation of the rules. Moreover, the need for ordering the rules clearly and simply imposes formal restrictions in a natural way.

We shall briefly describe the most recent ideas of the notion of transformation.

(1) *The original idea of Harris*, as later taken up by Chomsky in "Syntactic Structures", is rather well described by the use of the rules (C) in our example; however, gender and number would be treated as independent morphemes in Harris' method.

(2) *The new concept of Chomsky* is different. If we describe it in terms of a generative automaton, there is a grammar having a base component which generates structures by means of CF-rules; these structures are then specified, i.e., the subscripts of the kind described above are specified by means of context-sensitive rules. These base structures are transformed into surface structures, which are the trees, by means of transformational rules. The unary-binary distinction which we have made has no sense in this process, since the base structure contains all the elementary sentences which can be used for constructing a complex sentence.

A grammar of this kind that would describe L(A, B) would be made up of the grammar (A″) plus a rule for transposing into post-nominal position noun modifiers which consist of entire sentences:

$$NP = Art x x N x x \# S \#$$

(the symbols # are markers for the beginning and the end of an elementary sentence).

The base structure corresponding to sentences (1) and (2) is:

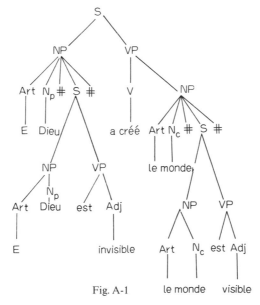

Fig. A-1

There are problems at this level: in this example, the lexical elements must be specified in such a way that the subjects of those sentences which will become relative clauses are identical to their respective antecedents. There are various ways of carrying out these operations of specification (Chomsky, 1965; Klima).

The transition from the base structure of Fig. A-1 to the surface structure below is accomplished by transformations:

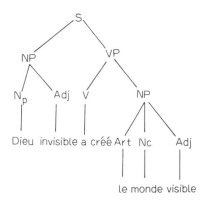

Fig. A-2

a first rule operates on Fig. A-1: it deletes the boundary markers # and replaces the repeated N by relative pronouns. The result of the application of this rule is the surface structure of sentence (2).

the rule (C 2) then operates on the surface structure of (2), deleting "qui est" and restructuring the tree. The result is Fig. A-2.

Certain problems related to the concept of a transformation have not been satisfactorily worked out. These problems become apparent when a transformation is defined in detail as a function defined on CF-trees and having its values in the set of trees. As matters stand at present, the notion of a transformation is much too complex for one to hope to be able to subject it to a detailed mathematical analysis.

(3) *The idea of Harris* (1964) has a more algebraic character: a first set of generators (morphemes corresponding to the various parts of speech) and operations of a finite nature generate the kernel sentences. The kernel sentences constitute a second set of generators which generate complex sentences by means of unary and binary transformations.

Consider the kernel sentences (3) (cf. § 1) and the transformations:

(C 1) $T_r(P_1, P_2)$, embedding of P_2 in P_1; P_2 becomes a relative clause.

(C 2) $T_a(P)$, deletion of "qui est".

Then T_r, $T_a(3)$ and (3) can generate:

$$T_r(3\,i, 3\,ii) = \text{Dieu qui est invisible a créé le monde.}$$

$$T_r(3\,i, 3\,iii) = \text{Dieu a créé le monde qui est visible.}$$

$$T_r\big(T_r(3\,i, 3\,ii), 3\,iii\big) = T_r\big(T_r(3\,i, 3\,iii), 3\,ii\big)$$
$$= \text{Dieu qui est invisible a créé le monde qui est visible.}$$

$$T_a\,T_a\,T_r\big(T_r(3\,i, 3\,ii), 3\,iii\big) = T_a\,T_a\,T_r\big(T_r(3\,i, 3\,iii), 3\,i\big)$$
$$= \text{Dieu invisible a créé le monde visible.}$$

Note that this last sentence can also be described as

$$T_a\,T_r\big(T_a\,T_r(3\,i, 3\,ii), 3\,iii\big) = T_a\,T_r\big(T_a\,T_r(3\,i, 3\,iii), 3\,ii\big).$$

These examples show the kinds of problems encountered when constructing an algebra of transformations. Thus, sentence (1) has four different descriptions. However, it is more interesting to reserve the idea of different descriptions for the case where the sentence is ambiguous; in that case, as many different descriptions are attributed to it as it has meanings. In the set given above, either the four descriptions of (1) must be made equivalent, or else we must so contrive matters that only one description is generated by the procedure. It can be shown, by empirical considerations, that natural groupings of the transformations exist; for example, that certain products of unary transformations (passive, reflexive, …) must be carried out before the binary transformations operate, or that certain unary transformations of a local (morphophonemic) character are applied at the end of the process of sentence generation. If the transformation T_a is of this last kind, then these considerations would suggest placing all the T_a at the "front" of the products. This can also be expressed by postulating a certain commutativity of products of T_a and T_r.

There are also certain problems of associativity for these products: the products of T_r are associative, but others are not. Harris also considered other formal properties of the transformations: the Kleene-like nature of sequences of transformations, and the definition of the inverse of a transformation, in certain cases.

It is to be noted that the problems of defining the concept of a transformation, which were mentioned in connection with Chomsky's notion of transformation, are also problems here for the definition of the T. Furthermore, the problem of the characterization of the permissible sequences of T, which is empirical at the present, is also important if Chomsky's point of view is adopted.

With these few definitions, we have tried to set forth the problem of formal syntax for natural languages. This problem is, above all, empirical.

15*

From numerous observations of syntactic phenomena of natural languages, in particular the distinction between allowed and forbidden sequences of words, certain formal mechanisms took shape. In some cases, these mechanisms could be separated from the data and studied independently of them, but for the linguist it is very clear that these mechanisms are far from adequate, and that numerous and difficult empirical studies will be needed before a comprehensive insight into the mechanisms involved becomes available. It is not even certain that such processes as CF-grammars or context-sensitive grammars have a linguistic or psychological reality. In effect, situations like the following crop up frequently in the course of the research:

at a certain stage in the linguistic study, a group of phenomena (α) can be described by context-sensitive rules ($\mathfrak{C}$);

at a later stage, the phenomena (β) compel the linguist to adopt the transformational rules ($\mathfrak{T}$);

the rules ($\mathfrak{T}$) enable the linguist to describe the phenomena (α) more naturally. Faced with this situation, the linguist is led to eliminate the rules ($\mathfrak{C}$) and to adopt a uniform description in terms of the rules ($\mathfrak{T}$).

In these conditions, which are only normal for a young science, it is not easy to see what the nature of abstract studies of models of natural languages will be like, but there is no denying that the systematic attempts at making abstract models yield adequate descriptions of natural languages are highly instructive, even when the results are negative, so that the linguist finds himself compelled to carry on his abstract and empirical research at the same time.

Bibliography of Transformational Grammars

Chomsky, N.: Three models for the description of language. IRE Trans. Inform. Theory IT 2, 113 – 114 (1956).
- Syntactic structures. 's Gravenhage: Mouton and Co. 1957.
- On certain formal properties of grammars. Information and Control 2, 137 – 167 (1959).
- A transformational approach to syntax. In: Proceedings of the 1958 Conference on Problems of Linguistic Analysis in English (A. A. Hill, ed.). Austin (Texas) 1962.
- Aspects of the theory of syntax. Cambridge, Mass.: M.I.T. Press 1965.
Harris, Z. S.: From morpheme to utterance. Language 22, 161 – 183 (1946).
 Methods in structural linguistics. Chicago, Ill.: Chicago University Press 1951.
- Discourse analysis. Language 28, 1, 1 – 30 (1952).
- Cooccurrence and transformations in linguistic structure. Language 33, 283 – 340 (1957).
- Elementary transformations. T. D. A. P., 54, University of Pennsylvania (1964).
- Mathematical structures of language. New York: J. Wiley 1968.
Klima, E. S.: Current development in generative grammar. Prague Colloquium on Algebraic Linguistics and Machine Translation-Kibernetica Číslo 2, Ročnik 1/1965 (1965).

Annotated Bibliography

Starting from certain results of structural linguistics, and in particular from those of Z.S.Harris [12, 13], N.Chomsky [4] has defined a typology of formal grammars and subjected it to mathematical analysis [5]. At the same time, the theory of "regular events", which had been created independently by S.C.Kleene, received a new impetus from the work of J.Myhill [19], N.Chomsky and G.A.Miller [7], and also M.O.Rabin and D.Scott [25].

The introduction by M.P.Schützenberger of the concept of a power series [28] as well as the ideas of linearity and meta-linearity [29] opened up the path to important advances in the theory of automata and formal grammars.

We list below the most distinctive works, some of which contain rather extensive bibliographies.

1. Bar-Hillel, Y.: Language and information; selected essays on their theory and application. Jerusalem: Academic Press, Addison-Wesley 1964. 388 pages, 155 references. (A collection of articles containing, in particular, the two references that follow.)
2. — Perles, M., Shamir, E.: On formal properties of simple phrase structure grammars. Z. Phonetik, Sprachwiss. Kommunikat. 14, 143 – 172 (1961). (Undecidable properties of CF-grammars, subclasses.)
3. — Shamir, E.: Finite-State: formal representations and adequacy problems. Bull. Res. Council Israel F 8, No. 3 (1960). (Grammar-automaton equivalence; problems of the representation of natural languages.)

4. Chomsky, N.: Three models for the description of language. IRE Trans. Inform. Theory IT 2, 113 – 114 (1956). *(Typology of grammars, linguistic problems.)*
5. – On certain formal properties of grammars. Information and Control 2, 137 – 167 (1959) (a). *(Mathematical properties of various classes of formal grammars.)*
6. – Formal properties of grammars. Handbook of Mathematical Psychology (ed. by D. Luce, E. Bush, E. Galanter). John Wiley & Sons, Inc. 1963. *(Contains a résumé of many properties of automata and formal grammars; an extensive bibliography.)*
7. – Miller, G. A.: Finite state languages. Information and Control 1, 91 – 112 (1958). *(Boolean properties of K-languages.)*
8. – Schützenberger, M. P.: The algebraic theory of context-free languages. In: Computer programming and formal systems (ed. by Braffort and Hirschberg). North Holland Publ. Co. 1963. *(Algebraic properties of CF-languages, formal series, Dyck languages; an extensive bibliography.)*
9. Davis, M.: Computability and unsolvability. New York: McGraw-Hill 1958. *(This important book contains the basic descriptions of Turing machines and combinatorial systems, as well as their applications in mathematical logic.)*
10. Gross, M.: Linguistique mathématique et langages de programmation. Rev. Française Traitement Information 231 – 253 (1963-64). *(On the use of languages and automata.)*
11. – Applications géométriques des langages formels. ICC Bull. 5-3 (1966). *(CF-languages and algebraic languages applied to combinatorial analysis.)*
12. Harris, Z. S.: From morpheme to utterance. Language 22, 161 – 183 (1946).
13. – Methods in structural linguistics. Chicago: Chicago University Press 1951. *(Axiomatization of the linguistic rules of natural languages.)*
14. Kleene, S. C.: Representation of events in nerve nets and finite automata. In: Automata Studies. Princeton. 1956. *(Definition of regular events; the structural characterization theorem of Kleene.)*
15. Kuroda, S.-Y.: Classes of languages and linear-bounded automata. Information and Control 7, 2 (1964).
16. Landweber, P. S.: Three theorems on phrase structure grammars of type 1. Information and Control 6, 2 (1963).
 (These two articles prove the equivalence of context-sensitive grammars and linear bounded automata.)
17. McNaughton, R., Yamada, H.: Regular expressions and state graphs for automata. IRE Trans. Electron. Computers EC-9, No. 1, March (1960). *(The relation between representing expressions and graphs of finite automata.)*
18. Matthews, G. H.: Discontinuity and assymmetry in phrase structure grammars. Information and Control 6, 2 (1963). *(Sub-classes of grammars, push-down automata.)*
19. Myhill, J.: Finite automata and representation of events. In: Fundamental concepts of the theory of systems (J. Myhill, A. Nerode, S. Tennenbaum). WADC Tech. Report: 57-624, ASTIA document No. AD 155741. *(Definition of the monoid of a finite automaton; standard K-languages, K-languages and graphs.)*
20. – Linear bounded automata. WADD Technical note 60-165. Wright Air Develop. Div. 1960. *(Definition and properties of linear bounded automata.)*
21. Nerode, A.: Linear automaton transformations. Proc. Amer. Math. Soc. 9, 541 – 544 (1958). *(Theorem of algebraic characterization by equivalence classes.)*
22. Nivat, M.: Elément de la théorie générale des codes. NATO Seminar on the theory of automata (Caïanello ed.), 1966. *(Properties of codes.)*
23. Parikh, R.: Language-generating devices. RLE Quart. Prog. Rept., No. 60, Cambridge, Mass.: MIT, January 1961, pp. 199 – 212. *(Inherent ambiguity of the CF-languages.)*
24. Post, E.: A variant of a recursively unsolvable problem. Bull. Amer. Math. Soc. (1946). *(Post's correspondence problem.)*
25. Rabin, M. O., Scott, D.: Finite automata and their decision problems. IBM J. Res. Develop. 3, 115 – 125 (1959). *(Boolean properties of the K-languages.)*
26. Rodgers, H.: Recursive functions and effective computability. Mimeographed, Dept. Math., Mass. Inst. Tech., 1961. *(Recursive functions and computable functions.)*

27. Scheinberg, S.: Note on the Boolean properties of context-free languages. Information and Control **3**, 372 – 375 (1960) (b).
28. Schützenberger, M. P.: Un problème de la théorie des automates. Séminaire Dubreil-Pisot, Paris, december 1959. *(Definition and use of the concept of power series in the study of automata.)*
29. — Some remarks on Chomsky's context-free languages. RLE Quart. Prog. Rept. No. 63, Cambridge, Mass.: M.I.T., October 1961, pp. 155 – 170. *(Definition of linear CF-languages.)*
30. — Certain families of elementary automata and their decision problems. Proc. Sympos. on Math. Theory Automata, Vol. XII, MRI Symposia Series, 1962. *(Definition and study of families of CF-languages using algebraic techniques.)*
31. — On context-free languages and push-down automata. Information and Control **6**, 3 (1963). *(Definition of the push-down automaton; study of the Dyck languages.)*
32. — A remark on finite transducers. Information and Control **4**, 185 – 196 (1961).

We have not been able to set forth certain "avant-garde" studies in the algebraic theory of automata. The following are the two most important articles on this subject:

Krohn, K., Rhodes, J.: Algebraic theory of machines, In: Mathematical theory of automata (J. Fox, ed.), pp. 341 – 384. Polytechnic Institute of Brooklyn Press 1963.
Schützenberger, M. P.: On finite monoïds having only trivial subgroups. Information and Control **8**, 190 – 194 (1965).

Additional Bibliography

Ginsburg, S.: The mathematical theory of context-free languages. New York: McGraw Hill 1966.
Harrison, M. A.: Introduction to switching and automata theory. New York: McGraw Hill 1965.

Typesetting and printing: Universitätsdruckerei H. Stürtz AG, Würzburg